WE ARE ALL
MADE OF SCARS

Christopher Morris

Cover design: Christopher Morris & @pro_design190

Author photo: Caroline Morris

ISBN: 9798364762399

To Josephine and Caroline,
for showing me that anything is possible and
how absolutely wonderful life can be.

PROLOGUE

Dearest,

Everything is fine now, but it didn't used to be. I could easily be dead already.

My childhood wasn't "normal." Maybe you are in the same boat. Maybe you were at some point. Maybe you know someone. Regardless, it's a little unfathomable and sometimes I can't even believe what happened during those years. This is my story, simply surviving in that world, doing the best and worst that I could.

These days, my mother isn't around, like other mothers are in other people's daily lives. What follows is a collection of memories that have taken me a long time to comprehend the scope and magnitude of. This is a story not often told. A peek behind the closed curtains of that one house on the block. It's time.

The best way to explain everything is to start at the beginning. The beginning of the end. My freshman year in high school until . . . well, how I got from age thirteen to nineteen is still a mystery. It's amazing that I did at all as you'll soon see in this catalogue of bad impulses. And I'm here now, twenty-something years later, full of scars, but I made it.

So let's fall back into my world. Crawl into the bottle a bit with my mom. A steady descent into the depths of my despair. Grab a life jacket. You'll want to grab my hand, but it's out of reach, slippery and unaware that I'm sinking too.

Oh, and yes, it's all true. Every last drop.

CAPSIZE

February 1992

I wake up to cold hands touching my arms and wrist. Beeping and strange noises. Light from the hallway bathes the bare, white room. Numbers spoken in stern voices. I answer a few questions from strangers dreamily. More poking and prodding. I pull up the thin blankets.

"Better get ready. Breakfast is in thirty minutes."

The door closes. Darkness.

I lift myself holding onto the metal railing beside me.

Every day is like this now. It doesn't matter what you dream or think of during the night. Waking up is always the same.

Nameless, faceless nurses. The white coats. The tests.

I suddenly realize, again, that I am, in fact, a real patient in a real psychiatric ward of a real hospital.

And then, of course, the angst hits. The anger. The sadness. The sick feeling as I wonder if everyone I know knows. The injustice of it all. The whole damn thing.

Because I'm not the crazy one. Nope. I just made a bad, impulsive decision. My mom on the other hand . . .

I think back to four days ago. It seemed like a good idea at the time.

My mom had been on the phone all night.

"I'll be off soon," she said over and over, playing with the long swirling cord.

No, I HAD to use the phone. What would Michelle think? I told her in World History that I'd call her at night. What would I tell her tomorrow? Things this year were finally clicking into place for me, since starting high school in the fall. Now this. Grr.

What would I tell her tomorrow? "Sorry, my mom was on the phone." Yeah, right. Then I look like an ass. She already kinda knows I like her. Who else sings Guns N' Roses' ballads to her during French class in a near perfect Axl Rose voice? I've been pretty much listening to *Use Your Illusion I* and *Use Your Illusion II* non-stop since they came out recently, which is why I've been serenading songs from it to Michelle.

Around nine o'clock, I was getting anxious. My mom was still sitting in her usual chair in the dining room, chatting away, smoking cigarette after cigarette at the glass dining room table and completely ignoring me. Up to that point, I'd been walking back and forth to the kitchen from my room asking for my turn. It was getting late, so I just leaned over with my arms on the kitchen counter that separated the kitchen from the dining room and stared at her.

"Just wait," she said, barely looking at me and waving me off through a cloud of smoke.

She wasn't getting the hint. I needed to make a point. A show. An act of defiance. Anything to get her attention.

It wasn't premeditated. At all. I just happened to be standing in front of the silverware drawer. So I took out an old steak knife from the silverware drawer underneath the counter that I was leaning on.

"Hey, Mom. If you don't get off the phone in five minutes I'll cut myself. And I am dead serious."

"CJ, c'mon, stop."

The drawn out way she said "CJ" irritated me. When I was a kid, most people called me "CJ" because there were always so many Chris's. Now it's just her.

"Mom, I've waited patiently all night. *It's my turn.* Five minutes or you will see blood."

It wasn't working. She just rolled her eyes and turned away from me.

"Four minutes, Mom."

And what was so important that she's on the phone all night anyway? She doesn't work. She doesn't do anything but spend my stepdad's money shopping, smoking and drinking really. She's got the perfect suburban Chicago life.

I thought about a few nights ago, coming home from a friend's house after dinner to find my mom sitting in the same dining room chair. Cigarette lit as usual, only she is just rocking back and forth. Mumbling. She points at me and tries to say something but it comes out like a choppy moan. I try and take her upstairs to bed. She shakes me off. Violently. Her demeanor is like a zombie. I give up and go up to my room and put on some music.

"Three minutes."

She wasn't even looking at me. I thought about her being fourteen. She was fairly popular and pretty in high school. Did they not have phones back then? Did she never go out with someone?

She wouldn't care anyways. I watched her drink from a mystery cup and I could tell that her speech has gotten slower and muddier. Just made me more mad. I thought about when I went downstairs this morning to make breakfast and found her sleeping in the family room by the dining room. Fully clothed on the couch. Must have passed out last night. I made a Carnation instant breakfast and just stared at her while I drank it. What is happening lately? I made sure my little brother was up and put his cereal on the counter. He took it from there. He's only eleven and we both seem to know we don't want to talk about what's happening.

"Two minutes."

I'd been picturing Michelle all night sitting by the phone in her bedroom. Waiting and waiting. Sighing. Long brown hair, with her little bangs curled down to her bright blue eyes. Next to her is a little stack of paper – all the notes I've passed to her in our two classes together. She's reading them over and over, laughing at all my funny drawings, witticisms and observations. I've had a crush on her since school started.

"Mom, one more minute. C'mon! How are you going to explain this to everyone? 'I wouldn't get off the phone when I said I would and now my son is scarred for life.' Seriously. One minute or this is going to happen. For real."

That was a bit much, but needed some dramatic effect. I looked at the knife. I can do this. I will do this.

I'll wear the scars like a soldier. I'll show them off and tell everyone I cut my arm doing something dangerous they couldn't even imagine.

I looked at her. Thanks for listening, Mom.

I cut six small lines lightly into the top of my wrist, dragging the knife slow as to not go too deep. It barely hurt. Scratches really. Each little one was about an inch long. She wasn't even looking. What the hell? Immediate regret. You can't see them now with this bandage around my wrist, which makes it look like a suicide attempt unfortunately.

They didn't bleed that much at all. It did look kind of cool at first, like a tribal tattoo.

"Are you happy now?" I showed her.

She got off the phone. It was stupid, but it worked.

"Run it under water! You're crazy, you know that? What if you cut a vein? Wait until your stepdad finds out."

I put a paper towel over it.

"Give me the phone."

She disappeared in her bathroom and I talked to Michelle for about a half an hour. I was so nervous I don't even remember what we talked about. I just spent the whole time not trying to sound like an idiot.

We still had some gauze on top of the refrigerator from when my mom fell down a few stairs around Christmas (I think she sprained her ankle or something). I put that over the paper towel on my arm until it looked like a badass bandage.

Everyone will wonder what happened to me tomorrow, I thought. And they did.

Hell, I did too.

* * *

"Mom, why did you wait until after a whole day of school to take me to this awful place?"

It was my turn to talk during "circle time", group therapy or whatever the hell they call this exercise where through "open dialogue" everything is supposed to be better somehow. I look at my stepdad with his head down and confused expression on his face.

Naturally, I asked the question that's been on my mind since I got here four days ago - why did my mom wait a full day before realizing, "Hey, my son is nuts for carving up his arm so let's put him in the psych ward." Thanks mom for your quick thinking and good judgment as always! Or - this has crossed my mind too lately and way more likely - she was being manipulative, and this was a signal to let me know she's ultimately in charge.

She straightened up in her chair and held her head back.

"I was worried. That's not normal behavior."

Normal behavior? My mom said that. Out loud. She should be the one in here. Not me. I have been asking the doctors about this, but they remind me that she would have to check herself in as an adult. Instead, I've been here four days, which feels like forever.

My stepdad is quiet, but that's not unusual.

I hear the pay phone ring and every time I wonder if it's one of my friends trying to call. I don't even know if they know I'm here, but being out of school this long? Come on. People have got to be talking. I told my best friends Andy and Dan that I was in the hospital. I lied saying I just got mono again, which gets you out of school. I'm pretty sure you can't get mono twice.

I'm half listening to the doctor and my mom, half regretting everything.

* * *

I kind of wish I didn't go to school that day to be honest. At first, there was an air of mystery around my arm with the bandage and all. I didn't say anything except a mysterious "Um, long story."

Then I made the mistake in study hall before lunch of showing everyone at my table.

"Ewww," Kelly said. Jenny and Brian just looked at me like I was crazy.

"What happened, dude? Did you get in a fight with a cat?" Brian said a little too loud.

"Yes, a huge cat," I lied.

This wasn't going as well as I'd hoped. Plus they had a point - the scars did look a little weird and out of place now underneath the harsh school lighting. A spotlight on the red lines against my bright white skin. God, I was stupid.

"C'mon, what really happened?" Kelly asked.

"Um, Brian was right. I got in a fight."

I had no idea what to say. That sounded dumb right after I said it. I had symmetrical scars almost all the same size. The only person who could've done that was Freddy Krueger or a very careful Edward Scissorhands, maybe? Damn.

They weren't buying it. It looked like they didn't know what to say. I took my books and asked to go to the bathroom where I stayed until the bell rang, reading the graffiti in the stalls. The rest of the day I wore a hooded sweatshirt I had in my locker for months. That covered up most of the bandage. I didn't show anyone else except Dan, because he wouldn't let up about it during Biology class.

After school, my mom was waiting for me by the front door. I knew something was wrong right away because she hadn't picked me up in months. I usually just hang out at Dan's until dinner or later.

"Hey, CJ. Hi, Dan. How are you, honey? Listen, CJ, change of plans today. We have to be somewhere. I'll tell you in the car."

She was focused. Intense. I knew something was amiss.

"What? C'mon, Mom, just tell me now. Dan and I have homework to do that we have to work together on."

That was a lie. Well, not actually a lie. We did have homework, but weren't going to do it. I usually didn't anyway. Dan always did after we hung out because he's smart like that.

"Don't make a scene. It's important."

We got in the van and drove off. Either someone died or I was in deep shit.

"So . . . how was school?"

"Mom, seriously. What the hell is going on? Something is up. You never pick me up from school and now you're acting like you're super mom."

"Who are you talking to? No, you're . . . um, going to see a doctor."

"What? Who? Why? This doesn't make sense."

"Self-mutilation."

"What the hell are you talking about?"

"Self-mutilation. I talked to the hospital today and you are going to see a doctor. Not one, but a few. I'm worried about you. I can't believe you did that to yourself. Or to me."

"Jesus Christ. So I gave myself a scrape on the arm? Big deal. Does my stepdad know about this?"

"I called him at work. He didn't even believe me."

Seriously? Wait a second. It's not like I tried to commit suicide. I shook my head. The idea was preposterous.

Okay, be cool, I thought. I'll probably get to the hospital, tell the story to the doctor and what? He'll laugh, I'll laugh and my mom looks like a fool. We'll both be home in a few hours and my stepdad will be pissed that we wasted gas driving around for nothing.

❊ ❊ ❊

Life here is . . . different.

It's a mix of ages, but thankfully there are a few other people my age. Will, Angie and Beth.

Will has an anger management problem and either beat someone up or did something really out of bounds at school. He also has the mascot of his favorite basketball team shaved into the back of his head. Sure, I shaved lines into my eyebrow like Vanilla Ice and even some bricks into the side of my head once at the beginning of the year. But a mascot? Dude.

Angie has long blonde hair. Tall. Cute. Quiet. She's bandaged up too on her arms, but not like mine. I'm pretty sure she legitimately tried to commit suicide. An air of sadness follows her. She always seems to be covering up her face with her hair.

Beth has longish brown hair. Pretty, but intimidating and slightly scary. I think she's older. I can't figure her out and not sure I want to. One minute she seems like the happiest, funniest person. The next she is screaming. For no apparent reason. I've seen her have a few breakdowns and they had to take her out of the room.

We don't mix much with the older folks, except for meals and during times when we aren't in meetings or other things. Almost no one is in their room. We're all usually in the "community area," which consists of a television and chairs at one end and a pool table and little kitchenette at the other. The nurses station is in view at all times. From there, two hallways branch out to the rooms. The payphone is right outside the station too.

At night, I call Dan or Andy for updates on the school

front. Occasionally, I talk to my dad in Chicago. I don't see him as much anymore and feel bad about it. Before high school, I would see him almost every Saturday after the divorce. Now it's just a Saturday here and there. I'm just so busy these days.

I call my mom sometimes. As much as I'm mad at her, it's still good to hear her voice. A piece of home, as dysfunctional as it was.

There are older folks in the psych ward too, mostly senior-citizen age. They're always huddled around the TV in the corner. I don't know what they're in here for.

A few seem genuinely mentally unstable. Not in a scary way, but like their mind just doesn't work right any more. I was playing pool with Will and one of the older guys got up, yelled "It's showtime!" then pulled down his pants. And just stood there. Nurses took him away. It should've been funny, but it wasn't. I overheard someone say that most of them have dementia or something.

I never watch TV here. I'd rather listen to music, which is always a great escape, but I can't of course. I would give anything to have access to a CD player. Instead, I read. I play pool. So much pool. The fridge by the pool table is stocked with little chocolate milks like they have in school. Will and I consume way too much until we feel sick. The nurses always yell at us because we drink all of it. What are they going to do though?

Will wasn't someone I would probably hang out with in "the real world," but here we are best friends or something resembling it. Almost like when you're a kid and are suddenly buddies with anyone your age at the playground for as long as you're there. Except we are in a psychiatric ward instead of a sandbox.

Every time we play pool, Will won't stop talking about the Chicago Bulls like everyone else, but he's obsessed. I've never been a sports fan and only collected baseball cards for a summer or two just to fit in and have something of value. I just don't get it or care that much. I just nod and let him talk while we play.

Right next to the pool table is the entrance. The exit. The very secure looking one. It reminds me of a prison door. It even has the little window near the top with thick, protective glass.

It's not just the door. The feeling is always there. The searches for contraband. The hospital smell and hospital sounds. The lack of color. Pastel paintings. An outburst here or crying there. The loneliness. The stares. The endless questions from the stereotypical white coats.

Of course, we talk amongst ourselves. I flirt with Angie, but I think she likes Will? It's hard to tell anymore. Beth told me she thought they had sex in the shower. But I doubt it. How could they with everyone watching all the time?

I don't look like myself anymore. My hair hasn't been cleaned up and shaved on the sides by my friends, plus the hospital doesn't let you bring any hair products for some reason. As if we are going to eat or drink them or something? Meanwhile, my hair is poofier than ever.

Most days the four of us get shuffled to a special room for a long stretch of time to do homework. The stale interior reminds me of being in detention. There are two windows, just high enough to let light in, but not low enough to let us look out. The walls are brown. Depressing. So I sit there, digging into my geometry book, half remembering last week's work and trying to sort things out and half thinking how strange this is. Everyone else I know is sitting in a normal classroom with Mrs. Tidds at the chalkboard, explaining everything and answering questions. All I have now are nurses and my new friends alongside me.

At some point, my mom must have went to the high school and asked for every assignment for the coming weeks. Does that mean all my teachers now think I'm crazy too? Awesome. I picture my teachers checking my work at some point. I wonder if I will get graded on some special psych ward curve. This feeling of humiliation never stops.

* * *

Dear Diary,
I'm writing to you because I'm bored and supposed to do this. Part of the therapy! Can you tell I'm excited? I hope they don't ask to read this, but I do need to fill up the pages. So here we are.

Anyway, earlier today was interesting. We've done a few craft activities since I've been here, but the one today was full-on school wood shop. A bit bizarre for a psych ward.

We each got blank wood plaques about ten inches long and had to stain them a shade of brown. Then we were handed a sheet of paper with the serenity prayer on it. I wasn't familiar with it, so recording it here for posterity:

> God, grant me the serenity to accept the things I cannot change,
> Courage to change the things I can,
> And wisdom to know the difference.

That's fine if you believe in God and all, but whatever. I get the message. I think so anyway. It reminds me of what the one doctor said when I talked to him about my mom's drinking. There isn't anything I can do about it, he said. I can't change or stop her. I've certainly asked her to stop before, which didn't help.

You know what we did next? We then burnt - yes, with real actual matches - the serenity prayer. We let the flames burn around the edges of the paper and blew it out once it got close to the words. That way the edges looked all cool for us to then stick it to our newly stained plaques. I have to admit, I was pretty proud of mine. I also have a feeling not everyone gets to do this activity - again, access to fire! - so it did make me feel slightly less crazy.

Speaking of, I have a feeling the people that work here are actually slightly demented themselves. Case in point: this afternoon they escorted us to watch the movie *The Hand That Rocks The Cradle.* I mean, really? I'm hoping they just didn't do their homework on that one. It's basically about a severely mentally ill woman who is nuts and gets more psychotic while trying to steal a nice lady's family. Pretty intense and people die. *Fried Green Tomatoes? Father of the Bride? Hook?* All contenders, funny with wide appeal. I hope they are just messing with us.

Oh, I say "escorted us" because instead of being on a tight lockdown, they also took us on a field trip today to the mall after the movie to do some shopping. What a group we were. Some recovering alcoholics or drug addicts, Will, two counselors, some other people that didn't look well and myself. I would've been embarrassed but I was too distracted being OUTSIDE for a change.

Similar to doing our schoolwork in the hospital, going to the mall knowing you are on a psych ward field trip just doesn't feel the same. We didn't stick together, which was nice. We just had to meet up in an hour so we could walk around. Again, like burning our serenity prayer plaques, this trip made me feel a little like finally the doctors were coming around and noticing, "Hey, this Chris kid is actually alright." We weren't supposed to shop, but I ended up buying a few CD singles that I've been looking for, like "Paper Doll" by P.M. Dawn and "Mysterious Ways" by U2 for the bonus tracks. I shoved them under my shirt when we got back to the hospital. Can't wait to listen to them. When I get out of course.

* * *

"Chris, you seem upset. What are you feeling right now?"

This doctor. Always with the feelings. It's not only annoying, but I'm also realizing I've never had a good handle on articulating what I'm "feeling" which doesn't help. Um, bored? Sad? Mad? All of the above?

It's only been fifteen minutes at circle time and it feels like an eternity. I'd give anything to just go out the door and knock some balls around on the pool table. Instead, I'm here looking at my mom, stepdad and this stupid doctor. It's been ten days since I've been at the hospital. Will got out and isn't here anymore to play pool with. Lucky bastard.

I've been answering questions from the therapists since I've been here, with variations on the same theme, but I haven't brought up things with my mom during these family discussions. I take a deep breath - thank you meditation and relaxation therapy - and decide to say what's on my mind.

"Listen, I've been here for ten days. I admit I made a mistake. It was stupid. A defiant spur of the moment decision with no thought of the consequences of my actions. I know that now. But I'm not the one who should be in here."

I point at my mom. My voice shakes and my stepdad looks like he's going to leap out of his chair.

"She's the one who needs help. It's her fault. Everything I did was a reaction to her behavior. Ask my mom about her drinking."

Just saying that out loud was hard. My mom starts to say something, but the doctor makes a motion to let me finish. My stepdad has his head in his hands.

Images from the last few months flood my head.

All night, usually beginning in the afternoon, I hear kitchen cabinet doors opening and closing. Sometimes hard.

I walk downstairs to the kitchen. My mom's voice fills the air along with the rich smell of menthol cigarettes. It's late. My stepdad is watching football downstairs, lying on the couch. My brother is asleep in his room, blissfully unaware that the house is almost always on the verge of burning down. I find a lit cigarette in an ashtray on the edge of the counter. She's holding another one in her hand. This goes in a circle all night as I keep checking on her to put them out. I can't sleep otherwise.

One night I ask to sleep over at Dan's house after a barely edible Hamburger Helper dinner and I get a mouthful. "What? You are never home anymore? Are you too good for us? Don't even want to eat here? Am I a bad cook? Is that it? You sit down and listen to me. I know what you are up to. Don't think you can fool me. I was thirteen too you know." And on and on. I don't say anything because I learned a while ago when she's like this, there isn't anything you can say to get her to calm down. She is just talking out loud to me or herself. I think. I just want to go over and play Sega Genesis at Dan's, not start any trouble. I grab a sweatshirt. "Mom, please stop. I'm leaving." The next day, she doesn't remember anything. Figures.

I sigh, then relay these events to everyone in the circle. They're all looking at me.

"It sucks, because when she's not like that, she can be mother of the year. All my friends think of her as the 'cool mom', always chatting, being funny, listening to good music, driving us to the mall or wherever, and just being generally, well, cool. Now I hardly ever invite my friends over.

"You know, I'm not stupid. My mom has always drank a little here and there, but the last year has been different."

"Oh, CJ," she laughs. "I don't think you are the sympathetic character you think you are. You are taking things out of proportion too. You know I love you . . ."

My mom continues to defend herself, but I can't listen. She's not drunk, so she puts on the charm. She's good at it.

She's clearly in denial. The doctors told me denial is often the hardest thing to overcome. Doesn't she see what we see? Does she realize it at all?

My stepdad doesn't say anything. I know he knows the truth too, but like me, what can you do?

❊ ❊ ❊

After the many different activities all day where I stubbornly answer questions from hospital staff, I have to attend Alateen. It's in the evening, somewhere in the bowels of the building. At first, I'm excited. Unlike Will, Beth and Angie, these are supposed to be teens more on my level. Apparently, Alateen is for teenagers who have a parent that has a drinking problem. And even though I'm sure nothing could become of it, I still hope that pretty girls will be there every time.

The teens all live nearby. I quickly realize that everyone's alcoholic parent is different. For example, I find myself feeling a little lucky that I don't have a drunk dad that hits me.

I don't say much during the meetings. I know they are in similar situations, but it's still embarrassing to talk about my mom and her drinking in front of other people my age. Plus, I'm wearing my clearly visible hospital bracelet and bandage, which doesn't send a clear signal that I have my own act together. I try to keep my hands under the table.

We talk or read about drinking, drinking and more drinking. The effects of drinking too. How it not only affects the drinker, but those close to them. I look down at my bandage. Yep. I quickly wonder what crazy things people here have done. Apparently, nothing too wild as I'm the only one coming down from the psychiatric ward.

We talk about how we aren't the reason our parents drink. I never think this, but can see why some would.

Frankly, I have no idea why she does. We were living the American Dream in many ways. After struggling for years, in poverty and moving up and down the state, my mom married my stepdad. We are finally middle-class-ish, living in a nice house in Oak Forest, a quiet suburb of Chicago. My stepdad works a steady blue-collar job in Aurora, while my mother spends her time shopping and talking on the phone to friends. We have two cars and a pool in the backyard. My little brother and I have our own rooms and are taken on at least one vacation a year, usually to the Midwestern Mecca that is Wisconsin Dells. Things were just getting good in some ways.

In the meetings, we also talk a lot about how we can't change our parents or their drinking. The alcoholic can't control it, so how could we possibly think to do so? It's a disease some say, as if the urge to drink consumes them.

This is a concept that's harder to swallow. Surely my mom really does love me right? And my stepdad and my brother? Wouldn't knowing that her drinking disrupts our daily lives get her to stop? Doesn't she know what it does to her? To us? Doesn't she know how damn hard it is to see her so drunk every night? We've never talked about it as a family so I don't know. I wonder for the first time if and when my stepdad and my mom ever talk about this stuff.

At some point during every meeting, we say the serenity prayer. The same prayer I have a permanent, burned plaque of now:

> God, grant me the serenity to accept the things I cannot change,
> Courage to change the things I can,

And wisdom to know the difference.

I still don't completely know what it means, but I make the connection again about not being able to change things.

After the last meeting I attend, on the way back to my room, I stop in my tracks in the hallway from the nurses' station. The air from the vents has always made a loud sound, but tonight I finally determine what it is that always sounds familiar. It sounds exactly like the screeching synthesizer-ish sound from the very end of "My World" by Guns N' Roses, which is the last song on *Use Your Illusion II*. An echo of my life a few weeks ago.

* * *

I'm sitting in Biology class where Mr. Willis is at the front of the room droning on about the functions of DNA. I can barely stay awake. Biology is my last class of the day and has been a constant struggle.

It's been a week since I returned back to "normal" life. I ended up being in the hospital about two weeks and everything feels a bit off since then. Almost no one says anything, but I get the impression that some kids knew I was in the hospital, but likely don't know why. I can't stop thinking about who knows what. I figure the safest thing is to act like it never happened.

I'm still mad at myself for showing off the scars like a lunatic after the fact. Shouldn't have done that. I wonder if Michelle knows. She's been a little cold to me in French class since I returned. My first day back at school, I awkwardly asked her to go out with me.

"Um, no. Sorry. I really don't want to see anyone right now."

Ouch. It hurts more after thinking about her constantly. There's not an easy way to say, "Sorry, I didn't call or see you for the last two weeks. I was admitted to the hospital. You know, self-mutilation and all."

The scars are still there. Faint, but there. Six white lines about an inch or so in a row.

I wear a watch now.

Mr. Willis is talking about RNA. Ugh, how much longer until I can leave?

This school year has been a whirlwind in all kinds of ways. As a kid, I always imagined high school a bit like the TV show *Saved by the Bell*, where I could be like Zack Morris, getting the girls and always up to something fun. High school is intimidating though and there is no way to prepare for it.

I always did pretty good in school and I'm in mostly honors classes this year. Except for Biology and Gym. I just can't get into it and frankly have stopped trying.

Why? New school. New friends and girls. Oh, the girls.

I think about the three horrible years of middle school as a complete dork. I went by for the most part unnoticed, probably because I was ugly and shy. I never fit in. I had all the wrong clothes. I was picked on for wearing cheap shoes from Payless. We couldn't afford the sweatshirts and other name brand clothes everyone was wearing, so I would settle for getting knock-off versions at the flea market with my stepdad. Some kids couldn't tell the difference. But I did. There were a few that laughed when I walked by. It was one thing eating generic food because no one knew, but everyone could seemingly tell when you were wearing "generic" clothes.

I never had a girl show any interest except a few that weren't my type. I was definitely interested in a few girls too, but nothing ever happened. Nothing could happen. The longing was unbearable. I would go over every awkward moment in horrible detail. I was way more like the nerdy Screech from *Saved by the Bell* than Zack.

Something amazing happened though right towards the end of eighth grade, where the stars aligned for once in my favor. First, puberty happened that year and by about April, my face finally grew into something remotely worth looking at. My big nose and cheeks didn't stick out anymore. Then my braces came off, which I had the entirety of middle school. Before that, my teeth were out of control, with the two front ones sticking out like fangs. Soon after all of these transformations, I had one of my first girlfriends - Crystal, a girl from another school that my middle school friend Jon and I met at the mall. He dated her friend Tracy. Nothing ever happened - I tried to kiss her on a double date at the movies and chickened out - but we saw each other a few times and talked on the phone a lot. I consider it practice.

The tipping point was the eighth grade school dance. I had never been to a school dance before, but this was to celebrate the end of the year and everyone was going. We were discouraged from bringing dates, so that took a little of the edge off of figuring out what girl to ask. If I was to even ask at all.

I was excited. I was also ready to dance.

Middle school was the time of Michael Jackson's *Bad* album. I was obsessed with *Thriller* as a kid and when *Bad* came out, I listened to it constantly and memorized all the dance moves from the video for the title single. I would even jump off the couch when Michael jumped from the turnstile. MC Hammer was big. C&C Music Factory too. I listened and danced to Bell Biv Devoe and the *New Jack City* Soundtrack all the time. "I Wanna Sex You Up" and "She's Dope (remix)" especially. I had worked up some good moves and was actually confident about something for a change.

I was happy about my outfit that night too, which helped. My mom took me to the mall to find an outfit, and when I asked for the black Z-Cavaricci suit that I knew would look awesome, she surprised me and actually said yes. I probably would only wear it once too. The pants were stylishly baggy with the little white Z-Cavaricci tag by the zipper and the jacket was high and tight. I had a nice green dress shirt to wear under it. I finally had some non-generic clothes.

At that point, aside from my little brother and mom, no one had seen me dance. I had actually meant to, once before. In fourth grade, I was ready to unveil some funky moves on some classmates in our talent show. Another kid and I worked out a little routine to an old song by The Monkees. But the day of, he was home "sick" and I foolishly told the teacher I'd do it anyway. Out of pride. I was so nervous by the time I had to go on, I blanked on what I was supposed to do and just held the microphone and mouthed the words to "Last Train to Clarksville," awkwardly bobbing from side to side.

Needless to say, that didn't build my confidence, but four years later I was ready to dance. On my own.

The dance was a Friday night and my mom dropped me off. The high school gym was dark and pretty much everyone was there. I found my friend Jon and we hung out on the sidelines. He also had a Z-Cavaricci suit, but his was grey. I remember being nervous about actually dancing. After a few songs though, I coolly walked up to the DJ and asked him if he had "Dangerous on the Dance Floor" by Musto & Bones.

"I do, but was going to save that one for later once things get moving," he said.

"Can you play it now? Please? I NEED to hear that song."

The song starts with some sexual-type moaning, so I wasn't even sure he'd play it, but he came through. As soon as I heard it, I looked his way and he gave me a nod of recognition.

I walked out away from the wall. There were some people dancing already, but not too many. They didn't acknowledge me. Then I started dancing. Like *dancing*

dancing. I tried to forget where I was and pictured myself just jumping around my bedroom like usual. I focused on the music while kicking from side to side, bouncing each leg up like I was kicking someone in the shins. I went through every move I knew and ended by doing "the worm," where you jump up and land on the floor on your upper chest and then move across the floor like a snake in a rhythmic pattern, making your body like a wave.

I killed it. People were clapping and yelling like on TV. I had a circle around me and I high fived everyone I could. I danced like that for the next few songs and took a break for the first slow one. Then I danced some more, this time with classmates. A few kids wanted me to show them what I was doing. When the next slow song came around, this pretty girl Sara asked me to dance. What was happening? By the next slow song, *I* was the one asking girls to dance. And they did! I was on an adrenaline high and didn't want the night to end.

Towards the end of the night, I danced with a girl, Jackie, that I liked on and off for most of middle school. She only held my waist though, because my back was soaked with sweat. By the time my mom picked me up, I was still in disbelief about it all.

It was a turning point though. A legitimate popularity breakthrough, fueled by the power of dance.

The following week, I got more signatures in my yearbook than the previous two years. Phone numbers even! That was nice, but who calls in July, "Um, yeah you said to keep in touch and I just wanted to see if you wanted to hang out at the mall?" Still though. Better than before. Almost everyone - boys and girls - alluded to my dancing when they signed it: "Keep dancing!", "Hey, MC Hammer!" and my favorite were a few that wrote in big girly curly writing, "Maybe over the summer you can teach me how to dance?" What?

Two girls in particular, Mandy and Janine, actually seemed serious about the whole teaching dance thing and invited me to hang out. They both were cute and were best friends. I had no idea what was going to happen, but I knew these opportunities never presented themselves before so why the hell not? Would I date Janine? Mandy? Both? I had no idea. If I could get even remotely close to either of them . . . it would be amazing.

Janine and Mandy conveniently lived down the street from my friend Jon, so the next time I was over at his house a week or so after school ended, I called Janine and we went over. Turns out that her mom, a chaperone at the dance, actually recorded some video of me there and we watched it. I got the impression it wasn't the first or second time Janine had seen it. The three of us went over to Mandy's and then walked to a park. We talked and they made me promise to call them both soon.

Then something strange happened. The next week, neither Janine or Mandy would return my calls. This went on for a few days until I decided to go over to Janine's house while hanging out at Jon's.

"Hey, do you want to take a walk?"

"No, especially not after what you did."

"Wait, what are you talking about?"

"Mandy heard that you told everyone about how you made out with both of us. Why would you say something like that?"

"Whoa, whoa. I never said that. That's insane. Who told you that?"

"I don't know who she talked to, but it's not cool. We can't hang out anymore," she said, closing the door.

What. The. Hell. Who said that? I racked my brain for every boy that liked either girl and couldn't come up with anyone specific. Some jealous jerk. I tried calling both again to see if it was some cruel joke, but could never get through.

It all happened so fast. Affection and then swift rejection. That was a dirty first entree into the wider world of girls and teenage relationships.

Over the summer, I had two quick and strange hook ups too that left my head spinning. I ended up making out with a girl from Holland by a hotel pool in the Wisconsin Dells. She was aggressive. It was all over before I knew it had started. Then I went to my grandfather's house in Indiana - we called him Papa - and I met a girl there. She lived next to the swimming area of the lake that I've been going to off and on since I was a kid. We talked. Flirted. Next thing I know we're in her room making out. Hard. She was aggressive too and putting my hands all over her. I had no idea what to do and I think she was expecting me to do something more, but I was stunned and overwhelmed. I felt embarrassed walking back to Papa's house, yet oddly satisfied that something happened. We talked on the phone occasionally, but it didn't go anywhere after that. She went to a Catholic all-girls high school and her mom was super strict.

This school year started on a good note though. There was a dance/open house/party thing for incoming freshman right before school started. I danced again. I think I even "battled" a few people, dancing aggressively to win. Winning what exactly I don't know, but it was nice to start the year fresh with new people. And the kids from my middle school seemed to hold me in higher esteem.

I started asking girls out almost immediately. We would be boyfriend and girlfriend for a week or two and then I'd find a reason to date someone else. I'd get bored sometimes or just jump at the next person I heard or knew was interested in me. They'd take it okay and move on to the next. Maggie was pissed though because I broke up with her for starting to smoke. C'mon. It's so gross.

Or they'd break it off with me and it would end quietly. We'd exchange notes and have awkward interactions in the hall, then suddenly whatever was happening was over. Other girls would say "I love you" after a week. High school was weird. Or I was. Or both?

One girl, Leslie, did break up with me though for being

"too pawy." It was another reminder I had no idea what I was doing, clearly reading her signals wrong in my room. She didn't say anything at the time. That was a bummer, because she was so pretty and popular. Plus, she had a Turbografx system at home, which no one had.

The girls have been a whirlwind and they take up most of my mental space. I love and crave the attention. I still can't believe it. I kissed a few. In the hallways even. I wrote notes and received notes in classes. I held hands. I went on "dates" to McDonald's and the movies. I spent time in a few girl's bedrooms. I talked to their moms, who usually seem to like me. I learned a bit more, even if it wasn't always the right things.

By the time of the "incident" and the hospital stay, I had already dated or went steady with about eight girls. A side benefit is now the guys think I'm cool because the girls like me. Even the jocks. It's crazy. I-

CRASH!

I look up to find Mr. Willis towering over me. I notice a metal garbage can lid on the ground. I must have been seriously daydreaming about girls again. Damn, another detention.

❉ ❉ ❉

Friday night. I'm in Dan's bedroom, playing Sega Genesis and listening to *Nevermind* by Nirvana. It's hard to believe we didn't know each other until this year, but thanks to a few classes together, Dan and I became fast friends.

Andy and Eric rounded out the crew. They almost all knew each other from middle school yet somehow I fit in. They were all Korean, with the exception of Andy who was from China. I wasn't the only non-Asian. Sometimes Matt or Jake from the neighborhood would hang out too. But Dan, Andy and I were the closest. We seemed to gravitate to the same music, girls and outlandish humor. We even cut each other's hair. Well, shaved the sides and back, which was still better than the cheap beauty school haircuts I got in middle school.

They were nice to me and only occasionally made fun of my "smoky shirts" since my family was the only one that smoked, so I was the odd man out that way. If they only knew . . .

Dan's parents welcomed me with open arms. They seemed like a pretty put together family. His dad and mom were quiet and super nice. Dan's brother was a year younger and often hung out with us too. Well, they shared a room, but thankfully he's cool. His sister was a few years younger and largely kept to herself. The siblings would have normal disagreements, but largely the family seemed so happy and . . . normal. It was a welcome change and since school started, I've found myself over here more and more on the weekends. Spending the night more and more too. No one ever slept over at my house.

I can't believe I even started going to church with his family on Sundays sometimes. At church, Dan was still fun to hang out with. He'd crack me up making fart jokes and strange sounds in the pews or sang wildly during the hymns.

I was waiting for Dan to come back while trying to beat Sonic the Hedgehog, endlessly spinning through loops and springs collecting rings. It seemed never ending, but Dr. Robotnik had to be beat as far as we were concerned. After playing Super Mario Bros. on Nintendo for years, this was a nice upgrade, even if the basic game was more simplistic. It was brighter. Faster.

Dan came in wearing a frilly dress and a bowl of cereal with an oversized huge cooking spoon.

"What did I miss?" He deadpanned, while trying to scoop up the cereal.

"What the -"

"Dude, you're crazy!" I laughed so hard.

"What? When's it my turn?"

That was Dan. He would do anything to make us laugh even if it meant putting on his little sister's clothes randomly on a Friday night. She wouldn't be happy about it either.

Dan put on *Dangerous* by Michael Jackson. This never got old. We had all the album's singles so far too on CD, playing the remixes over and over. This album was quickly becoming the soundtrack to freshman year along with *Nevermind.*

"Man, put on 'Remember the Time.' No, put on 'In the

Closet.' That's my new jam."

We turned it up. We sang loud. We were not Michael Jackson, but we were in that moment. Until Dan's dad banged on the door.

"I'm so sorry, Dad, it won't happen again. It was an accident . . ."

Dan was funny, even talking to his parents.

"So what happened with Jenny?" He asks.

Jenny. We were a couple for a few weeks. I think.

"I don't know, man, I think she's with Troy who's on the football team. Who cares, I think Kristina in my French class is cute and she's been talking to me more lately. Next week, I'm going to make a move."

Just by looking at my grades, it was clear I was spending more time maneuvering and flirting with girls than actual school work. I knew I could do okay if I put the time in, but OH MY GOD, THIS IS WHAT I WAS WAITING FOR THE LAST FEW YEARS. Girls talked to me. Looked at me. I finally felt seen a little bit. It didn't make sense most of the time, but even the mistakes were worthwhile and gave me a rush.

Second quarter this year I flunked French, probably because of singing to Michelle most of the time, but then after the French teacher scolded me about it, I got an A the next quarter just to spite her. My other grades were in trouble and I'm probably going to flunk Biology thanks to sleeping or daydreaming in class.

Dan and I stay up late talking. During breakfast the next morning, we talk about possibly going to the mall or riding bikes around the neighborhood. As I'm getting ready, I hear a voice from downstairs.

"Chris, your dad is here."

Shit. It's Saturday. I totally blanked. I've already missed the last few Saturdays with him for Dan or Jenny. But, do I hang out with my friends today or my dad?

"Can you tell him I'm not here?"

"Um, okay . . ."

I watch from the window upstairs and see my dad waiting on the sidewalk near the front door. I see his shoulders crumple a little as Dan's brother tells him whatever he tells him. I'm sure my dad knows I'm here, but he doesn't push it. He drives off with my brother in the car. My stomach sinks. I tell myself that I've seen my dad forever on Saturdays, but I've only had friends like this for months.

"That was cold, man. Are you okay?"

I turn from the window and shake it off, trying to not think about my dad driving away, slighted by his own son. I grab my wallet and check my hair in the mirror.

"It's fine. You almost ready? We can take the bus at eleven to the mall."

❋ ❋ ❋

I'm beginning to think I have superhuman senses. Granted, not the type that I can put on a suit and cape to go out and help others, but a heightened sense for sure. When I'm at home and I walk into the kitchen or when I come home at night from Dan's or wherever, I can tell that my mom has been drinking before even encountering her.

The house sounds different. Smells different. It's hard to describe. It's like everything is the same, just tuned to a slightly different frequency. I can almost feel it in the air.

There isn't a pattern to my mom's drinking, but it's like I've cracked some code to when she actually is drinking. She might not even be drunk yet, but at least I know it's underway.

A few weeks ago, when I was doing the dishes - one of the house chores I do sporadically - I found a jug of wine underneath the kitchen sink. That was new. Over time, it's in various states of emptiness. At this point, my mom could just keep this right on the dining room table for easy access, but the charade continues. Instead, she still tries to hide it. Maybe it's working in some respects because we are the only two people that use this cabinet, but still. It at least explains why I always hear kitchen cabinets slamming at all hours. I find some more wine hiding in the bathroom cabinets too.

My stepdad has his routine and is unchanged - works all day, eats dinner, then watches TV until bedtime downstairs. I wonder how much he knows about my mom's drinking and just doesn't know what to do. He seems to just ignore it. I wonder again if they've talked about it. We certainly never talk about it. The only change between us is that I start to let him know where I'm going instead of my mom. He never says no.

He sees my stepsisters - his daughters - less and less now that they are my age and also spending time with friends I'm guessing. Or maybe he doesn't want them to be around my mom? I don't ask.

One benefit of the girls being over less is my stepdad decided to give me their bedroom in the house. My brother and I have been sharing a room while the other was the girls' room for when they visited. I always thought it was weird since they weren't over much, but it was so nice to just live in a house instead of an apartment and have a larger room to share. Plus, we had a TV and Nintendo in our room! What more do you need? Since middle school, I did start to yearn for my own space. It was great. No more fighting over what to watch or listen to. No more negotiations over posters on the wall.

What's funny though is that even with all that, I'm hardly home. Dan's parents have almost adopted me and I interact with them more than my stepdad and my mom. When I'm home, I check in with my brother or talk on the phone with girls.

The phone is free a lot more these days.

One convenient aspect to my new bedroom is having a window right above the fireplace downstairs, where the brick sticks out from the house, making a little stepladder of sorts on both sides of where the chimney is. I realized quickly how to remove the screen and get in and out of my room without anyone noticing. This comes in handy a few times when I come home late. I come downstairs like everything is normal.

"When did you get home?" My stepdad or my mom might ask.

"What do you mean? I've been home for a while. Didn't you guys hear me come in?"

They don't say anything and return to the TV. It's one benefit of hardly talking with them.

I pushed it too hard the other night though, which is why I'm grounded this week. This cute girl Lisa invited me to her house saying she was having a few of her girlfriends over. She's two years older and we chat during lunch from time to time, so it seemed worth the risk.

The idea was way more exciting than the reality.

At eleven, I stuffed my bed with clothes to make it look like I was sleeping and left through the window. I biked to her in the dark through the quiet streets.

Her parents were in bed so I had to climb through her basement window. Before I knew it, I was being stared at by five girls that were all a lot older than me. It felt like a mistake immediately. I didn't belong there.

They grilled me with questions.

"What music do you like?"

"Do you have Mr. Mullen for math?"

"Do you have a girlfriend?"

They laughed a lot and I couldn't tell if they were making fun of me or that's just how older girls act. It was a bit terrifying.

Lisa and I barely got a chance to talk. Nothing good was going to happen. At two in the morning, I was getting tired so I lied and told them I had to be home.

"Please stay, Chris! Let's play a game!" They pleaded and pleaded, while giggling.

When I got back home to my window, it was shut. I knew I was in trouble. I snuck in through the back sliding glass door, which was usually unlocked because my mom often opened it to let smoke out and forgets to close it.

My mom was half asleep in my bed. I told her I was just out with friends but it didn't matter. I was grounded for the first time in a long time. She must have checked on me for some reason or needed something. I think my stepdad screwed in the screen afterwards because now it won't budge.

I'm still mad about it all, but only at myself for getting caught and agreeing to meet Lisa in the first place.

I'm thinking about all this when my mom comes in my room. I can sense she's been drinking immediately.

"CJ, I'm on my last cigarette. Can you get some? I'll write you a note. It's okay, I promise."

"What? Why can't you go? And aren't I grounded?"

"I'm not, um, feeling too good. It's fine. You can go out just for this. It's important."

I'm grounded, but can go out to get cigarettes? Noted.

"Fine, I'll go. It's not like I'm doing anything."

I know her. It's probably easier to go than to push back.

I follow her downstairs where she writes a barely legible note that looks as if a child wrote it. I'm feeling nervous, but we've done this before. This reminds me of going to the grocery story by myself as a boy when we lived in a trailer park.

I ride my bike to the liquor store I know she goes to, which is about ten minutes away. I'm hoping they recognize her name.

I walk in and take the crumpled piece of paper out of my pocket along with a five dollar bill. The old, bearded man behind the counter takes both and looks at the note.

Hi,
Please give my son a pack of Benson & Hedges Menthols.

Call me if you need to.

- Linda

"You know my mom, right? She comes in all the time. She isn't feeling great right now."

He takes a drag of his cigarette and looks down at me for a long time. I watch him call the number my mom left at the bottom of the note.

"Lynn, your son is in here buying cigarettes. These are for you right? Don't you go getting me in trouble."

I nervously pace around the store while he's on the phone. All I hear at the end is something about hoping my mom felt better.

Her ruse works. I take the cigarettes and go, hiding them in my pocket.

The next day, my mom asks again and I don't even need a note.

The day after that, she asks me to get wine too. The cashier calls her again and looks at me with a sad smile. I feel nauseous.

She's probably telling him how much sicker she was. I imagine her flirting with him on the phone saying how a little bottle would go a long way. I know it won't.

"I can't be doing this all the time," the cashier says and hangs up.

"Take it easy, kid."

I grab the bottle and go.

While slowly riding home on the gravel next to Central Avenue, I try to balance the brown bag on my knee with one hand, gripping my handlebar with the other.

* * *

We're at the Orland Square Mall. Dan, Andy and me.

To the outside observer, it looks like we are aimlessly wandering, but we have a routine - a precise plan - to walk around the mall. We start at the big department store by the food court to each put on a cologne sample. Drakkar Noir is popular or Eternity by Calvin Klein. Then we walk in a circle, stopping at Sam Goody for any new CDs or maxi-singles. I don't need to get any today, thanks to my new system with the music clubs through the mail that advertise "twelve CDs for a penny." I sign up under different names and get a batch of CDs every now and then. I pay the first bill for shipping and that's it. Ignoring the mailings after that is easy. So far, so good.

We then go to our favorite clothing stores, Merry-Go-Round and Dejaiz. I rarely have money for clothes, but Dan and Andy do. I've got some good stuff on clearance though. I had a good job last summer at the Midlothian Country Club nearby as a caddy and then on the driving range, but now I just cut the grass for a few neighbors here and there. I take some money from my mom's purse now and then. So far, she hasn't noticed. It's an allowance of sorts.

I don't think my mom's watching money as closely. When she seems sober enough, I beg her to take me shopping. She's been better about buying me Nike shoes and a shirt or whatever here and there so I can fit in as much as possible. I have a rotation of my three to four decent things that work for me and some passable counterfeits from the flea market, spacing them out in a way that I think makes me seem as if I have more cool clothes than I actually do. Of course, my mom goes shopping all the time on her own when she can, sometimes never wearing the clothes, just piling them up, tags and all, around her bedroom.

As always on our mall route, my friends and I make eyes with any pretty girls and try to act as cool as possible. Very occasionally, it works, but never goes anywhere. Maybe an awkward conversation or two. We have better luck with girls at our own school. Well, for the most part.

"What's wrong, man?" Dan asks.

I'm clearly in my head too much. They can tell.

"So Katie . . ."

"Oh no! Katie. Yes?" Dan says.

"So even with all the girls all year, her and I have been flirting in English class on and off. She's so cute and way out of my league."

"Okay. So what's the problem?"

"Well, the other day in class she was particularly flirty

so I called her that night."

"Have you ever called her before?"

"Nope, but I just had a feeling. Plus, I was bored being grounded and all. Anyway, we talked and I can tell she feels a little weird that I called. But we chatted and it seemed to go well. To me anyway. Then I asked her out."

"No!"

"Yes, and it was horrible. She waited for what felt like forever and said something like, 'Chris, I like you, but you're kind of a player now. If you asked me at the beginning of the year, I would've said yes, but now . . . I'm sorry.' Shit, I didn't think girls thought of me as a player these days."

I shake my head. I always thought of a player as someone having sex all the time. I've dated a lot of girls this year, but I'm still a virgin. The make-out sessions are usually pretty tame. At this point, I know so little about what happens before, during and after sex, that I just want to get it over with. I've never talked about the actual mechanics of it with anyone. I can't discuss it with my friends either because I'm pretty sure they're virgins too.

"Man, sooner or later you'll be dating. Just wait. What about Tracy?"

"Yeah, that will probably happen. She wrote me a note the other day that was so nice. And long too. She's really sweet. We'll see. I need to write her back. When are we gonna get picked up by the way?"

"At two. So what did you do all week being grounded? I feel like we haven't been over to your house in forever."

That's true. My stomach sinks.

"I know, but your house is so much better. I don't have a Sega Genesis! And my mom has been pretty sick you know."

"Is she alright, man? You've said that before. What does she have, like cancer or something?"

I think fast and realize I should've come up with a better story about her. I mean, things haven't gotten better. The truth is too embarrassing and they wouldn't understand.

"No, I don't think so. I'm not a doctor, but it's just like one of those types of things where you are sick all the time and they don't know what it is. It's like that."

"Oh sorry, man. I hope she gets better. Sorry for bringing it up."

I hate lying to my friends, especially Dan, who is so kind to me.

I guess she is sick though, just in her own way.

❋ ❋ ❋

As part of being released from the psych ward a few months ago, I have to see a therapist as part of "outpatient treatment." I hated it immediately.

It's annoying because it's my mom that needs help. When are these people going to get that? The first guy I saw was terrible. He looked like a bodybuilder, which was mildly threatening too.

I hated his questions.

"How does your mom's drinking make you feel?"

So happy. I'm glad you asked because I feel like I've won the lottery every time I see her drunk. What a stupid question. Here we go with the feelings. Again.

"You said your self-harm was really a reaction to your mom's behavior. I'm wondering if there other ways you have maybe acted out similarly to seek attention?"

Attention? It was an isolated incident. I'm mostly fine. I hate thinking and talking about this stuff because no one seems to get it.

"What do you expect to get out of seeing me or a therapist?"

Hmm, answer all of your questions so I don't have to see you anymore and we both can go on with our lives? Have I aced this test yet?

"I'm hearing that you are largely focused on girls, friends, etc, but how invested are you in your own recovery?"

And so on. It was exhausting listening to him and answering his questions the way I feel like I should answer them and then thinking about what he's thinking. I was truthful about my mom's situation though, hoping that he could somehow get her help through his magical therapy network.

I complained to my mom and she found me a different guy but he asked the same questions. I gave the same answers.

He told my mom I should go to Alateen, so I went a few times. It was better than before, since I wasn't a patient at a psychiatric ward, but it still was awkward. Once again, I realized that my mom's drinking could be way worse after hearing other people share. I heard stories of violence, stories of sadness, stories of repeated hospital stays. Stories of shame. I always passed when it was my turn to talk, even though I had so many stories of my own. The covering up. The lies. The denial.

Strangely, for tonight's meeting, my stepdad decided to take me. After the hour was up, he picked me up and turned down the radio.

"Chris, I'm taking your mom to the hospital tonight."

I knew there was a reason he drove me. He's usually quiet, so when he talks or does something, it's with purposeful intent.

"What do you mean? Like treatment? Help her to stop drinking? Do you think -"

"Yes, well, we're going to try it. Unless your mom is a harm to herself or others, she has to consent and sign the papers to be admitted. I talked with her today and she said she'd do it. I don't know how long the whole thing will last, but probably a few weeks at least."

I was stunned. This was big. It was going to be different with my mom not home, but this was good. She wouldn't be home drinking. Yes, this was good. Will it work though?

He shifted in his seat.

"You're going to need to help out a little more. Around the house and with your brother. And anything else that comes up. I have work and all that, and then I'll be with your mom when I can."

"Can I visit her too?"

"Of course. I don't know all the details yet, but I'll let you know tomorrow."

The rest of the night was a blur. When we got home, my mom was already packed. She said goodbye to my brother and I. He looked so sad. My brother only knew she was going away to get help, but I'm not sure he fully understood what was happening. I didn't either really. "This is good," I kept telling myself.

I stopped my mom before she walked out the door and she pulled me close while stumbling. She looked like she hadn't slept, smelling like wine and perfume.

"I love you, CJ," she said in between tears. "I'm so sorry. I feel terrible. I didn't want this to happen."

"I love you too, Mom. I -"

They were already out the door. My stepdad probably wanted to go before my mom changed her mind. I was at a loss anyway. What do you say when your mom goes off to rehab for the first time?

* * *

We go to visit my mom a few days later. As we drive up to the hospital, I'm dumbstruck.

"Woah, that's . . . are you serious . . ."

"What?" My stepdad asks.

"Are we going to Palos Community? No . . ."

"Yes, that's where your mom is. Sorry I didn't mention it. What's the difference?"

We park and after signing in, I start to sweat as I realize where we were going. No, this can't be. Of all the hospitals. Of all the places to get help.

Before I knew it, we were walking through the very same door I was so happy to walk out of a few months ago. The very same psychiatric ward. I follow my stepdad and start to shake. Don't pass out. Jesus.

It looks like nothing has changed and everything came back to me. The sounds. The doctors. The ringing phones. The feeling of hopelessness.

I spot my mom on a couch and she rushes up to hug us. She seems . . . good? She has more color in her face, but she's sweaty and seems nervous. Probably the withdrawal symptoms that one of the nurses mentioned when we checked in. I see some kids around my age by the pool table. Other people stare at us. I can't believe I used to be one of those people.

She talks and I hardly listen. I should be happy. The whole time I was the one here, I asked anyone that would listen to change places with her. She was the one with the problem, remember?

Yet, here we are. She is the patient. I am the visitor. I feel sick. Numb. I feel sorry for the first time in a long time. I feel bad.

I think I knew before that my mom had a drinking problem by her behavior, but in this moment looking at her with no make-up on, standing in the common area of the psychiatric ward, I truly feel the weight of it all. This somehow makes everything very, very real.

It's official. My mom is an alcoholic.

BREACH

So much of high school is pretending to be someone you're not, holding back as many secrets as possible.

Even if I could be completely honest with people at school, they probably wouldn't get it. Most of them have grown up in the same house with the same parents and same friends for their whole lives. I'm a tad envious of their normalcy. Their stories seem predictable yet stable.

My story starts in a suburban strip mall.

My parents met in the mid-seventies in Oak Lawn, Illinois. My dad was eighteen, fresh out of high school and delivering pizzas. Free food and the money was good. Money for cigarettes, guitar strings, records and concerts.

Linda, my mom, was twenty and going to Morraine Valley Community College, studying early childhood education. She dabbled in art and worked nights at a White Hen convenience store.

This particular White Hen was located in the same strip mall where my dad worked. He used to stop in to get cigarettes and fell hard over this Irish looking, pretty brunette who even smoked the same brand of smokes as he did. They went on a fateful date to see James Taylor sing about fire and rain, getting married months later.

At the time, my dad was living with his younger brother and mom - my Nana Madge - in Palos Hills. His own dad had been out of the picture since he was three, leaving my grandmother with two kids while he was off starting a new life in Las Vegas, remarrying and having two more boys. My dad had little contact with him, but he grew up with a loving single mother who was supported by her own stern German parents.

My mother was living with her older brother and mother - my Nana Dody - in Oak Lawn, who was recently remarried. When they were teens, Papa and Nana Dody's marriage unraveled into divorce. My mom and uncle were close with him and I could see why because Papa was a charismatic guy. Handsome, funny and full of stories and wisdom. At that time, he was a Vice President of Sales at Philip Morris, known mostly for selling cigarettes such as Marlboro, which of course was the brand I saw him smoke years later. Although he lost that job around the time of the divorce and I only remember him in landscaping . . . but I'm getting ahead of myself.

After my parents married, they fled the suburbs for southern Illinois to the small town of Charleston. College town. Small. Cheap. It was a perfect place to start a brand new life for themselves.

They bought a trailer home, found friends and then in the Spring of 1977, I came along. My mom stopped working at a daycare provider to take care of me while my dad was driving a Pepsi truck to pay the bills.

My brother was born three years later and things were about the same, maybe just a little tighter. At some point, we moved into a different trailer. My dad would come home from work and we watched the old Batman TV show from the sixties together, which I was obsessed with. Afterwards, we played with Hot Wheels and action figures until dinner.

I had friends in the trailer park, like Max, whose parents were friends with my parents. Well, Max's mom Maria was friends with my mom. Max's dad was quiet while Maria was loud.

My mom talked a lot about missing her family by this time, so we moved up to a two-bedroom apartment in Tinley Park, closer to both of their families. It was a welcoming building and a group of older girls that lived downstairs used to babysit me. It was a good year for the most part. We went to church most Sundays, which was new for us. My dad got a job as a metal fabricator. I won a coloring contest and won my family fifty dollars at a local clothing store.

A year later, we moved to an apartment in Chicago Ridge. I started Kindergarten and would go to movies with my uncle - my mom's brother - and dad a lot. My uncle relentlessly teases me for running out of *Raiders of the Lost Ark* in the face of many scary moments throughout the film. I also ran out of the theater when a babysitter took me to see *Snow White and the Seven Dwarfs* because I couldn't bear to see Snow White bite into the poison apple. If it was potentially unsettling, I didn't like it.

We lived in Chicago Ridge for about two and a half years, and it was pretty memorable. We lived right next to a highway underpass with train tracks, and just like in the movies, I tended to hang around there with my neighborhood friends. We found a dirty magazine there once, which confused me. Why were the people in it naked and what were they doing? I learned to ride a bike. I saw my extended family a lot. I attended my first funeral for my great-grandfather on my dad's side and remember visiting my dying great-grandmother on my mom's side in the hospital. You don't forget those things.

More shards of memories: I had a birthday party at McDonald's. I was bullied by some older kids for having longer hair because it wasn't cut regularly. They'd yell, "Ooh, aren't you pretty Christina," before throwing me in the bushes on the way home from school. Either in retribution or to act cool, I brought a steak knife to my school bus stop, then at the last minute, realizing the magnitude and possible repercussions of bringing a knife to school, I ran home and threw it into the kitchen sink. My mom grounded me.

A friend fell out of a tree one day and landed on the top of a chain link fence. I got his mom and she took him to the hospital. I made an Indian friend my age who had nothing in his living room but a TV and some pillows. His bedroom was more like mine. I played doctor with a girl I liked who lived in my building and I threw up when she was doing a check-up on me. The same girl invited me with her dad to go bowling and I got gutter balls the whole time. I loved going to Brookfield Zoo with my family. Like most of America, I watched music videos all night on MTV with my dad and loved everything about Michael Jackson's "Thriller" video. I still wet the bed to my dismay.

I read a lot too, devouring books. I don't remember many books before *Charlotte's Web* though. That one changed me and I cried so hard when Charlotte died. I didn't even know books could do that.

First grade was easy. When we read aloud in class, I was awestruck by just how slow kids read! I did so well that year that my teacher wanted me to move up to second grade early. My parents declined as my dad skipped a grade in elementary school and was teased about being younger than everyone else. The same thing happened in third grade at a different school later on. I found this all out sometime later and still wonder what my life would've been like if they'd let me move up.

※　※　※

In just those few years, in hindsight, so much changed for the worse. I was becoming more aware of things too. I was realizing we didn't have much and wondered if we were poor. There was the whole issue of not getting my hair cut. Our car was brown, rusted and old. I didn't have a lot of toys or clothes. I had just enough ("Hey, I got a couple G.I. Joes and a couple more knock-off ones!"), but it always seemed like everyone else at school had more ("Oh, Seth has the G.I. Joe vehicles, Cobra Commander and all the He-Man figures I wanted…").

My belief in God started to falter too. We were still going to church and I was in a bible group one night a week, but I didn't understand the rules I heard. Even at that young age, I had too many questions. I'd go to hell for murdering someone. Sure, that made sense. But for swearing? Or not listening to my parents? No one ever had a satisfying answer.

My parents were too busy fighting at this point to answer my endless religious quandaries. Divorce always sounds like it is something that happens at one particular point in time, but it's really just a culmination of sad, angry or terrible moments. First, I noticed we stopped watching TV as a family after dinner. My mom yelled more. Once, my dad - who was rarely angry - upturned a huge plant in the middle of the living room after an argument with my mom. My little brother screaming and crying at dinner while yet another argument erupted. Me staring off, unsure of what was transpiring.

Then one day my dad left and didn't come back. That's all I knew. We started seeing him here and there until starting regular visits on Saturdays, where he would pick us up around late morning - after our cartoons of course - and drop us off after dinner sometime. We'd usually eat at McDonald's or a pizza place, go to the zoo, see movies, play games at an arcade or visit my Nana Madge's house where he was living. This routine lasted until I was in high school for the most part. We didn't talk to him much during the week unless it was a special event.

The divorce became final. It was hard for everyone, but it seemed as if my mom was suffering the most. She acted that way for sure. But I spent more time with her and it's possible my dad was silently suffering. She started to complain out loud to us.

"Your father didn't give us much child support so we can't get the dinner you wanted," and so on. She told me she would get the police involved if he didn't give more. Who knows where the truth lies with my mother, but she always knew how to make a point.

I think they were still figuring out life. My dad was only twenty-five when they divorced and he worked throughout the marriage as they lived paycheck to paycheck. Were they rich? No, but we got by, even if it was in a trailer or small apartment. And we had each other, which was enough for him. My mom however, aspired to be the model suburban housewife and all of her high school friends would tell her about their fancy new car, vacations, clothes, house furnishings and whatever else women talk about. My dad couldn't provide that, nor did he want to live that life. Sometimes I wonder how they were ever married given how different they were.

My mom started dating. I can still feel the awkwardness of a strange man sitting in our living room, my brother asleep and me having to make conversation with a guy who is probably equally as uncomfortable. My mom never made things better.

"CJ, why don't you show John your dance moves?"

Ugh. I would do an embarrassing breakdance routine. The guy would feign excitement. I quickly learned it was easier to just do it than to fight back. Get the whole situation over with as fast as possible. That way I could go back to reading in my room, on the floor next to the lights peering out of the slates of the louvered closet doors.

One guy had a small house with a pool, where we all visited one Sunday afternoon. My brother and I were spoiled with candy and soda. It was fun but felt like a show. Plus, would this guy be my stepdad someday? You never knew. I knew my mom. Linda liked to be courted. Linda liked new things. She relished the attention and excitement.

To help pay the bills, my mom "moved" into the living room - my brother and I kept our shared bedroom - and we rented out the other bedroom. It felt odd to have a stranger in our home all the time. The young woman stayed out of our way for the most part. She did have an interesting boyfriend who decided to draw the cover of Def Leppard's "Pyromania" on the wall next to the bed. It actually looked pretty good, but my mom wasn't happy about it. When they weren't home, I used to sneak in to stare at the picture of a building blowing up. We left the apartment pretty soon after that.

* * *

My mom moved us back down to Charleston. We were back in the trailer park off of Eighteenth Street, this time without my dad. I was only a few months into second grade. I felt distraught and lonely even. I had good friends before we moved, both in the neighborhood and at school. I would never see them again.

For some reason, the second bedroom of our two-bedroom trailer my mom rented was completely filled with building materials and random items, which made it unhabitable. So like our last year in Chicago Ridge, my mom slept on the couch, while my brother and I shared the only bedroom. This time it was a queen bed and since we both still wet the bed occasionally, we did a lot of laundry.

Maybe it was because I was older, but I felt the smallness of the trailer more and the dozen or so other trailers seemed more run down than before too. I felt the cold in the winter. Bugs would come in and we always had flies. We were the last trailer on the lot. From our living room area I could watch people smoking outside of the laundromat next door. Sometimes my mom joined them. She would put a load of clothes in to wash and walk back and forth to our trailer. This was much better than us all sitting in the laundromat, waiting hours for our clothes to be clean.

You could also see a Chinese restaurant in the little strip mall beside the laundromat, but we never ate there. Behind us was a little field that bumped up to a middle school, a community pool and a parking lot. There was an abandoned service station next to the laundromat in front of the field. I spent many hours, alone, just kicking a soccer ball off that blank wall after school.

Right in front of our trailer, where we parked, was a little supermarket. To get into the trailer park, you'd have to drive between the supermarket and laundromat. We were hidden from the street in that way.

I went to Mark Twain Elementary nearby. I felt like an outsider right away, especially since we moved after school already started. Everyone had known each other there too since preschool. I was the only one from the trailer park as they all lived in nearby houses. I started to feel even more poor. I made friends quickly, but we only played and talked at school. I almost hardly ever went to anyone's house and I certainly never had anyone over to my "house." Wetting the bed made me too nervous to go to a sleepover anyway.

The one time I was invited to a friend's birthday party, I was mortified. I sat there as Pete opened up He-Man figures, G.I. Joes . . . and then the embarrassing coloring book my mom bought.

"Um, thanks?" Pete fake smiled.

I felt shame over and over that year.

At school, a girl was gone for two weeks and she came back filled with stories about Europe. Other kids went to Disney World. I had never been on "vacation" before. The idea seemed inconceivable.

I knew we used food stamps in the past to pay for items at the grocery store. We relied on them more now. We also started going to a church nearby for blocks of cheese (which I grew to like), powdered milk (I grew to hate) and peanut butter (indifferent, as long as it was creamy) among other things. We almost never bought name-brand food and if I saw Oreos cookies or Lay's potato chips at school or elsewhere, I would have to pretend to not be that excited, even though I couldn't wait to eat as much as possible. I wondered if kids in my class were grateful or knew how lucky they were to afford real food. I was jealous.

In Charleston, I found a friend I could relate to, a boy named Justin. He lived right next to the trailer park in a brown row of "apartments." They were smaller than trailers, put together in a brown strip of four or five little living areas. I never was invited inside and it was always dark when I peeked behind the door when Justin came out. His mom was always hidden. I met his dad once, but then he was gone. Justin mumbled about him being in jail for something he didn't do. We didn't talk about it. He had a little brother and sister. We'd kick around a ball, playing in the nearby field or park. Throw rocks. Justin had more of a temper than other kids, but I had to take what I could get. We made the best of it.

My mom worked at the same daycare she worked at before. My four-year old brother stayed with her there and I'd go too after school sometimes, playing board games with other kids. I learned to cheat at Clue, even though I didn't have to since most of the kids were younger. It was boring otherwise. My friend Max from when we were little was there too, but he seemed "off" and I didn't like playing with him as much. I'm pretty sure he had special needs, but as a kid I just thought he was rough and loud. My mom was still friends with his mom, Maria, so he was in my life whether I liked it or not.

We didn't see my dad that much since he was three hours away. And when we did, it wasn't like before, where we could drive up to Chicago and have a wealth of things to do. We'd go to the park. We'd visit Abraham Lincoln's relative's house or graves. We'd go to the woods. I didn't mind though because it was good to see him, even for a short time. We hardly ever saw the rest of my family, so I missed both of my Nanas and Papa.

During the cold winter in the trailer, we had needles everywhere from our sad Christmas tree. Talking to my dad on the phone was a nice escape. He always had such a tender voice. So much so that when I'd lie in bed at night, I'd replay him in my head over and over softly saying, "I love you and miss you. Good night, Chris . . . good night." It soothed me.

To help with his absence, my mom did sign me up for a "Big Brother" through Big Brothers Big Sisters. Basically, Dave would pick me up once a week or so and we'd get something to eat, go to his apartment, play Atari and just generally hang out. He was a nice guy in his twenties. He used to be in the Army and even gave me his camouflaged hat, which I almost exclusively wore for the next year, because I thought it made me look cool. A highlight with Dave was seeing my first R-rated movie, *Witness* with Harrison Ford, which also had some surprise nudity. Thanks, Dave!

I only hung out with Dave for a few months. He gave me some neat books, but he also introduced me to *Mad* and

Cracked magazines, which blew my mind at that age. They were smart, funny and I loved every inch of them, even the secret little drawings in the margins of *Mad*.

More than those magazines, I loved *The Adventures of Huckleberry Finn* by Mark Twain around this time. That one I got from school, which was having kind of a banner year being called Mark Twain Elementary and all. It was also 1986 and the return of Halley's Comet, which only appears every seventy-five years or so. The last time it was visible from Earth was 1910, the year Twain died and it just so happened that Twain was born a few weeks after the Comet's previous return in 1835. The two were intertwined mysteriously. Of course, around the time of the Comet's return, my classmates and I gathered in the gymnasium to chant or sing something related to it like kids do. Clearly, the world was talking about Mark Twain, which got the school into its namesake and I was swept along with it, reading a book that changed my life.

I felt alone and adored Huck Finn. Huck was alone like me. Sure, he had Tom Sawyer and Jim, but he was poor and largely on his own left to his own wits. He was funny. He was brave. That moment towards the end when he decides not to turn in Jim, who was a slave on the run, but more importantly his friend, just broke my mind and heart wide open. He was fiercely independent.

"You gotta read this book. It's an older one, but the story is awesome . . ." I started to tell Justin, but in the middle of relaying the story, I slowly realized he was at a remedial level in school.

"Why are you reading outside of school?" Sneered Justin. I shrugged.

I was independent, whether I wanted to be or not. I used to walk to school alone, which took about fifteen minutes. I'd get home sometimes and my mom would give me money to go to the grocery store next to our trailer because she was "too tired or sick and couldn't leave." It was a little scary the first time, but I powered through. It felt like a secret mission to get some staples like milk or crackers. Plus, with the money left over I could buy myself a magazine, scratch n' sniff stickers, Garbage Pail Kids or Wacky Packages trading cards. Every now and then, the cashier would look at me and my little note like, "What is this seven year old kid doing here shopping by himself?" I would let them know it was okay and lived right behind the store. I don't know if that reassured them all that much. I felt like a grownup. I felt like Huck Finn.

One time, I was over swimming at my mom's friend's house in the late Spring, and this girl Shannon sat with us on the pool deck. She was a neighbor and I adored her. Shannon went to leave and out of nowhere said, "You both are cute, but Chris, I've always wanted to do this."

She kissed me on the cheek, gave me her white ponytail hair band and walked home. Nothing ever happened after that between us and I'm still bewildered by it. Of course, I held on to that hair band for an embarrassingly long time.

Later that day, my mom's friends had cable TV and let me watch *Purple Rain*. I had always liked Prince. My mom had his first records, and we listened to the *1999* album constantly, plus the video for "Little Red Corvette" was on all the time in Chicago Ridge. But *Purple Rain*? Those songs changed everything. We got the soundtrack from the library and I never stopped listening to it. "When Doves Cry" was on non-stop on the radio too. Like Prince's heels from his videos, the lyrics about his mother and father on "When Doves Cry" always left me mystified. It stuck with me. My mom's favorite from the record was "Take Me With U." I liked "Darling Nikki" even though I didn't know what it meant either. My favorite was "I Would Die 4 U," which made me think of Shannon and that first kiss.

I didn't have to wait long though for Shannon to leave my mind. One day in the summer of 1985, everything changed again.

✳ ✳ ✳

My mom suddenly declared we were moving to Tinley Park from Charleston, just like we did years earlier with my dad. This time was definitely different. We were moving in with my Nana Dody and husband Hal in their house in a suburban community by 159th and Harlem. I was only eight and this was the fifth time I was uprooted. Even at that age, I got the feeling like every time I started to settle in and get comfortable, cementing some friendships and finding a sort of stability, everything shattered and I had to start over.

However, I was okay with leaving the trailer in some ways and moving into a more "normal" environment. A house! Up to this point, I had never lived in a proper house, just trailers and apartments. My brother and I still shared a room, but it was on the second floor - the house had two floors! - and we had separate beds. Also, Nana had this big framed picture in the room already of an old timey street scene. At night if you switched it on, all the windows and light posts would light up. We also had a television to ourselves and an Atari to play games.

Plus, while Hal was quiet and strict, my Nana was always loving and kind to us. Hal was kind in his own way, but kept to himself. He was an auto mechanic and a WWII veteran who apparently saw some serious action in the Navy. I never was told the whole story, just bits and pieces. My childhood brain remembers a tale where his ship was blown up and he was one of the only survivors, which is probably partly true. That's why he was so quiet. He did give me an allowance to water the garden and help him with other odd jobs, which was the first time I received money for work. I'd still get in trouble eating all his pretzels, but they tasted so good with the Canfield's Chocolate Fudge soda Nana would give me.

Life seemed good for a moment. Sure, we were living with my grandma, which wasn't like other kids at school, but my brother and I finally returned to fun Saturdays with dad. We saw my other Nana more. We visited my Papa at the garden center where he worked. My uncle got married and I was in his wedding.

My brother and I not only had our room to hang out in, but also the basement largely to ourselves, where we watched cable television, including the Disney channel and Nickelodeon every morning and after school. We watched MTV at night. We also had a backyard, with fun neighbors behind us. At some point, we even had a sandbox.

I started third grade. I was hesitant to make new friends, fearing we'd be moving again, but at that age, you can't help it. I always tried to fit in by making kids laugh and before I knew it, I had friends again, at school and in the neighborhood. School was easy and like I mentioned earlier, they wanted to put me in fourth grade, but my parents vetoed it again.

One day, my classmates and I all sat in a gym watching the Space Shuttle Challenger unexpectedly blow up and the shocked teachers tried to explain what happened. Another day, I lost a tooth during a school assembly, which left me with such a bloody shirt that I had to leave early.

* * *

My mom was dating again, but not as much as before moving to Charleston. My dad however, never talked about other women after the divorce, until he met someone playing music at a club on the north side of Chicago. Nancy. They both played a few songs at an open mic and hit it off. We didn't meet her right away, but after a few months, she was at Nana Madge's house and we all had dinner together. Nancy was nice, with kind eyes, long brown hair, always smiling, and walked with a cane, her hips dipping with each step. My dad said it's due to cerebral palsy as a child. She had never been married or had kids and lived in Chicago with a roommate. Nancy taught English at community college, played music and clearly loved my dad. We didn't see her every Saturday, but definitely a lot more.

One time, my dad, Nancy, my brother and I were out on a Saturday and my dad dropped us off at Maria Mueller's apartment for a sleepover. This was the same Maria from Charleston, who now lived up in Palos Hills with her two kids since her husband died a few years prior. My mom was going to pick us up the next morning since she had a date that night.

I played with Max, which was fine when we were two and three years old, but now I had a hard time adjusting to his mental handicap. I tried to just get us to watch TV. We went to sleep and when I woke up the next morning, I was packing my things to leave and couldn't find the Transformers action figure my dad had bought me the day before.

"Have you seen it?" I asked Max and Maria.

"Nope."

Maria didn't seem that concerned.

I was sure it was with me and called my dad the next day to see if he had it. I sometimes left toys in his car. He didn't.

It made no sense. It wouldn't just disappear! I had this on my mind the next time we slept over, because I had a brand new *Return of the Jedi* shirt my dad had bought me at the flea market. I was excited about the shirt and was considering sleeping in it, but I didn't want to be that conspicuous. Instead, I strategically put it right next to my bag where I slept.

The next morning, it was gone.

I asked Max. He didn't remember even seeing it.

"Are you sure you brought it over?" Maria asked.

Max was a nice kid and frankly, I don't think he was smart enough to take it. Maria though? It just upset and confused me. Why would my mom's friend steal my toys and clothes?

I told my mom, who brushed it off.

You can't trust anyone, not even grown-ups sometimes.

Soon after, my dad and Nancy got married in a small ceremony. It was during the week and my brother and I didn't go for some reason. I found out about it from my mom when I got home from school. I was a little sad about it, but mostly confused.

The next Saturday, we went to Nancy's - and now my dad's - apartment in Chicago to see her. She was friendlier than usual and over pizza for dinner, it sunk in that she was my stepmother now. Did I have to call her mom? How does all that work? On the drive home to Tinley Park from Chicago with my dad and my brother,

I contemplated my new "mom."

"Dad, now that Nancy is technically my stepmom, do I have to call her Mom? I mean, it's not like I don't like her, but it would be weird I think."

"No, you can call her whatever you like. Is that okay?"

"I'll call her Nancy then."

I took a breath.

"Why couldn't we go to the wedding? Were kids not supposed to be there?"

"No, your mom said you couldn't go."

✻ ✻ ✻

Marriage. It was in the air apparently.

Around the time that my dad and Nancy got married, my mom started dating someone new. We didn't see him much during that time, except for when he picked her up. I gleaned bits and pieces over the months. He drove a black SUV - a Chevy Blazer - before they were called SUVs. He was tall and bald except for short dark, hair around the sides. Big guy, but not fat. Worked at a factory. Liked sports. Had a three-bedroom house in a nice part of Oak Forest, about ten minutes away.

He also had two girls, one a year older than me and the other was a year younger. They lived with their mom in Mokena, which was about thirty minutes away. He didn't have the same visitation schedule as my dad and saw them every few months.

I didn't go to their wedding either, although I was told it was happening. My mom got married at the courthouse and just like that, my brother and I had a stepdad.

We slowly moved out of Nana Dody's house, waiting until the school year ended to move in completely. I said goodbye to all my friends. Again. I would miss Nana, but I know she was happy for her daughter. It made sense.

My brother and I shared a room at our new house, as we were told the other belonged to the girls. It was about the same size as before, but we got bunk beds for the first time, which made it seem bigger. I started fourth grade at another school, nervous as usual, but hopeful this would be my school district for many years to come, which made the transition easier. After four elementary schools and four years in a trailer park in poverty, this was another upgrade.

The neighborhood had lots of kids. We played kickball on the street. Skateboarded on every surface. Swam in pools. Explored the creek and forests around the houses. Played freeze tag all over. Everything kids in the suburbs did, we did it. I started sleeping over at my friend's houses, regardless of the fact that I still wet the bed, which made for some embarrassing mornings. I had to sleep on the floor at my best friend Jordan's house, as his mom was tired of washing the sheets every morning and it was easier just to scrub the pee out of the carpet. No one slept at my house because I shared a room with my little brother, which I was still embarrassed by.

Jordan had much older siblings so he was almost like an only child. His family had money too, since his dad had a good construction job. He was spoiled and I loved it, even though it just reminded me of how much we didn't have at our house. Sure my brother and I finally had our own Nintendo, but Jordan had Nintendo, the Power Glove and the fancy controllers along with every game you wanted. I had my few G.I. Joe action figures, but Jordan had the actual eight-foot-long G.I. Joe aircraft carrier. More importantly, he had a finished basement that he used as a playroom and a fridge stocked with name brand soda and snacks. My mom still used food stamps, so we continued to buy almost everything generic at Aldi or the grocery store.

✳ ✳ ✳

My stepdad was unlike my dad in almost every way. Not in a bad way. Just different. Where my dad loved his guitars and rock music, my new stepdad didn't own any music and only listened to "soft rock" or "lite rock" music, the kind of in-offensive songs made for dentist's offices. Where my dad went through a (sometimes very) used car every year or so, my stepdad had his nicer new SUV and bought a minivan for my mom. He even had a boat.

My dad was curious and thoughtful, and my stepdad didn't seem to have many opinions on anything but football, food and our house. I don't mean that negatively, but he literally went to work, came home, changed into sweatpants with no shirt, ate dinner (rarely would we eat as a family - my brother and I would eat at a table downstairs and my mom and stepdad upstairs) and then he'd lie on the couch watching TV until he went to bed. He went through the motions of life, no more, no less. I don't remember a time that my dad and stepdad ever talked to each other. I'm sure they had to at some point, but I only remember awkward pick-ups and drop-offs with my mom and my dad at the front door on Saturdays.

My dad was soft spoken and rarely was provoked to any type of anger. My stepdad had a temper and had a wooden curtain rod he kept on top of the fridge that he'd break out like a bat if we misbehaved. I don't remember him actually using it and if he did, it was on my brother, not me. If he got really upset he'd take his belt off and make a whip-like sound that snapped you right back in line. He was a towering figure, so even without the stick, he intimidated us. If he raised his voice, that would be enough to shut you up. My mom tried once or twice to use the curtain rod to keep us in line, but it didn't suit her, so she'd use a wooden spoon to threaten us, one time breaking it over my head for swearing.

Although my stepdad wasn't "rich," he was good with money and stretched it as far as he could to provide as much as possible. We eventually went on our first vacation ever when he took us to the Wisconsin Dells. He didn't see his girls that often and my mom would tell us that he was a little disappointed to never have sons of his own. He put in a basketball hoop in the driveway. He had a pool built in the backyard. He wasn't overly involved in the lives of me and my brother, but if you asked him to drive you somewhere or if we could use the TV to watch something special, he'd oblige. Just don't touch the damn thermostat.

I finally stopped wetting the bed when puberty hit. Otherwise, puberty hit me the same as everyone else and I became even more obsessed with girls. My locker in middle school had rotating pictures of the young female TV stars of the time like Alyssa Milano or Danica McKellar. I would wait all day, agonizing for that little moment to see a secret crush in the hallway at school. I hardly ever did anything about it.

I had fun birthday parties at the local roller rink and other places around town. I had mono in middle school, missing school for two weeks. It's known as the "kissing disease," but I never kissed anyone really before getting it. Of course, I didn't tell anyone that. Why sink my status even lower?

I wasn't popular. It could've been the braces. The social anxiety. The knock-off name brand clothes from the flea market or Payless shoes. The fact that my mom only took us to beauty schools for cheap haircuts. The visible awkwardness of puberty. I was shy and insecure. Big surprise.

❈ ❈ ❈

I was settling into our new suburban life nicely and it flowed out of my fingertips.

Even though my brother and I shared a room, I had my own desk. I would spend countless hours listening to music from a little boombox on the end while I drew pictures from comic books. I didn't draw much from scratch and got pretty good at recreating pictures of the Teenage Mutant Ninja Turtles, Daredevil and Batman from posters and comic covers.

I would spend time writing too. I always wrote little plays and stories, but in seventh grade, I had a teacher, Mrs. Egli, who tapped into a part of my brain I didn't know I had for some fun writing. Every week, one of the exercises was to write a one-page story in our spiral notebook based all around a short writing prompt, which would be a phrase like "If I Were President," "We Interrupt This Program," "A Christmas Fantasy" and so on. On Friday, anyone who wanted to could stand up at the front of class and read their story. Almost from the beginning, it became standard that I would kick off the readings. It was the only time I was comfortable talking in front of other students.

I wrote the most ridiculous, dark, funny, crazy stories, trying to fit in as many unexpected twists as I could to get laughs from the class. Santa was murdered. There were epic battles between vengeful sorcerers. In one story, I was God. I took the prompts as a challenge to write the most outlandish things I could.

Not only was I still into comic books, but I was still yearning for more cassettes and now video games more than ever, especially as I moved into middle school. I was into trading cards and baseball cards for a short while. Mostly ones for movies like *Batman* and others, because I still didn't follow sports. All of these habits cost money and it didn't help that the desire was never ending, but my resources were. There were always new comics, music and games. I would mow the lawn for our neighbors and make about ten dollars each, but that would only get me a few cassettes (and CDs later on). I even babysat here and there.

My mom suggested that since I liked riding my bike so much, why don't I deliver newspapers? There was a free *Penny Saver* paper that almost everyone got on Monday and another subscriber-based one that was delivered on Mondays and Thursdays. I started delivering both around my neighborhood, each taking me about two hours to wrap the papers at my house and then deliver them. I suddenly had more money to spend and it felt amazing.

And when it wasn't enough, I stole. I felt awful about it. But it was so easy. I would buy my comics at the store and on the way out, hide a graphic novel I wanted behind my bag while the owner was distracted. When I was at the store with my mom, I would slide some trading card packages into my coat while she shopped on the other side of the store. A little bit here and there.

I didn't think much of it until I got a little cocky for my own good. I got caught stealing comics at a comic book convention when I split off with my friends. I barely got away and gave security a friend's phone number when they asked for my parents' number. I knew my friend didn't have an answering machine so it would just ring and ring. They kicked me out and I made up some story to my friends about knocking over a box of comics and some asshole getting upset and kicking me out. They believed me and we left soon after. My secret was safe, but I didn't steal again after that.

I worked harder instead. In the summer after eighth grade, I got a job at the country club nearby, caddying and then working on the driving range picking up golf balls. It was good money and a little surreal spending the day with the more well-to-do folks in town figuring out what club to give them and listening to them talk about middle-aged life. We got free food at the halfway house. We drove golf carts all over, racing from the driving range to different holes on the course. They let us play a game on Mondays and hit balls any day if the range was free, but I would rather sit around with the other caddies trying chewing tobacco and talking about girls. By that point, the eighth-grade dance gave me some solid ground to stand on with the opposite sex.

On the home front, my mom drank, but not to the point where I noticed it every day. We spent a lot of time together. Driving me to soccer practice - the only sport I played for a few years - or to the video store and comic book store. Singing to Prince in the car. Helping me study for tests when I needed it. Belting out "rise and shine" annoyingly in the morning when she woke us up. Asking me about girls I liked and talking to them on the phone as if they were her friends when they called. It wasn't all bad.

This was the suburban life she always wanted. The life she desired that my dad couldn't or didn't want to provide. A life where she talked for hours on end with friends lighting cigarette after cigarette in the dining room. A life where she was perpetually looking for jobs, but never needing to work. She shopped when she wanted too. She could spend afternoons working on her tan in the backyard. She made it. Plateaued, in a sense.

My brother and I still saw my dad on Saturdays. On other days, my mom, brother and I visited Nana Dody and Hal at her house and Papa at the garden center. I relished when Papa came over as he always had good stories. I idolized him and the mysterious air around him, never quite understanding what he used to do at Philip Morris, but could tell it seemed important and he was successful. I did wonder why he was working at a garden center now instead of still meeting celebrities at his old job. My mom was always happy too when Papa was around. She lit up.

Papa also spoiled us. Most notably, after finding out I aced my school's test on the Constitution in seventh grade, he took me on my first trip on an airplane to Washington, D.C. for a few days. It was an unforgettable experience, but I was confused about why he had a big bottle of vodka in his suitcase and why airport security was asking him about it. I found a bottle in our hotel room too.

A year after our trip to see the real Constitution, right before I started high school, Papa died of lung cancer. He was sixty-three years old. It was hard and the first death I really felt. It left a hell of a mark on my mom too. When she got the call that he had passed, I was in my room and I instantly knew what the call was. She let out a loud, chilling wail as if she herself was dying.

She was never quite the same after that.

DIVE

November 1992

I wake up later than usual. The house is quiet. I put on the *Mama Said* CD by Lenny Kravitz that I've been obsessed with lately and the song "All I Ever Wanted" fills the air.

I stretch. No school today.

Well, there is school for everyone else. I'm suspended for a few days. The good kind: two days of out-of-school suspension.

I've had in-school suspension before, known as Model Disciplinary Program, but everyone calls it MDP. This beats that. You not only have to go to school for MDP, but you are quarantined in a room with other no-gooders. There is a window looking out to the library hallway, serving as a portal to the world where you do your work and watch the whole school day go by. It feels like jail and kids treat you as such.

"Oooh, saw you in MDP the other day. What did you do?"

The first few times, it's cool, but now it's just annoying. Sometimes I don't mind getting away from everything. And even though MDP is technically supposed to be the next level of disciplinary action after detention, I'd prefer MDP. Saturday detention is four long hours in the morning. I bring a book, the latest *Rolling Stone* magazine, or just doodle, but it's still painful. After-school detention is only like forty-five minutes and I haven't had it in a while. I'm usually late enough or miss a class or two - or three, okay, fine, sometimes the whole day - which brings me right to the next tier of fun on the dean's list of punishment.

Being told to stay home is a rarity. This whole situation is rare.

I mean, I didn't plan on getting into a fight.

My head hurts thinking about the whole situation and I'm transported back to yesterday morning. I'm talking to my girlfriend Kim by her locker. Since she's a year younger and a freshman, her locker is in a different area and one reason I'm late so often. She's telling me about this kid Lucas that is in one of her classes and keeps bugging her. She thinks he likes her, so he's annoying about it and been writing notes.

"What an ass. Doesn't he know you have a boyfriend? Want me to talk to him?" I say, not really knowing how to handle this.

I'm aware of Lucas because he has a brother in my grade, but don't actually know either of them that well. They are neither that popular or athletic. They are just there. They both are about my height, but slightly skinnier too.

"No, it's fine. I'll figure it out."

We kiss quickly and she's off. The bell rings and I'm late for American Literature. Awesome.

After class, I run into Chad, Lucas's brother. Well, he runs into me.

"What's up, man? I hear you been saying shit about my brother?"

Damn, okay. Word travels way too fast! I don't say anything. I immediately think that Kim said something way too harsh to Lucas. But what could she -

"Yeah, man, my boy heard you talking in the hallway like you're all that. Lucas is pissed. You ready for that?"

Now I'm pissed. I barely said anything to Kim in the hall about this dude and now someone is gonna step to me? I just want it all to end. I can't back down in front of everyone, so I laugh and make myself seem taller.

"Oh, I'm ready. For your *punk-ass* little brother. Is *he* ready?"

I'm shaking and my heart is racing. I walk past him, making sure to bump his arm and shoulder. The wheels were officially in motion.

What the hell was I doing? Aside from a small slap in the face here and there in eighth grade, I don't know a thing about fighting except for what I've seen in movies.

The next two classes are a blur. I see Kim and she's worried that this might actually happen. I don't tell her I'm worried, I just play it cool. Right after that, there is

Lucas hanging by my locker.

Shit.

"So what's up, man? I hear you are talking smack and you say you're gonna take me down?" Lucas says with his arms up like he's in a damn teen movie or something.

A crowd is gathering. Of course. I walk up close to him.

"Yeah, so what? I didn't care about you yesterday and now you're a pain in my ass. Let's go."

I don't even think about what I'm saying. All pure adrenaline. The crowd is gathering. This either needs to happen now or a teacher will be here any minute to stop it. I'm not that stupid.

"No, no. After school. Three thirty. Across the street behind Oak Foods."

He smiles and walks away. The crowd murmurs and I feel hands on my back.

"Oh, I can't wait to see this."

"Morris, you're gonna kill that kid."

"I hope you change. You're too dressed up to fight."

I am wearing my one nice pair of Girbaud pants and shirt, along with a long, thin black jacket. I look way too preppy to fight. There's no way I have time to change though. I'm scared, but everything seems heightened and I know I have to go through with this.

Kim begs me to not do it, but I think she secretly wants me to fight. After all, in some weird way, aren't I fighting for her?

Kim's older sister, Alicia, and her boyfriend, Dale, drive me over to the Oak Foods parking lot across from the school before the fight. They are both juniors and Alicia has a car. It's close enough to walk, but Kim wants a car there in case something bad happens.

"We barely know them. What if Lucas brings a whole bunch of guys and they all jump in?"

She has a point. I haven't been in enough fights - well, any fights - to know how things go down.

Lucas is already there with his brother and some other kids that I assume are his friends. Some of my friends are there too and I nod at Dan and Andy. Of course, there are gawkers.

I put on some light fleece gloves earlier just to protect my hands on top of being a bit cold. And aren't you supposed to wear gloves to a fight? I walk to the middle of the parking lot and punch my hands together.

"So what's up? You want to actually do this?"

He walks up and before I know what's happening, he pushes me and punches me in the eye as I'm falling down.

Sucker punched. What a dick.

I get up and just start hammering him in the face, back

and forth in a rage.

I can feel my hands start to bleed underneath my gloves. I don't even see Lucas anymore, just a blur as I try to focus every ounce of anger into his head.

He stops trying to push back or anything else. When he hits the ground, I'm about to jump on top of him, but his brother steps in and I can feel Kim trying to pull me away.

"It's over, man. It's over. Just let him be," Chad says.

I finally see Lucas's face and his forehead is a bloody mess. My fists hurt and I catch my breath. I don't know what else to say so we get in Alicia's car. The whole thing is over in minutes.

We drop off Dale and while Kim and I are waiting for them to say their goodbyes. I see Stan, a junior I kind of know from Biology summer school, walk up to the car. Does he live near here?

"Hey, what's up? I just heard about that fight. Man, people are ready to throw down. Chris, let me see your hands."

"What? Why?"

Throw down? Didn't we just end all this? I take off my gloves anyway. Stan is a big guy. Like football big.

"Aw, man. They all think you were wearing rings under the gloves. His face is all fucked up. Huh, your hands are bruised, but I don't see anything. Damn, man. Fists of fury!"

"So what's that mean? Are people looking for me?"

"Man, Lucas knows Nate and some other guys that are some wanna-be gangsters and maybe a couple real ones. Just be careful."

Shit, I don't know Nate that well, but he's a scary dude. Definitely dresses like a gangster too.

"Thanks, Stan. If you see anyone, please let them know all is good and it was a fair fight."

Alicia is back in the car now and we drive off. Just when I was starting to relax, I'm more scared now than I was this morning.

Rather than go back to Kim's as I usually would, I just have her take me to my house. I just want to lie down in my own bed and chill out. I'm not sure if any of those guys know where I live anyway.

My stepdad isn't home yet and my brother is upstairs in his room. I heat up a breaded chicken patty in the microwave as I do most nights.

Mom is in the kitchen though. Half sober. Lately she starts drinking in the afternoon and is a mess by the evening. Around dinner time, she has a foot in both worlds. Part mom, part zombie.

"What happened?"

Apparently, I have a black eye. I hadn't looked yet.

I tell her I was sucker punched after school. She gets the

sanitized version where I'm the victim.

"It's fine. I did fight back, but he punched me first. I did what I had to do."

"We'll see at school tomorrow. I have a feeling you'll be in trouble regardless. I can give you, um, some concealer though for your eye so it doesn't look so bad."

"Like make-up? I don't know."

"CJ, it's skin-colored. No one will know and you'll look totally fine. Don't you trust me?"

Worth a try. She shows me how to put it on upstairs and she's right. You can hardly tell. Huh.

At school the next day, I get hard looks by everyone and I'm in the dean's office area before my first class. The teachers must have had a warrant out on me or something.

I sit outside the dean's office. In walks Lucas. His face is bruised and has a band-aid over one eye. He looks like he was in a fight. I don't. Thanks, Mom!

"So what's up? Are we good?" I say, trying to break the ice. What else can we do at this point?

"Nah, man, that wasn't cool. Look at this." He points to his face. "You were wearing rings, man. That ain't fair. Normal hands couldn't have done this. You're gonna get yours."

"Dude, I wasn't wearing rings. I - "

The dean comes out and then we're both sitting in his office. We hear a speech about no fighting on or off school grounds between students. We both apologize to each other in front of the dean. Next thing I know, I'm walking home.

*　*　*

Even though I'm suspended, I talk my way into going over to Kim's for dinner. I don't even think my stepdad knew I was suspended and my mom probably forgot already and just thought I was sick. I don't care. I just need to see Kim.

Immediately, in her living room, Kim starts telling me about the aftermath. Lucas has Nate and other guys out looking for me, apparently to kick my ass in retaliation for an unfair fight. He has connections with the Vice Lords and the Kings too? Great. It could all be rumors, but I still fade out a bit.

I'm having a hard time taking this all in. It doesn't help that as I'm eating dinner in the kitchen with Kim and her mom, I see a car drive by in front of her house. It stops for a moment, then drives off. It's odd, but odder when in about twenty minutes, it's back again and does the same thing. I recognize Nate in the passenger seat this time.

"Oh no, I think they're waiting for me to leave."

"Should we call the police? This is getting too scary, Chris. I don't know . . ."

"No, let's think about this. That might just complicate things even further or make them worse."

We talk and make a plan. I can't fight Nate and his friends. I sure as hell am not taking on any Chicago gangs. That's out of the question. I need to somehow prove that I wasn't wearing rings in the first place to stop all this. Stan is the only outside person to see the truth. Stan! The missing piece and the guy is invincible. I just needed to get Stan on board.

I call my stepdad to pick me up. He protests, but I tell him it's important and he does. He doesn't ask why I plead with him to specifically park in their driveway as close to their front door as possible. I jump in the van and we are off and home in ten minutes. I don't see any cars by my house, which is good.

The next day, I walk to school and take only side streets, looking everywhere. It dawns on me that I don't know where Nate or any of these guys live. Even Lucas.

I know I should be okay once I reach school. As crazy as these guys might be, almost no one actually fights at school as it's too risky. Suspension. Possible expulsion. Police.

I don't even go to my locker. Instead, I walk straight to the junior wing of the school, looking for Stan. He's tall so I spot him right away.

"Hey, Morris, what's up, man? Heard things are -"

"Yeah, Stan. I need your help. Since that fight, you were

so right! They are all acting crazy for no reason. They've got Nate Ashton and some other guys after me because they think I was wearing rings."

"I heard. That's messed up -"

"Listen, you were there. You saw my hands. I'm not about to fight a bunch of dudes for nothing or get beat down. Can you help me out?"

"I'll talk with Nate. I'm sure it's nothing. But if it is more than this, that's on you."

"Of course, of course. It's got to be just this. I don't know what else it could be. Thanks, man."

I am so thankful Stan plays football. I am so thankful we sat next to each other in Biology last summer and I made him laugh. I might've even gave him an answer here and there. This just might work.

I see Kim and tell her everything is going to be fine. I go to class and try not to act like someone is going to pounce on me right after I walk out of the door. That doesn't last long. Right before lunch, I see Nate who runs towards me. Shit, this is it.

"Hey! I just want to talk to you for a sec," he says, seemingly out of breath.

I look around nervously.

"Yeah, it seems like you've been wanting to for awhile. What's up? I thought I saw your car the other day too. Starting to scare my girlfriend."

"I know, I know. Look, I'm sorry."

Wait, what?

"It's all a big misunderstanding. I talked to Stan and it's good. Lucas must've been talking shit because he lost. We okay?"

Stan the man. This is crazy.

"Yeah, it's all good. Just glad we can all move on. So no more drive-bys?"

"No, no . . ."

The bell rings and he's off.

Kim's relieved when I tell her. She was about to tell her parents I think, which would've added to the drama, but I get it. It's scary when people are circling your family's house because of your boyfriend's antics.

I run into Stan as he is leaving the lunchroom.

"Yo, I just saw Nate and he apologized. I don't know what you did, but you're awesome. Thanks, man."

"Ha, yeah, he started acting hard, but once I picked him up against the lockers and all that and told him I was there at the fight and saw with my own eyes that you didn't have no rings on, he had a change of heart."

"Damn. Thanks again. I owe you one."

I'm happy, but still annoyed at the whole thing. You win a battle but somehow start a small war. Story of my life.

I'd give anything for one normal day.

* * *

I'm at dinner again with Kim and her family. I look at Kim and smile, thinking about how I got so lucky. Kim has been my longest relationship so far. Four months since August. She's fourteen, brunette, brown eyes, prettier than most girls and half Mexican from her dad's side. Her parents seem to like me, which is great since I'm over here after school most days and even before school sometimes. I'd rather walk the forty-five minutes than be in my house. I don't like being home unless I have to be.

Her dad works in a manufacturing plant and her mom works in an office. Kim shares a room with Alicia. Their older sister, who we never see, lives downstairs off of the living room. They have a gentle Rottweiler who likes me too. As time goes by, it feels more like home than my own, similar to Dan's last year. Before I could sense danger inside our house, now I feel it even in the neighborhood, coming down the street when I'm close.

Kim and I have only kissed and that's it. She's pretty adamant about taking things slow and that's fine. We're together so much outside of school, I'm sure the whole school thinks we've done it already.

Kim's family must've picked up about my mom, because they started to treat me like their own and didn't complain when they had another mouth to feed at dinner. I was grateful, even if I didn't say it loud.

"How's work going?" Kim's mom asks me, handing me another slice of pizza.

"Not bad, the cash every night is great."

I started as a waiter at Ponderosa, a steakhouse on 159th, a couple weeks ago. It's been better than my last job so far.

"I like it a lot. It's a good gig, because aside from the entree, you know everything else is served on a buffet, so you end up just refilling sodas and dropping off their steaks! It's a little bit more money in tips and hours than I made as a busboy at Jack Gibbons steakhouse. I'd work more if I could, but I'm not sixteen yet, so my hours and jobs are limited. Also, they have an ice cream bar, which is awesome at any age."

They laugh.

The pizza is good. Homemade. I think about work while I eat and I'm actually doing alright so far, even though I was nervous to be a waiter for the first time. I only messed up once when two tables ordered the exact same thing. I was busy and after delivering the first order of steaks, the second came up and I thought, "I just put these out, the kitchen must have messed up." And promptly ate both steaks. Fast forward to ten minutes later and an angry couple asking why their T-bones are taking too long. Whoops. Blamed it on the cooks.

Ponderosa is close to Kim's. Only a ten-minute walk. Sometimes she meets me after and we walk back together with some ice cream. It's pretty great.

Across the street is the Jewel grocery store, where I can cash my paycheck. The fee is a little less than a currency exchange, which is nice too. At Thanksgiving, where my mom was absent or "not feeling well," my stepdad's mom kept telling me to open up a checking account, but I don't know why. She said I could cash checks for free, but I never could figure out how it all worked. I had an account for a while, but I hated just having money locked away like that. I ended up closing it after a month and just stuck to what I knew. No one taught me this stuff.

I think about last Saturday. I had just refilled a family of four's soda and in walked my dad with my brother. It had been a while since I'd seen him as Kim fills most of my waking hours lately. We talk on the phone every now and then, but that's it. I know he wants to see me more. When I'm home, my brother fills me in on any news and how they fill their Saturday adventures. Around Christmas, when I saw my dad, he sat me down with my stepmom next to him and asked exasperated, "What do you want from us? What do you need?" I just looked at him with a blank stare.

My Nanas I see even less, just on holidays. I miss them all, but I don't know what to say or do.

Unfortunately, it was busy at Ponderosa and I didn't get enough time to chat with him as I'd like. I watched him leave and felt a moment of sadness and jealousy for my brother. But then I was flagged down by the manager because the dishwasher called in sick and I'm suddenly in the back loading dishes into trays while he covered my customers.

Dinner is over and we go upstairs. I wonder what Jack is up to. Or Dan or Andy. I hardly ever see Dan or Andy anymore. I know they're upset about it too, calling me "whipped" every chance they get at school. Jack is a different story.

Jack and I started hanging out in July. He's tall, thin, freckled and while we are in the same grade, we didn't hang out last year. We both started working at Jack Gibbons steakhouse as busboys and then started riding our bikes all over the city, sometimes even miles away to Orland Square Mall or Brementowne Theatre to see a cheap movie. We fell into a routine where we'd meet up at Taco Bell for lunch, plot out our afternoon and ride off. Jack and I had the same sense of humor and soon we were hanging out more and more.

Dan was and is outlandishly funny, but Jack wasn't afraid to act wild at all times, appropriate or not. No dare was off limits. Want him to ride his bike through the Jewel grocery store real quick? Done. He'd ask any girl out at the register at McDonald's, even a grown woman. He'd pretend to fall asleep on the mattresses at the stores in the mall and seemed to actually like being chased out of the store. He killed me.

We were thick as thieves. Well, until I met Kim. He isn't shy about reminding me about it either.

I think it's because Jack was a big help in one of my first big romances earlier in the summer. It came out of nowhere with my friend Ann. We were friends all year. Just friends. Since she struggled with body issues, depression and other stuff I can't remember, we had "group" together, which was when they pulled all the "not normal" kids out of class to gather round and talk with a school counselor, Mrs. Clark.

Like Alateen before, I didn't talk much in the sessions. I would let out a little bit now and then. It helped that Ann was the only person I could open up to about my mom. The truth. I felt like she understood because of her background and her own issues with her dad, which were complicated. She seemed fragile and cried more than anyone I knew. But that was part of what I liked about her. We both were broken in our own ways.

Towards the end of the year, her dad got a job in Lockport, so she was moving in June.

"You have to come be my date to my cousin's wedding in June. Promise?"

"Of course. And I'll call you before then too."

We stayed in touch and she wrote two full pages in my yearbook, longer than anyone else. Not the jokey, stupid stuff about how boring such and such class was or getting laid during the summer. No, she encouraged me to stay strong and stop messing around. With girls, friends, school . . . everything. I know Ann understands it's easier said than done.

I missed her and apparently she missed me, because at her cousin's wedding, sparks flew. The DJ played "Lady in Red" and we slow danced. The whole room slowed. My body felt weak and hot. We almost kissed right there, but knew we couldn't in front of everyone. After the song, we held hands and walked out of the ballroom and kissed in the hallway. It was electrifying.

We talked on the phone after that almost every night. Then we made plans to see each other. After a few more nights of long phone calls, suddenly I was sleeping over somehow.

I told my stepdad and my mom that Jack was staying at his cousin's in Lockport and they dropped me off in the afternoon. But it was actually Ann's house. We hung out, taking long walks, meeting her family again and sometime after dinner, I pretended to wait outside for my ride home. I re-traced the path from the afternoon with Ann, but just myself, walking and waiting for her parents to go to bed.

At about ten o'clock, I walked back to Ann's. The light was on in her room, which was our signal that the coast was clear. I found myself crawling through another basement window, but this time, instead of girls waiting to tease me, I was greeted by a smiling one in her pajamas who kissed me and pushed me down onto her bed.

"Shhh," she said.

"Are you okay?" I could tell she was distracted.

"Sorry, I'm just so nervous someone will hear us."

"We should be good," I said. "If they hear us, I'll just tell them my parents didn't come and we were too embarrassed to say anything, so you let me stay on your floor."

I was getting good at this. Jack had an alibi too in case my parents called for some reason. He'd say we ended up back at his house because he wasn't feeling well and then he'd call Ann's, letting it ring once. That was my cue to go. I didn't think through much after that.

We kissed all night. We didn't do much more as we both got tired. I didn't want to push it and to me, it was liberating enough to just be in another girl's bed when I wasn't really supposed to. My parents didn't know. Her parents didn't either.

At seven in the morning, her alarm went off and I quickly put my shirt on and fixed my hair. I had to go to the bathroom so bad, but couldn't risk it. I could hear footsteps upstairs. Ann looked at me with her big, beautiful eyes.

"Okay, be quiet and be careful. I had so much fun with you."

We kissed again and I held her for a long time. I could feel her crying a little.

"I'll call you tonight," I said.

"I can't believe we did this! We're so bad!"

I snuck back out and quickly ran to the bushes on the side of her house. I peed immediately where no one could see. Then I walked nonchalantly to the sidewalk, towards the little lake we were at yesterday. About a mile away was a gas station with a payphone. I got some chocolate donuts, a Coke and called home.

"Hey, Mom, I know it's early, but Jack's cousin got sick and they ended up taking him to the doctor. It's crazy. Anyway, can you get me? I'm at a Mobil station by their house. I didn't want to be in the way, so I just took a walk."

Too easy. Hey, if my mom can lie all the time, why can't I?

Soon after that, Ann met someone. An older someone that lived closer. I couldn't compete. It hurt, but at the time I was already flirting with girls at work and would meet Kim in August anyway.

Kim is great, but I can't talk to her the way I could with Ann. She knew my mom drank, but I didn't talk about much else. All the dirty details.

Kim and I argue like high school couples do, but we always come back to each other. I'm jealous. She's jealous. What are you gonna do? I still spend almost all my free time with her.

It's nine p.m. and I start the long bike ride home across Oak Forest, wondering what awaits me at home. I ride my normal route through side streets and then on Central Avenue, which is a lot busier, darker, no sidewalks and not a lot of room on the side of the road to ride. But it's the only way really.

I bike on the right side of the street so I can tell when cars are coming behind me by their headlights. This time, I could see lights . . . but they didn't pass. Next thing I know, a car was right next to me with some teens or adults reaching out trying to grab me, either to pull me off my bike, into their car or both.

"Haha! What's up? Get over here, kid," someone yells, while the others laugh in the car.

I'm able to quickly get off my bike and run into the dark forest on the other side of the street, pulling the bike behind me. My heart is pounding out of my chest. I walk deep into the woods, sit and wait. I hear the car stop and them walking around the woods for awhile and finally leave. I leave the bike, run home and call the police. I'm relieved to find my mom is sober-ish and with the police, we go into the woods to get my bike. I don't remember anything about the car as it was so dark and happened so fast. I make a mental note to ride my bike on the grass as far from the road as possible when I have to go down Central. Nowhere seems safe anymore.

* * *

I wake up for school like any other day, dreading the walk to school. My sixteenth birthday is coming up in April, which is after the arbitrary date the school set to take "behind the wheel" classes after our regular drivers ed in the beginning of the year. So now if I want to get my license on my birthday, I'll have to pay two hundred dollars for private classes. My mom has already said that when I get my license, I can drive her minivan sometime. Given the state of things, will she even be awake to ask?

For the first time in a long time, I save a little of my money from work each week so I can take the required number of hours for behind the wheel. I get my permit, a money order and then I'm in a car driving on the highway with someone I just met. It goes fine.

I ask some of my friends at school what they are doing: in-school or private classes? Some of their parents are paying for them to get private classes. Others say they are too busy with track, tennis, homework or other extra-curricular activities. I have none of those complications. Not even a part of my world in the least. What's the point? I'm a little jealous though of my friends with a permit that drive around with their mom or dad. I haven't had either my mom or stepdad yet in the passenger side of the car, only the driving instructor.

I can't wait to drive. I'll have a faster, easier way to get to Kim's, work and other places. No more long and sometimes scary bike rides. I've got another way to escape.

I throw on some clothes quick and I'm about to go downstairs for some waffles when I see my mom asleep at the bottom of the stairs. Well, on the stairs. She's lying there like she meant to go upstairs, but just passed out on the first step. She has her head in her arms on a stair like a pillow. I wake her up and she just grumbles. After five to ten long minutes, I half drag her to her bedroom. My stepdad is already gone and I wonder if he saw her or she passed out very recently. I eat and wait to make sure my brother is up before I go on with my day as I usually do.

This put me behind, so instead of going to Kim's in the morning and walking with her to school, I just walk to school by myself. I'm not in a good mood to say the least. Right as I'm near my locker, I pass Jenny - who I recognize from my math class - talking to her friends in an agitated voice.

"I know! I mean, yeah, thanks for letting me drive all weekend, Dad, but you don't give me any gas money? Ugh, what the hell?"

Yeah, what the hell indeed. I don't think anyone at school realizes how goddamn lucky they are.

* * *

I've got the car tonight and am over at Kim's. We're looking at the paper, trying to figure out what movie to see. She's making the case for *The Sandlot* and I'm trying to talk her into *CB4*.

For all the anticipation, actually getting your license was pretty uneventful. The DMV is not glamorous at all. I aced all the tests and next thing you know, I'm driving back home. Kim and I drive out to Orland Park and all over Tinley Park. My mom's been drinking pretty heavily lately, so I was glad that I could just take her van and leave.

I saw my dad last weekend too, for my birthday and the first time since Christmas. I insisted on Kim coming along. He gave me the book *Breakfast of Champions* by

Kurt Vonnegut for my birthday. I've never heard of the book or Vonnegut, but he said "I was ready for it," which I liked. Even though I don't see him much, I know he loves me and we both love good books. I devour it and am enthralled by the meta-storytelling, witticisms, humor and insights. The drawings are amazing. Thanks Dad. It also makes me feel bad for not seeing him in months.

The phone rings and Kim answers.

"Sure, hold on."

She gives me the phone and shrugs.

"Hello?"

I can tell it's my stepdad immediately by the way he clears his throat.

"Hey, Chris. I'm gonna need you to come home."

"Why, what's up? We were just going to a movie and -"

"Sorry, you'll have to go another time. It's important."

He sounded tired. He hardly ever called or asked me to do anything directly. Something must've happened.

"Okay, I'll be home in a bit." Kim takes the phone back.

"What's wrong?"

"I don't know. He wouldn't say. Probably something with my mom. I'll call you if I can."

I hugged her goodbye. I wanted to kiss her, but her mom

was in the kitchen in the line of sight. Eight months now and that's still where things were at, but I don't have time to think about that now.

My stepdad is in the kitchen when I get home. Usually at this hour, he's comfortably laying downstairs, watching TV for the rest of the night. Something is seriously wrong.

"What's up? Where's mom? Is everything alright?"

"Well, I'm going to need you to do something. With your mom."

Hmm. This is news.

"Okay, I'm listening."

"You know I've been taking her to rehab every few months for the last year right? I can't do it anymore. Now that you can drive, it's your turn for awhile. You know your mom needs to go again. It's time."

Shit, no. This is not how I planned my evening to go. Eating popcorn in a theater watching a bunch of kids play neighborhood baseball with my arm around Kim sounds a hundred times better than whatever is about to happen.

"Can we talk about this? I don't even know what to do."

"You'll be fine. The only thing is remember your mom has to sign herself in. She's done it before. Just take her to the ER and go from there. Don't worry about bringing anything except her purse. Packing a bag will just make her anxious and we can bring that up later." He pauses and looks upstairs. "She just got up. Lynn!"

I don't hear anything upstairs.

"I'll go get her," I say as I walk upstairs.

She's sitting on the bed smoking a cigarette, not quite awake. The room smells like wine, sweat and cigarettes. I notice that she's been wearing the same black top and jeans for a few days now.

"C'mon, Mom, we gotta go."

"Go where? Get out of here! I'm trying to sleep."

"We need to go to Palos, Mom. It's time. You've been drinking too long."

"What . . . are you talking about? I'm fine. I just had a little bit with dinner and some yesterday . . ."

Right, right.

My stepdad eventually comes up and gives me a look to leave. I check to see if my brother is home. He isn't. Probably over at his friend's house. I don't blame him. I wait in the living room.

The next thing I know, my mom is downstairs with her coat on. Crying softly with her head down. I don't know what he said to her, but she seems ready to go all of a sudden. My stepdad has her propped up in a chair, putting her shoes on.

He puts her purse in her lap and walks away, yelling out, "Call if you need anything. All our insurance info should be current."

I guess this is my responsibility now.

I hold my mom's hand until we get to the van and drive off. I put a Prince tape on that I know she likes. "Diamonds and Pearls" fills the air. I look around and wonder what our neighbors think. Surely, they must know something is up. She hardly leaves the house anymore! For a moment, I long for the times when she just hid it and we all pretended this wasn't a thing.

By the time we get to Palos Community, she's asleep. I shake her and get a wheelchair to take her to the ER. I pass a clock and see it's almost nine p.m. On any other night, I would start walking home from Kim's about now.

I go to the front desk unsure what to do or say.

"Hi, I'm Chris Morris. This is my mom Linda. She's an alcoholic and needs to go to rehab upstairs. Sorry, um, chemical dependency treatment."

"Fill this out and we'll be with you in a minute."

I'm handed a clipboard with paperwork. I take my mom's purse and slowly fill in as much as I can. I feel a little thankful that she actually has her license, insurance and other info. It takes me a while because my mom is also trying to get her purse back and grunting at me.

"What are you doing? I want to go smoke," she says a bit too loudly.

"Mom, you're going to have to wait. We need to get you checked in."

She starts talking, but I get up and hand in the paperwork. After a long thirty minutes, we are ushered to a hospital bed in the ER surrounded by curtains in a long hallway. I hear someone moaning. It's coming from the bed next to us on the other side of the curtain to the right. Someone is speaking Spanish on the left side of us.

My mom refuses to change into a gown.

"That's fine," the nurse says, sensing my frustration. "We do need to take her vitals though."

"No!" She screams. The whole floor gets quiet. I'm mortified. I don't know what to do except stand up.

"I'm sorry. Can you all come back in a bit? I think she needs some time to calm down. I'm so sorry."

They give me a look like they've seen this before and silently leave.

"Mom, you have to cooperate. Otherwise, they can't help you."

"I don't need any help. I wanna go home. I wanna cigarette . . ."

She grabs for my arm.

I sit back down. I'm half worried she is going to run away, but I can tell by the way she's deepening into the bed, she isn't moving anytime soon. You never know though.

More moaning next door. I hate hospitals. One of my first memories is getting a bad case of pneumonia when I was three and spending days sitting in a tent at the hospital. I was scared and apparently, I could've died. But I didn't. Instead, I spent evenings in a plastic bubble, surrounded by the beeps and machines, watching TV, with my dad sleeping in a chair nearby.

I wait. I look at my mom and stare. She used to spend what seemed like hours in front of the mirror, applying makeup, constantly checking her hair in between going to tanning salons. Now her face is pale, her hair frazzled and dry. Her eyes are darker than I remember.

She looks thinner. I don't know when she eats, sleeping most of the day and drinking or smoking the few hours she's "awake." I wonder where she gets her cigarettes and wine now. Do friends bring it over? They must. I haven't for awhile and I don't think my stepdad does. Maybe in the weeks here and there when she is sober, she stockpiles some? It doesn't make any sense.

I think about the times in the last couple of months when she wasn't drinking. This past summer - after her first time in rehab - was good. I think we all thought it was all over. It worked. As it should. She was fine for months! Well, not drinking at least, which is fine. She wasn't exactly the same for sure. Irritable. Mopey. She seemed even melancholy at times.

Then one day, without warning, that other mom was

back. The blacked out mom. The mom who talked about making sure I was home for dinner, but then was asleep or "forgot" by suppertime. The mom who started yelling more and more. For cigarettes. For talking. For just being there at the wrong time. The innocuous lies about this friend or my stepdad or Nana or what happened that day. There was no rationale to the madness that I could figure out. I missed talking with her. Not talking at her.

It's been almost a cycle of her being three weeks drunk and one or two weeks sober. The longer she's drunk, the more I miss my "cool mom" or just mom. The mom who talked to Kim on the phone. The mom that actually followed through on promises to take me shopping for clothes or music. But even those days are few and far between. I never know when she hugs me if I'll be greeted by the mom who's "sorry." The mom that's going to "work to be a better mom, but it's just so hard sometimes," she'll say casually, as if our lives were so easy before.

The few times she's been in rehab since the summer, it's the same story. We get together as a family in therapy there, and after the third or fourth time, it's excuses like how alcoholism is a disease or apologies or declarations of love, but nothing changes. I often wonder what else she does in therapy and the big question, why doesn't it work?

A half hour later, the nurses come back. My mom looks like she is going to spit at them. I wave them away. The nurses motion for me to follow them, pulling back the curtain. My mom kicks at the air in their direction. A delayed response.

"Is this your mother?" The nurse asks with an exhausted look on her face.

I nod.

"You know that we can't take her upstairs until she signs herself in voluntarily."

"I know, I know. She just needs to sober up a little. Please keep coming back. I don't know what else to do."

I go back in and wait. I try to talk to my mom, but it's no use. She goes from sad to angry to confused quickly. Eventually, she passes out. I try to stay awake too, which is easy thanks to all of the other patients around me. I hear more moaning, beeping, screaming, crying, talking and more beeping. It's creepy and I'm tired.

I think about what my friends are doing right now. At the movies probably, where I should be too. Some are at home, watching TV with their family. Together. Some are doing homework or studying. Some are playing video games.

I try to picture myself sitting at our glass dining table with my stepdad, brother and mom all about to eat a big ham. Carefree. Smiling.

No, wait. Who made dinner? What do we talk about? What is my mom drinking? I'm suddenly jealous of my friends, but more upset because I don't see how my family can ever be like their families. It's probably too late for that.

An hour or so later, the nurses come back in and take my mom's vitals. She wakes up and is much calmer. She's not a hundred percent, but she's obviously better and more accommodating. I don't know what happened. Maybe she thinks she is dreaming.

"Linda, are you ready to go upstairs so we can help you? We just need you to sign these forms, okay?"

My mom hardly moves, taking the pen slowly. She makes a somewhat legible signature on the clipboard.

"Thank you, Linda. Sir, does she have everything?"

I look around for her purse and put it on my mom's bed. I sigh.

"Just that. Someone will bring up her clothes and anything else soon."

Probably me.

"Okay. It looks like she's been here before. Do you have any questions?" The nurse asks me with raised eyebrows.

"No."

I do, but I'm exhausted. My stepdad knows what he's doing, right?

"Thanks. Say bye to your son, Linda."

My mom just stares at me, still somewhere distant, not sleeping or awake. I just wave and half smile.

"Bye, Mom."

Then her bed is wheeled away, out of the curtain and down the corridor.

I glance at a clock on the way out. It's after midnight. I find the van in the parking lot and turn up the music for the road home.

For the first time in a long time, I drive through the darkness and let the tears come.

* * *

Things have been off with Kim. There is another guy that likes her apparently. Sam Murphy in her Algebra class. He's not as nerdy as Lucas was, so I'm even more jealous. Plus, she won't admit that he's ugly when I ask her. One day at our locker we share now, I catch her staring at him across the hall, where of course his stupid locker is.

When I tell Jack all this during American Literature, he's done with it.

"Man, you need to shut this whole thing down. You act like you're married. You're obsessed. And she's a freshman with three more years here! You think you're gonna date forever? Gimme a break."

He's right. When I'm with her, it's comforting. Sitting with Kim in her house, surrounded by her family, we do act like her parents. Of course, grown-ups go past second base, but anyway. When I'm not with her, it does become clear how much of my life is wrapped up in hers. I think I'm in love, but is this what it's like? She doesn't even act the same way towards me.

"Plus, c'mon, man. It's been all year and we've hung out like, what, three times? You need to see the signs and start living life again. Think about this summer."

Jack isn't afraid to call bullshit. I know he's right. With a car now, we could have some pretty good times and there's still so many "other fish in the sea" as my mom used to say.

After school, I bring up Sam Murphy again and she says she's bored in our relationship.

"I'm sorry, Chris. Maybe it's time to move on ..."

The rest is a blur. We both cry, hug and I leave her house. I take the long way home, through side streets, which takes almost ninety minutes. The whole time I think about the past year, visiting her relatives, hanging out with her sister Alicia and Dale, snuggling and watching old movies on her couch.

I don't say anything to my mom or stepdad. My mom has been sort of okay lately, but I'm not in the mood to talk about it. The next day, instead of going to Kim's after school, I go to Dan's. We haven't hung out much this year, but still joke around in class when we see each other. Back at his house, it's just like old times. I'm eating dinner with his family and realize how much I missed this. Yeah, I made a good decision. It's fine. The next few days it's just like old times.

Well, until Andy comes over to Dan's and lights up when he sees me. Not in a good way either.

"You won't believe what I saw. I was just at McDonald's and there was Kim and Sam Murphy. Together! They were with a group of people, but still. I'm sorry, man, but I had to tell you."

"For real? She didn't waste any time."

I replay all the fights we had and all the lies she told me, while all she really wanted to do was be with him anyway. I feel physically ill. I think about part of what she wrote in my yearbook literally a week ago. She made sure no other girls signed it that she didn't pre-approve.

"You're a very special person in my life and if I lose you, I'll never find another love as true as ours! I don't want to see you with anyone else ever! It'll break my heart! I'll love you forever . . ."

Love. I don't trust that word anymore. If Kim loved me so much, why would she be over me so fast? Why did she choose Sam over me?

I think about going home. But that hurts too. If my mom loved my stepdad, why does she keep drinking? Why did she pick the bottle over him? Over me? My dad years ago?

I'm so confused and don't know how to feel about anything or anyone anymore.

* * *

I'm sitting in the Oak Forest police station. Jack and Matt have already been picked up an hour ago, but either my mom forgot or she is too drunk to come get me. Or she's punishing me by making me sit here. I'm too young for jail, so I was put out by a bunch of policeman's desks.

This wasn't how this night was supposed to go. I don't think we thought about where it would go, which might be why we got busted.

At least one cop is in here at all times. Watching and working. The light in here is far too bright. I need a cigarette.

It's hot in the police station. Yesterday, it was hot, but we killed the time by filling up water guns and driving around in my mom's minivan randomly shooting people. It was awesome. We had the sliding door open like a mail truck and Jack just sat in the seat shooting anyone on the street, especially older kids. Some laughed. Some ran.

It was a little crazy, but this whole summer has been like that. It started with harmless bike rides to different malls and different girl's houses. After Kim and I broke up, I've met a bunch of girls at the mall and have started dating them, sometimes two or three at the same time. It's become like a game to me and Jack is even seeing a friend of one of the girls. Some nights we'll go to one girl's house, hang out for a bit and then go straight to another's. I've given girls gifts that others have given me. It's like juggling knives. Dangerous, but exhilarating.

I thought being a so-called player during freshman year was dating a lot of girls, but that wasn't at the same time like this. I've only been caught once so far by dating Stacy, a friend of Kristin's I know at Dejaiz, the clothes store in the mall I work at now. That was a mistake. Kristin saw me talking to this other girl I was seeing and asked me who it was.

"No one. Just a girl from school."

Somehow, Kristin knew this girl from somewhere, not school, but some sport she played, and next thing you know I'm being confronted in the front of Jack's house by an angry Stacy.

"Why? Why? I don't understand. Do you know how this makes me feel?"

I apologized and apologized and said everything I thought she wanted to hear. As she drove away, it felt like we might actually still be okay. We ended up not being together anymore, but did remain friends.

I was bad, but so was Jack. We were worse when we were together. We'd start many days by taking turns calling 950 AM, this dope hip-hop radio station we loved, and pretended we were working from a local White Castle, giving shout-outs to all "our homies behind the counter." After Jack and I would talk about something wacky to do, Jack would be the one to light the match and before you know it, he'd be getting two pizza parlors on three-way calling together to listen to them try and figure out who rang who. Or Jack paying for someone to buy us Mad Dog 20/20 from the liquor store or knocking on the door of our English teacher's house asking if his daughters were home. He even got caught stealing a Starter jacket from the mall on a dare and somehow talked his way out of it. He never failed to impress me. It was pushing boundaries, but I've never laughed so much and I loved breaking the mold of surburbia. It was never boring. Besides going to the mall or the movies, what the hell else was there to do anyway?

We started smoking cigarettes sometime this summer. Camel brand specifically. It was inevitable for me. I've grown up with it. Pretty much my whole family has always smoked. Mostly menthols, which taste gross. Except for Papa and his Marlboro cigarettes.

It started on a dare to buy a pack at the gas station by my house one day, but the older Indian man didn't bat an eye when Jack bought two packs of Camel Wides. So we kept buying them. Wides were thicker than regular cigarettes, which made them even more badass.

Jack had to work to hide the smell of the cigarettes. I think his dad is a little suspicious, and I can tell by his disapproving looks that he probably thinks it's all my influence. Whatever. I have nothing to hide. When I was home and my stepdad wasn't, I would smoke on the back porch or in my room with an ashtray hidden in my desk. Even if my mom wasn't drinking, what could she say? Don't smoke?

We couldn't smoke in public that much. It's okay though, because there was something magical about riding our bikes to another town, finding a quiet spot and having five minutes of bliss. A wonderful, forbidden release.

I look out the window of the police station and wonder how many cigarettes I have at home and how fast I'm going to smoke them. I think about the cop earlier asking us where we got fireworks.

If he only knew. It was a Works bomb. You fill up an empty plastic two-liter bottle with a little bit of shredded aluminum foil and some Works toilet bowl cleaner. Quickly screw the cap on and wait. About thirty seconds later, it explodes like a bomb. Except you have to be careful, because it releases a bunch of acid basically when it goes off. More dangerous than fireworks.

We had to try it. Our first attempt was made and thrown in the middle of the pond by the apartments behind the Jewel grocery store. It was so loud! Louder than a bomb. We ran faster than I ever remember running because I'm sure someone called the cops. They had to.

We met Matt after dinner and immediately bought three more bottles of soda. We still had enough foil and the Works.

"Alright, so what could we blow up?"

Talking through the options, it was clear it had to be something where people weren't nearby since we didn't want to burn anyone. Once one of us brought up the idea of mailboxes, it seemed perfect. They are right by the street and the bottles were made to fit in there!

We rode off and gathered the supplies in plastic bags, being careful to keep the different components separate. I carried the bottles, Matt had the foil and Jack had the Works.

It couldn't be by anyone we knew, so we crossed 151st into a few interconnected streets where we never went before. It was also less than a mile to Jack's house, so we had somewhere to retreat to.

The sun was coming down. I took out the first bottle and we made the first bomb after a truck drove by. Jack inserted it into the wooden mailbox of a two-story house that looked like any other house. All three of us rode off looking backwards.

BAM! The mailbox exploded into what looked like hundreds of little pieces. I could hear a little frying sound afterward.

"Holy shit! Quick, let's do another one."

He was right. It was so loud, people had to have heard it. We turned a corner and made another one. I put it into another wooden mailbox and right when I closed the little door, I saw the front door of the house open up and an older man step out.

"Hey! What are you doing?"

The homeowner started walking towards me. Jack and Matt were already riding off. I started pedaling and yelled back.

"It's okay! It's okay!" I shouted at him. "Just stay away from the mailbox!"

BAM! The explosion ended my sentence for me as it blew up all over his front lawn. He ran inside. I took off after Jack and Matt, who were already a block or two ahead of me. Once they crossed 151st Street, I lost them.

I heard sirens. It dawned on me that the police could've been on the way before we even made the second Works bomb, since the first was so loud. I kept riding.

Just as I was making a plan in my head on what roundabout way to take to Jack's house, I realized a brown van was close behind me. I remember seeing the van turn the corner right after the second mailbox blew up. I was being followed!

I saw an open field nearby behind an elementary school and turned into the parking lot. The van turned too and I noticed an older man driving it, the light from his headlights brighter and brighter in front of me. I rode across the grass and baseball diamond as fast as I could, hoping to make it to the other side thinking he couldn't possibly follow me there. But he did! It dawned on me that of course he did. It's only grass.

I could hardly think straight. I was sweaty and scared. At that moment, a police car turned onto the street I was aiming for and as my wheels hit the pavement, I could feel a hand on my shirt.

"Stop! Stop now! There's nowhere for you to go," the policeman said.

I was slightly impressed that he could drive and pull me off my bike. Then it hit me that things were about to get turned sideways. I wasn't going to take the fall for this. That's messed up.

He ushered me in the back of the car and my bike in the trunk.

"Where are your two friends? It will be easier if you are honest with me. We know it was three of you that were blowing up mailboxes."

Without hesitation, I told him to drive towards Jack's house. They left me, so it was only fair. As we got closer, I saw Jack and Matt walking their bikes on the sidewalk. They stopped.

Jack talked the cop into dropping his bikes at home. Luckily, his parents weren't home yet. Next thing I know, they were in the back of the car with me while the policeman talked on the radio. Matt was crying a little. Jack was quiet. I remembered that I had cigarettes and a lighter on me, so I hid both in the seat as best I could.

"Why'd you narc on us, man? That's fucked up," Jack said as we pulled out of his driveway.

"Hey, you guys left me! I was chased by a van and then a police car. You guys would've done the same!"

I didn't know that, but again, we didn't think about getting caught. We never did.

At the station, they took all of our information and phone numbers and our parents were called.

"So, where did you boys get the fireworks?"

Fireworks? We looked at each other. Do we lie about fireworks or do we talk about making a chemical bomb? Which is worse?

"We found them," Jack said without too much of a delay. We were both on the same wavelength. I nodded at him.

"Right . . ."

The policeman squinted his eyes at Jack. I could almost see him wonder how hard to push us about the fireworks, but clearly the more important thing was the damage.

"Well, they are illegal. And what if you or someone else got hurt?"

I stayed quiet. We didn't think of that either. This whole summer I felt invincible. In reality, we could've blown off a hand or burned someone's face off. Matt started to cry again.

It was clear after a little while that since none of us have a record, we weren't going to be charged with anything, but we do have to pay for the mailboxes at some point. The details will be given to our parents.

Matt and Jack got picked up almost right away. Their parents looked pissed and Jack's dad just shook his head at me.

I'm still here. Almost an hour or so later. I lost track of time. My mom arrives and it looks like she just took a shower. I can tell immediately by her walk that she's a little drunk. Even more so when I hear her voice. I think for a second that the police officer knows too, but he smiles and gives some paperwork to her and motions for me to leave.

"I don't want to see you back here. You stay out of trouble, alright?"

SINK

November 1993

We're parked in a forest preserve by Bachelor's Grove Cemetery, listening to *Midnight Marauders,* the new CD by A Tribe Called Quest. Jack gets the aluminum foil ready in the passenger seat of the van, wrapping it around a pen to make a tube about the same size. He pulls the pen out and turns the end up about an inch in to make a little open-ended pipe, or bowl as we call it. Jack grabs the dime bag of marijuana out of his coat pocket and puts in some of the dried, stiff plant, being careful not to get any seeds mixed in. I give him my lighter and he turns it sideways to light up the bowl. He inhales, holds it in and blows it slowly out the window. I take it from him and do the same. We go back and forth until the bowl is cashed.

I light a cigarette, get out of the van, crumple up the foil and throw it into a nearby metal trash can. Jack gets out and we sit on a picnic table, smoking and talking about everything and nothing, laughing too much. I get paranoid for a bit realizing how close we are to Bachelor's Grove Cemetery, but Jack insists we walk over to the famously haunted place and see "what's really going on." As we cross 147th Street and our shoes hit the path down to the cemetery, I realize I can hear the wind rustling the trees. The crunching of the pebbles under our feet. The moonlight lighting our way. I've never been more present.

It's almost dark and when we hit the actual gates of the cemetery, we both look at each other like, "Are you sure?" I was suddenly hit with paranoia again, but as soon as we walked around and started seeing the overturned headstones while hearing the cars go by nearby, it seemed less scary. Just an old, forgotten place where stoned teens like us come to fight boredom and feel alive.

* * *

I'm in MDP and restless, so I stare out the windows thinking about how good it will feel to smoke after school. I can't believe it's only been a few months since we started smoking pot. Tammy, a girl I met at Orland Square Mall and dated for a month, gave us a little bit of her stash. We didn't want to admit we never smoked before and then suddenly we were smoking it every few days. I also got my new friends, Scott and Corey, smoking it too. We had some classes together and Scott also worked as a busboy with me at the Charley Horse, a restaurant in Orland Park. Corey was his best friend, so I soon rounded out a fun, fast trio.

I've spent a lot more time with them and didn't see Jack as much. It was hard to shake him as a friend and he was trying too hard when we did hang out. The last few times he kept bragging about smoking weed with Swisher Sweets and blunts nonstop. I know he is trying to emulate his favorite rappers, but in reality, c'mon, we are just white kids in the suburbs. I'm probably making excuses too, when the reality is I've just moved on. How do you break-up with a friend?

Besides, I was listening to a lot of different music these days. It used to be just R&B, pop and rap, but Scott and Corey turned me onto their world of alternative music, which I dove into immediately. The Pixies, Sebadoh, The Breeders, Weezer, Radiohead, Pavement, The Flaming Lips, Matthew Sweet, Sonic Youth . . . the sounds all filled whatever car we were in. I also started to appreciate Q101, the alternative radio station in Chicago, much more.

Part of the alternative scene was to look casual. Lots of flannel, along with thrift store or vintage clothes. The first two years of high school had me pining for and buying expensive jeans and shirts with my hair meticulously styled. Now I was wearing ripped jeans with a used bowling shirt embroidered with a name patch that says "Bob" on the front. My hair is much longer on top, slicked back with the sides and back still shaved.

"Where did you get that old shirt?" My mom sneered when I saw her in the kitchen last night.

My mom has been saying I don't look good and shakes her head at me almost every time I see her. She should talk though. I try to stay out of her way. Having access to a car - and friends with cars - means I'm home even less than before. Scott, Corey and I drift around town and up to Chicago when the spirit moves us.

We drive to the record stores around town looking for the latest imports with bonus tracks and good used CDs. The suburbs are even duller now than they were before. It was one thing to go shopping at Orland Square Mall, it was another to go to "The Alley," an epic and unique alternative store in Lincoln Park downtown.

Unlike when I'd be at Dan's or Kim's house, where I inserted myself as part of their larger family unit, Scott lives with just his dad and older sister in a condo/apartment type set-up and Corey has a crowded house with two younger siblings and a very strict mom. His dad works long hours at a plant in Joliet and is hardly home. So it's not just me that wants to escape. We all want to get away, explore, listen to music and smoke the night away.

Corey has to be home at a certain time, but since Scott's dad works odd hours doing something with finance downtown, he doesn't have a curfew. I can't remember the last time anyone at my house told me to be home at a certain time. I come and go as I please. I didn't realize how abnormal this was until a few weeks ago, when we were at the house of one of Scott's friends, Adam Robertson, stopping in after dinner to play Super NES.

"Do you guys need to use the phone to call home?" Adam's mom asked us.

"For what?" I replied, a bit mystified.

"So your parents know where you are? Do they know you are over here?"

I didn't even know what to say. Is this what other kids do? Call home so their parents don't worry? Scott got up and called home. I thought for a moment.

"No, it's fine. I told them earlier we were stopping by and I just have to be home by nine so I get enough sleep for school tomorrow. I'm already caught up on my homework too. Thanks though."

She nodded. It must've sounded normal enough so she walked back in the kitchen. I looked at Adam and wondered how we can be so similar yet so different.

Every now and then, if I've run out of money for pizza, Mr. Subs or whatever, I'll venture to my house to make some Rice-A-Roni, macaroni and cheese or heat up whatever I can find in the freezer that my stepdad got at Aldi. I've been teaching myself to cook using the back of whatever box we have in the house. The only time I've messed up is when I decided I wanted breaded shrimp like they have at Mr. Subs. I heated up some oil to fry the shrimp and they turned out okay, but I put the pan full of oil under water to wash it. Rookie mistake. Apparently, you can't mix water and hot oil so it exploded all over the kitchen. I burned my arm and ruined a shirt. Lesson learned.

If my brother is around, I save him a plate. Now in middle school, he's been at his friends' more and more. My stepdad is working longer hours and hardly home either. It's as if we are all avoiding the harsh reality of my mom doing her usual cycle of drinking heavily for weeks and being half a mom the other weeks. From the outside you'd never know it, but the light in the house has definitely dimmed. My new friends have only been over once or twice. I tell them that my mom isn't feeling well and asleep in the bedroom, which isn't lying. It's sadly a lie I'm very used to telling at this point.

The bell rings. I grab my notebook and nod at the teacher assigned to MDP whose name I can't recall, hoping I don't see her anytime soon. Deep down, I know I will.

* * *

I stop home after school to grab something to eat quick and leave for the night. No plans but to drive around, get high and listen to music.

I notice a big brown envelope on the counter, seemingly waiting for me. What is this? Are the Marines sending me stuff at home now too?

I think back to the career fair in the gym a few days ago, where I ended up talking with a few guys from the Marines. Their brochures looked like something straight out of G.I. Joe. It all sounded exciting yet completely crazy at the same time. Action! Adventure! Free college! Or stay in the Marines for life and move up the ranks to fortune and glory! Seems so foreign. I gave them my contact information, almost to see what would happen and yesterday, Sergeant Williams left a message.

"Hey, just wanted to know if I could pick you up from

school to talk about Junior ROTC and some other things to make you more money after graduation?"

Whoa, slow down, dude. They don't mess around. I didn't call back.

I open it up and see an itinerary and the 7 Up logo all over everything, along with plane tickets to Miami from Chicago? I sit down.

"Holy shit."

My mind wanders. I recall a few weeks ago, in a halfway sober moment, my mom waiting for me after I came home from a long night of cleaning tables at the Charley Horse.

"CJ, come here," she said, shaking her head. "You won't believe this! While you were gone, someone from 7 Up called and you won a cruise! To the Bahamas!"

Is this another lie? Wouldn't doubt it. Sometimes it's about being sick. About my stepdad. Or about little things and strange things. A week ago, she told me she was pregnant again, which did shake me a bit, but when I asked about it the next day, she looked at me confused. This winning a trip thing seemed oddly specific and random. Even for her.

"Mom, what? I don't remember entering anything. Are you sure you're okay?"

"CJ, I swear. He said that we'll get everything in the mail soon and we are leaving in December! Well, you are leaving. You can bring one person. And you know if you bring me, I'll let you do whatever you want. Smoke - yes, I know you smoke now - stay out late, whatever. I don't know if your dad will do the same."

I was half listening as the 7 Up promotion finally hits me. Something about the bottom of a 7 Up can and you won if you saw a special cruise logo. Did I see one? I've been so stoned lately, it's possible. But I feel like I'd remember that.

"Alright, Mom, calm down. I'll believe it when I see it. And then we'll talk about who is going and not going. This sounds pretty far fetched."

"CJ, I swear it's true! Just wait."

Now I'm holding it all in my hands and in mid-December, I'm going to the Bahamas. What the hell? Did I really win though? I still don't remember a can, but I have a vague recollection of filling out one of those cards somewhere or being bored in the kitchen sending in something to enter.

It still doesn't feel real. Sure, my mom is a habitual liar, but I don't know how she'd find the time to falsify plane tickets. Finally some good luck?

❊ ❊ ❊

"Just one night, Linda!"

The door is open to my room as I listen to my stepdad and my mom argue downstairs. What I've picked up so far is that my stepdad wants her to not drink today so they can go over to his parents for Thanksgiving dinner in a few hours.

"This is a big deal," he kept saying. Or, "Just one night, that's all I'm asking."

I wonder if his parents know about my mom's drinking. I doubt it. The dinner will be a charade. Surely we can pretend to be normal for a few hours, eating turkey and stuffing in silence? I look forward to my stepdad's mom asking me how I can have "a job dressed like this or a haircut like this."

There is silence downstairs. I suddenly hear the TV, which means my stepdad gave up. My brother asks me what's going on and I tell him that Thanksgiving is a "maybe." We wait in our respective rooms, watching TV. I take a walk around the block and smoke a few cigarettes.

When I come back, I see it's after five now and my mom's not in the kitchen. My stepdad is dressed. He looks pissed.

"You're going to have to take your mom to the hospital again. She doesn't want to come with us. Your brother and I are going to my parents."

"What's the point? Can't she just stay here? Let me come."

"No, I gave her a chance and clearly she'd rather drink. She needs help."

"Can't we call an ambulance like last time? I don't want

to take her."

A month ago, I was at work and my stepdad called an ambulance to take my mom to rehab. It's clear that we've all given up on caring about what the neighbors think.

"No, that's too expensive. Plus, you're here. You know she probably doesn't want to go and someone has to stay with her until she can sign herself in. Sorry."

Great. Another long night in the ER. And on Thanksgiving. I think about just leaving, but where can I go? All my friends are somewhere with their families.

I sigh.

"Fine. I'll deal with it."

My brother comes downstairs, gives me a little smile that seems to say "I'm sorry" and they both leave.

I need a plan. I light a cigarette and sit at the dining table, smoking as slow as I can. Then I light another one. I sit for an hour or so, knowing I can't just pack a bag, snap my fingers and get my mom in the car. Not that easy.

Finally, it hits me.

I wake her up.

"Mom, let's go see Nana. It's been too long and she wants to see you," I say, cringing because I know that last part is true.

"But I look like shit, CJ. We can't go now."

"She won't care. She just wants to see you. Besides, you look fine," I lied.

I help her get dressed, happy her pants aren't wet this time. I grab her purse and cigarettes. She's sober enough to walk and get in the van at least. I think about putting Prince on, but I don't want to arouse suspicion, so I just turn on the radio. At a stop light, I light a cigarette for her and one for me. She takes her coat off for some reason.

"I'm hot. Are you sure this is the right way? Do you know where you're going?"

"Mom, I know how to get to Nana's. Just relax."

I realize that I didn't think through what to do when we actually get to the hospital. I hate this.

We're about ten minutes away when the gas light comes on. I didn't even look when we left the house, being so focused on what my mom was doing. Shit. It's dark, but I pull into an Amoco station.

"Sit tight, I'll be right back."

"Where are you going?"

"I'm just getting gas, Mom. It will only take a minute."

My mom's face starts to redden.

"CJ, don't lie to me. I've never seen this gas station

before. Where are we really going? Don't lie to me!"

She's almost yelling. Thank God this place is empty.

I don't know what else to do.

"I'm sorry, but, we're . . . we're going to the hospital. It's time again. It wasn't my idea, it was . . ."

I didn't want to, but I might as well deal with it here as opposed to sitting in the ER surrounded by sick strangers and nurses.

She doesn't say anything, just sits there. I get out to pay and pump the gas, but as I'm about to hit the twenty dollar mark, I hear the door open and see the blur of her shirt running past the station.

What the hell?

I quickly put the nozzle back and go around to close her door. I drive away, spotting her running towards a strip mall across the street. I pull into the deserted lot, park and jump out. She bobs and weaves in between the pillars, past a dollar store and Walgreens. I finally catch her and grab her by the shoulders.

"Sit down, Mom!"

We're both winded. I feel like I'm going to throw up and surprised my mom doesn't. She just lays on the pavement.

"Let me get your coat, Mom. It's freezing out here."

"I'm fine, CJ! Just leave me alone. I just want to stay here.

I'm not going to the hospital again."

She's at least wearing a long sleeve shirt, but she's shivering slightly. I give her my coat.

I light two cigarettes and hand one to my mom.

"Why do you do this? Running away, drinking . . . we could be eating turkey like everyone else. This whole night sucks."

"You don't understand. There is so much you don't see. You're never home."

"What are you talking about? You have a husband that's hardly home and the fact that he lets you just sit around and drink your life away is a miracle. You should be thanking him."

She sits up and jabs her finger at me.

"No, you don't know shit. A few days ago he got so mad, he tied me up around a tree in the backyard and left me there for hours."

Jesus. I know my stepdad has a temper, but he's not crazy or stupid. I haven't seen him do anything close to spanking my brother in years. I only hear about these things secondhand, but never see them with my own eyes. My mom lying was nothing new. She's always the host at the pity party.

"You don't get it. You don't understand. I'm all by myself and drinking is the only thing that helps. You think it's easy being a mom? To two boys? You think I've had it easy?"

I don't say anything. There's no point. We both smoke in silence. She occasionally shakes her head as if she's continuing her monologue to herself. I stare at this ghost of my mom and try not to remember who she used to be.

After what seems like an hour, but actually is only fifteen minutes, I get up.

"Mom, we can't just sit here in the middle of nowhere in a strip mall. Let's go. Please, for me?"

She gets up and I help her in the van. She cries softly as we drive to the hospital.

"I'm sorry, CJ. So sorry. It's just so hard."

We sit in the ER as we have before. Even though she's more willing to help this time, things still move slow and we wait two hours until they take her hospital bed up to rehab. Again.

On the way home, I don't cry this time. I'm just mad. Mad at my mom. Mad at everyone else I know sitting around a TV, bellies full. Mad at all the normal sixteen year olds. Mad at the world for being so damn unfair.

✳ ✳ ✳

It's December ninth. "7" by Prince is on the radio. Yesterday, my mom got out of rehab and she's coming with me to the Bahamas. I love my dad and know this probably isn't the best post-rehab idea for my mom, but at the end of the day, it's my cruise and I want to do whatever I want. And I want to have fun. I deserve it.

Someone at school told me that U.S. drinking laws don't apply once you're on the ocean, so I'm extra excited. I know I can't get high during the trip, so this will have to do. I'm also skeptical about these claims, so I haven't shaved my face for the past week, hoping to appear a little older. Just in case.

My mom is sober. Typical post-rehab sober. Cranky and a little unpredictable. We fly to Miami early and I realize this is only my second time on an airplane. I'm carrying all the cruise documents with me and I'm still waiting for the whole thing to fall apart, but so far so good.

We're standing in line on a pier with all the other winners to board the M/S Seaward. I'm sweating. It's not just the heat, but I'm so nervous about handing over our boarding documents or that our names aren't on whatever list they have. There has to be a mistake right? But then it's our turn.

"Hello! Congratulations. What is your name?"

"Um, Christopher Morris."

We wait. I swear I think I'm going to pass out.

"Ah, here you are."

He shows me as if he senses my anxiousness. Christopher Morris is listed twice and suddenly we are ushered into this big, beautiful ship. We're given keys to our cabin, which is like a glorified closet, with two beds, almost no room to walk, a fridge full of different 7 Up products and a little bathroom with the loudest flush I've ever heard.

It's gorgeous. I've never been on a cruise ship or seen the ocean. My mom wants to walk around, but I just want to hang out by the pool on the top deck. There has to be girls up there. Plus, I can work on my tan. In December! Suddenly, I feel the ship start moving. We go our separate ways.

I find a nice lounge chair by the pool and I turn it to face the ocean. I get up and look overboard and it feels like we are comically high above the water, almost like a moving building, which we are in a way.

A few minutes later, after I'm comfortable and wondering if it's okay to smoke, a waiter stops by.

"Drink, sir?"

"What do you have?"

"The usual, but we have a special right now for guests. It's the Bahama Mama, since we'll be in the Bahamas tomorrow."

That's gotta be some sort of grown-up, fancy alcoholic drink. This is my chance. Act cool.

"Oh, sounds good. I'll have one of those."

He smiles and disappears. I suddenly wonder if I have to pay anything? I don't want to ask too many questions.

The waiter brings a big orange drink with an umbrella

and a slip of paper. It just asks for my name and room number. Phew. We'll figure that out later.

"Thanks!"

If only my friends could see me now. They wouldn't believe it. Being able to casually order alcoholic drinks by a pool, right out in the open. What a world.

I take a sip. It's fruity. Also, very alcoholic. After a few minutes, I'm buzzed. Between that and the sounds of the sea, I fall asleep for a bit.

*   *   *

Later that night, my mom says she's tired and I feel out of it. I slept longer than usual and my head hurts. By the time I get dressed, I realize it's too late to attend whatever official dinner was happening tonight. I walk up to the deck and find a little restaurant.

"Are you guys open?"

There is hardly anyone there. I think the dinner downstairs was still happening.

"Of course, take a seat wherever you like, sir."

I sit down. The menu is a little nicer than I expected. I order ravioli.

"Oh, would you care for a Bahama Mama, we have a special -"

"No thanks. Just a Coke."

I clearly need to slow down on acting like an adult. At least until later.

After dinner, the deck is empty and I look out at the ocean. It's just black. I can barely see the ship moving against the water. I hardly hear it either. It's trippy.

When I go back downstairs to the cabin, my mom is gone. Hopefully she's just getting food, but I know she's likely at a bar somewhere. I sleep.

The next morning, we arrive in Nassau. We dock and are free to explore the mainland for a while. My mom is passed out. I ask a question I already know the answer to.

"Mom, we're here. Are you gonna leave the ship at all? I want to go down."

She barely moves. What was she doing last night? When did she come back to the room?

"Uh-huh. You go. Have fun. I don't feel so good," she says out one side of her mouth.

I leave the ship and am immediately accosted by aggressive taxi drivers. I light a cigarette, don't say a word and just keep walking into downtown Nassau in the Bahamas. I suddenly get an impulse to see a beach, any beach since I've never been to one.

Walking down the streets, kids, women, men . . . pretty much everyone has something to sell. I'm used to people asking for things on the streets of Chicago, but this was on another level. Some kids even wanted some money with a promise to dance for me or sing a song. It's wild.

I don't see any beaches, but I walk through a hotel and sneak onto their private beach. I sit for a bit and look at the water, which is spectacularly clear. I had heard that it was like this, but seeing it up close is pretty amazing. I quietly stare at the sparkling, small waves.

On the walk back to the ship, I realize that openly smoking cigarettes is a terrible idea because I end up giving out most of my pack to people on the street. So much work just to get a little glimpse of paradise.

In our cabin, my mom is awake and I'm surprised to find her getting dressed in an actual dress.

"Where are you going?"

"Tonight's the Captain's Champagne Party. Put on your nice clothes."

I put on a shirt and tie I bought at the mall and sit through dinner with other passengers, who are all so darn happy to be here. They are in awe of everything. My mom and I are too, but I think we are both hungover in different ways and barely speak. I order a screwdriver and my mom smiles, which all still feels a bit weird. After dinner, we take an awkward formal picture in the Crystal Court.

"So, have you met any girls yet?"

"Mom, really?"

"C'mon, I'm not stupid. It's fine. That's why you brought

me, remember? If anyone asks, I'll just say we are brother and sister, so you have more options."

I laugh. In this moment, I'm grateful for my mother, even though I know this is all very wrong.

My mom wants to go to the casino, but I have no interest. I'm already out of my league acting like I'm twenty-one, so gambling - even for me - sounds like a bad idea. Plus, no one under eighteen is allowed in the casino. I don't know how or if they check, but it's not worth risking the ruse.

I pop into a cabaret show, but it's boring, so I go back up on deck. While smoking a cigarette and staring out at the water, I see two women talking. They look like they're in their early twenties. The brunette is cute.

With a little vodka in me, I find myself talking before realizing it.

"Hey, how are you two?"

"Good! We're just waiting until the club opens. Are you going?"

"A club? Sounds awesome. I didn't know about it, but do now. I'll follow you guys."

The night goes on and we dance in Boomer's, a disco on the ship, which thankfully is playing a lot of music I know. I still have some of my old dance moves. Sue, the brunette, introduces me to Jack and Coke, which I like far better than anything I've drank so far. It's just Coke, which I'm obviously familiar with, but with some

Jack Daniels whiskey. Much smoother. Screwdrivers just taste like funky orange juice and make me nauseous.

Sue is smiling more and more. This is good.

"So . . . who are you with? Girlfriend, family, friend, what?" She yells above the music.

"Yeah, I just brought my, uh, sister with. She's older. By a lot."

Jesus. I involuntarily cringe saying that. By this point, her friend Jackie went to bed, not finding anyone to dance with and it's clear that Sue and I have a connection. She's wearing a short red dress, which looks amazing when she dances.

"That's nice you both get along so well. So where you from? What do you do? Who is Chris?" She laughs.

"Well, I - "

I realize I didn't think of a back story until now. She must be older since she's traveling with just a friend. Over eighteen at least.

"You first," I say, hoping to buy me some time.

"Fine," she says with a smile. "I work at a clothing store near Seattle. In the office. It's okay, but I'm thinking about going back to college. I'm twenty-six."

Twenty-six! What? Keep it together, man. Don't think about how she's ten years older than you. Or knows what it's like to take a college class. Just play off her answers with something you know something about.

I just say the first thing that comes to mind, which instantly sounds ridiculous.

"Oh, that's crazy. I work at a store too. I help manage a bike store outside of Chicago. I just turned twenty-two. I know, everyone says I look young for my age."

I immediately regret saying that. It doesn't matter because Sue leans in and kisses me. I can taste the whiskey on her breath.

"I like you," she says.

She seems pretty buzzed. I know I am. This is all a lot to handle.

Sue takes me by the hand and then we are on her bed. In her cabin. With Jackie - hopefully sleeping - a foot or two away in her own bed. We kiss for what seems like forever. I'm so nervous, knowing she's older. She's probably done this a hundred times. I just reciprocate whatever she does. She looks at me half serious for a second.

"So, do you have a condom or what?"

Shit. I don't. And even if I do, do I tell her I'm a virgin or just have sex as cool and casually as a twenty-two year-old does? Whatever that means. I think about the stash of condoms I do have in my top drawer that my stepdad put there last year only saying, "Yeah, I'm too young to be a grandfather." That was the extent of any sort of birds and bees talk. But here I am.

"Um . . . no. I don't. I'm sorry. I wish I did."

She looks disappointed.

I'm relieved in a way. We kiss for a while longer, but I can tell she is getting tired and falling asleep.

"You can stay over if you want," she says with eyes closed.

I look at the clock. It's almost four in the morning. I think about waking up in this strange bed in this strange room with these strange two people. It's too much.

"No, it's fine. These beds are so small. I'll see you tomorrow?"

Sue nods and I walk back to my room, collapsing onto my bed. I look over and my mom's bed is perfectly made up. Ugh. I'm too tired to care.

* * *

I wake up. My head hurts and I drink a 7 Up, which doesn't help. It's almost noon and doesn't feel like the ship is moving. I sit up and see that my mom is asleep.

Where are we? What day is it? Okay, it's Saturday. I find the itinerary.

"Oh my God! Mom, wake up!"

I look out the window and see an island. Treasure fucking Island. This was supposed to be the climax of the cruise, where we all go out on the island and have fun while winning actual treasure courtesy of 7 Up. Prizes, prizes and more prizes. According to the itinerary, the treasure hunt left at eleven o'clock.

"Mom, wake up!"

She rustles and looks at me. I can tell she is still a little drunk.

"What is it?"

"We're missing the biggest part of the trip! Everyone is at Treasure Island right now."

"Okay, well, whatever. It's probably too late. Can I go back to sleep now?"

"I guess. Where were you last night anyway? I got back at four and you weren't here. I know most things closed before that."

"Me? Where were you? I should be asking you."

"Uh-huh, one minute you're my sister and the next you're my mother. Did you meet someone too? You had to."

She lifts her pillow and turns her head away.

"It's none of your business, CJ. Just leave me alone and you don't have to tell me where you were."

I leave and just go up to the deck, lighting a cigarette. I can't help but wonder if she really did meet up with someone. And if so, was it intentional or was she drunk? I don't know what to do or think. I start to blame myself for bringing her along, but remember this is what she does. She drinks. She makes bad decisions.

I hear music and cheers from the island while I smoke in silence.

✳ ✳ ✳

It's cold. January is my least favorite month in the Midwest. If it's not freezing, it's the snow that gets to you. Or both. I turn the heat and music up then drive off. Matthew Sweet's "The Ugly Truth" blares from the minivan's speakers. I don't even ask to take the van anymore. My mom wouldn't notice anyhow and I can't remember the last time she drove. She got in big trouble with my stepdad for the four hundred dollar bill we were presented with at the end of the cruise, so she's been a bit more reclusive.

As the rest of the *Altered Beast* cassette plays, I try to figure out my way home. When I drove to Natalie's place it was still light out, but now this seems foreign. It's a part of Midlothian I don't go to much. It was worth it though, making out in her room. She's so pretty and kind, but something is off about her. I think she's using me as a rebound. I guess I don't care all that much. The affection is amazing and I can never get enough.

I think about how Natalie is already the second girl I've met working at the dollar store. The first girl, Heather, seemed cool, but she either cheated on me or blew me off on New Year's Eve. I still don't know what happened there. Sure, I had that little fling with Sue on the cruise ship last month, but that didn't count. She was so much older and none of my friends really believed me. I forgot to even get her phone number or anything.

Heather lived in Orland Park and in a different world. Her parents were strict, had money and let her do what she wanted. They didn't seem to care for me much. She went to Catholic high school and liked to get high and have fun. To rebel. She was picture perfect with thick eyebrows and long brown hair. I loved the way she looked at me. She knew her parents didn't like me and that made the attraction even hotter it seemed.

Then for New Year's Eve, she told me and Jack to meet her at her friend's house whose parents weren't home. Jack and I rode our bikes way out to Orland Park - I just had my license suspended for not paying a speeding ticket and Jack couldn't get his dad's car - and arrived at this girl Jessica's house. We listened to music, smoked on her back porch and waited. Heather never showed up.

Towards the end of the night, I was getting more and more upset and finally Jessica broke the news after I kept asking her. It was clear she knew what was going on. Heather was meeting some guy named Brian at a party. Why didn't she just break up with me? Why would she set her friend Jessica up like that? Just a shitty thing to do. I stopped juggling multiple girls a while ago, because it was too much work, but to be on the receiving end feels awful. I haven't talked to her since. Then I met Natalie.

When Natalie came into the dollar store soon after, her

friend told me she liked me and they giggled, and next thing you know I'm at her house. Now I'm here.

I somehow find 147th Street and can find my way home. Wait, was I supposed to be at work tonight? I don't miss driving to work at Orland Park to my old job at the Charley Horse, plus my friends didn't work there anymore either, so what's the point? I just remember it's Thursday and I have school tomorrow.

I light a joint, drive and finish it in the driveway of my house. All the lights are off. I go inside, already making up my mind to sleep in tomorrow and just start school around fourth period.

* * *

It's the day after Valentine's Day. We can all hang out finally since everyone was with their girlfriends yesterday. I hung out at home since I'm single again. It became clear that Natalie was just using me to get weed. She wanted to get high almost every time we hung out, but then she would call me just to meet up to get some weed.

"Hey, let's meet up tonight. Can you bring an extra dime bag?"

I don't mind helping out here and there, but I'm not a drug dealer. She still had one of my flannel shirts too. Ironically, she broke up with me because one night when we were high, I kept calling her Heather by accident.

Scott is driving, Corey is in the front seat and I'm in the back with Tom, Corey's cousin, who is a year younger than us and goes to a different school since he lives in Tinley Park. We just picked up Tom in Tinley and are aimlessly driving.

I wanted to drive, but my license is still suspended and I only drive for quick trips to see girls or go to work. Stupid speed trap. I tried to protest the ticket by not paying, but apparently that just makes it worse. I'm scheduled for court in a few weeks and I'll probably pay so I can drive again. Legally for a change.

"Dude, just park somewhere so we can smoke this bowl!" Corey yells.

"There is a quiet street right next to the school near my house. Go back that way," Tom says.

We drive and pass the elementary school and park in front of someone's house by their mailbox. Doesn't look like anyone's home.

Scott turns the car off and Corey gets the first hit from the bowl.

"Let's hotbox this. Don't roll the windows down!" Corey commands. He likes to talk when he smokes. Almost too much.

"Man, this is so good. I was so high last night, it was insane. I wish you guys could've been there. Veruca Salt was awesome and Julie was high too. When they played 'Seether' it was like . . . electric. The place went nuts. I bought weed from some guy outside the Riveria, it was so much better than this suburban shit," Corely says breathlessly.

"Right on, man. We need to get some of those fancy Chicago drugs more," I say, laughing as he keeps talking.

After awhile, it becomes hard to see as we pass the pipe around through all the cigarette smoke.

"Roll the windows down, I'm going to smell horrible. My mom will know. Again," Tom says, rolling his eyes.

I roll mine down just a little to let some smoke out. Scott can't stop coughing. I'm pretty buzzed and roll the window down more to get some air. Where are we?

"Guys, guys! Be cool. Cops," Scott shouts at us.

What? We all turn around and a police car is driving towards us. No one says anything.

"Scott, start driving," Tom says, saying what we all are thinking.

The police car slows and stops right behind ours.

"Corey, whatever weed you have, throw it out the window. Or drop it out, whatever. Just don't have it on you," I say from the backseat.

Corey discreetly throws the weed and the pipe on the grass.

No one says anything as the cop walks up to the car. I put my cigarette out. The car is unbelievably smoky.

"What are you boys doing? One of the neighbors called and said you all have just been sitting here. She wouldn't have called if you lived here."

No one says anything. Finally, Scott clears his throat. I'm hoping he's not as high as I am.

"Oh, sorry, officer. We just wanted to go somewhere and talk. Corey here just broke up with his girlfriend yesterday - Valentine's Day of all days - and we were just trying to help."

"That's right. We went to see Veruca Salt and next thing you know, it's all over. So messed up," Corey pipes up.

I wonder if he can smell the smoke. The weed. The very illegal weed. There is still a faint cloud in the car.

The officer peeks his head towards the back and Tom and I smile awkwardly.

"Well, you can't just sit here. Why not go to one of your houses or something? Alright? Hope things work out buddy. Women are complicated."

He walks back. We roll up our window and before he drives off, we are laughing uncontrollably.

"Holy shit, how . . . how did that happen?" Tom says.

"I know, it smells like we've been smoking weed in this car all day. Maybe he's just cool?" Corey says laughing.

"Scott! That story was so cheesy, yet I don't know, he seemed like he bought it," I say. "Corey, don't forget your pipe and stuff before we leave. But be careful, someone is clearly watching us."

Corey opens the door, jumps out and is back seconds later. Scott drives off and I can tell he didn't smoke as much as us by how calm he is. He's good like that.

"Women are complicated," we say in the officer's voice, giggling.

Everyone is in a great mood. We escaped the impossible. Corey or Scott turns up the Flaming Lips and we just take it in.

I start to think about all the other near misses in the last few months.

I've learned my own lesson about smoking pot in cars, at least when I'm driving. A couple weeks ago, I took out my stepdad's SUV, since it's so much nicer than my mom's minivan. I didn't ask. He was just home and went to bed early. I took his keys so Jack and I could go to Orland Square Mall before it closed at nine. We smoked on the way and I was fine driving, but when making a left turn at a light near the mall, the truck slid in the snow and we smacked into a snow bank. We turned into the parking lot to get out and inspect for damage, but there was none. We laughed even though it was a little too close for comfort. My stepdad would've killed me. Twice.

Two days later, Corey picked up Scott and me. We drove around in the snow getting high, this time driving outside the burbs. Not towards Chicago, but out south towards Lincoln Mall. Corey had just passed the joint to me in the back seat, when I noticed the light ahead turning red and Corey not slowing down.

"Dude, the light's red!"

Corey hit the brakes hard and we slid across the snowy street right through the intersection, narrowly missing a few cars. We never stopped. Corey decided to keep driving since we were on the other side at that point. We all got quiet and rode in silence for awhile.

That was two crazy car experiences in two days, sliding in and out of disaster. Was I invincible?

Nope. The following week I was snowboarding on a hill at a forest preserve with Jack. There was a lot of other people there sledding and having fun. We got high in the car ahead of time and I foolishly decided to impress some of the kids with my skills, using the little ramp someone had made of snow at the bottom of the hill for sledding. It turned out to be ice, not snow, and when I spontaneously decided in the air to do a backflip with my snowboard, I landed right on the ice and blacked out for a second. When I opened my eyes, Jack seemed scared. I got up and saw blood on the ice. I felt the back of my head and looked at my fingers. More blood.

"Man, we should probably go to the hospital."

"Okay. Actually I don't feel that bad, take me home and my mom can take me. It's fine."

It would've felt weird for him to take me. His dad already hated me too so I didn't want to get him in trouble. I knew my mom was actually in one of her rare sober periods for a week or two and this would give her something motherly to do.

She didn't seem that surprised when I got home. I just told her I fell on the ice, which was technically true. She made an appointment with our doctor and we were able to get in right away. I was relieved because having *her* take *me* to the ER would've been strange at this point. A few stitches later and I was out on our deck, smoking a cigarette thinking of the badass story I'd tell everyone the next day. In reality, I knew it was dumb and I made a decision to not snowboard ever again.

I rub the back of my head and snap out of it. Tom is reaching across to turn the music down.

"Hey, Corey, I gotta get home," Tom says. "Almost getting arrested is fun and all, but it's dinner time."

After we drop Tom off, I light a cigarette as Scott drives onto I-80. The suburbs fall away. I take a big drag and wonder where we are going.

* * *

I just had a not very filling Snickers bar for lunch in MDP. It's Tuesday. No, Wednesday? I don't even know. I look up and see Mrs. Harper grading tests or something. I missed most of last Friday because I just got to school and after a class or two, realized I didn't want to be there and just left. Instead, I smoked a joint and watched game shows all day while my mom was passed out upstairs.

I watch the guy next to me punch numbers into his calculator, with his math homework all over the desk. No thanks. If it weren't for grades, I would enjoy high school a lot more. Most of the students laugh and wave at me through the window as they pass by in between classes. I'm lucky to be able to navigate through most of the social circles. Since I was in honors classes before, I can talk to the smart or "nerdy" kids. Since I smoke pot and dress in thrift store clothes, I can talk to the outsiders. Since I've dated a lot of the girls in the school, I can talk to the jocks.

I'm still in a few honors classes, but my grades have been slipping. Slipping slowly like everything else since freshman year. I've been good about hiding my report card and when my stepdad or dad asks about it, I just say I'm getting Bs and Cs. I've flunked gym already this year just because I didn't feel like changing for swimming, not wanting to mess up my hair the rest of the day.

I stare at the chalkboard. School seems like a habit at this point. When am I going to use all this stuff? Where is the class on managing money? Where is the class that tells me how to deal with my mother? Where is the class on keeping a job? I look forward to MDP more and more just because it gives me a day at school to do what I want. Read, write notes to girls and just take a little break.

Sometimes, I don't have to ditch. Just last week, my mom was up in the morning and asked if I wanted to stay home and go shopping with her. Um, yeah? When she was sober, she could still be a cool mom. It was rare, but it was great too. After the mall, we hung out in the backyard, smoked a few cigarettes and talked about girls. She told me about dating my dad and some other boyfriends in high school. My brother got home and the three of us had dinner together.

Other times, my mom was sober enough to call school so I could stay home with her, but then she'd drink herself to sleep in her room soon after. I'd watch TV or hang out instead. It was still good, but not the same.

She's so unpredictable. I think about the other night where she called the cops on my stepdad after an argument. The next night she was certain I took her cigarettes, swearing she saw me take them. It didn't matter that I just got home or don't smoke menthol. She was snarling at me. I was annoyed, but then she pulled a knife out of a kitchen drawer and pointed it at me. The same knife I had used to get her off the phone almost two years ago. I ended up just running out to the gas station to get her some more. It was easier than getting stabbed. When I got back, she didn't even remember what happened. All she knew was she had cigarettes. She's living in an entirely different world.

She'd sometimes give me vague reprimands and lectures about MDP, my grades and everything too.

"CJ, you are so smart. What happened to my boy who was on the honor roll every semester in middle school? You can do better."

I've been hearing that from everyone my whole life it felt like. Whatever. Nice try.

I never talked to my dad about school either. He probably has no idea how much I've been in trouble at school. I doubt he would call out for me like Mom does so we could go do something fun. Maybe he would, but I don't really talk to him much lately, so I don't really know.

I learned the hard way that my mom had to be the one to call school. Jack and I were going to ditch a full day a few weeks ago and ride our bikes around after getting high. We decided to just pretend to be our parents and call the school office ourselves. I went first, called the number and cleared my throat.

"Hello, this is Chris Morris's stepfather. Unfortunately, he's not feeling well and won't be in today."

I tried adding bass to my voice, but it just sounded like I was impersonating a grown-up.

"Okay, sir, just one question before I get more info. Who was president when you were born?"

"Um . . ."

I stuttered and hung up. We still ditched, but I ended up in MDP again.

It wasn't all bad. Sometimes we'd read interesting stuff in English class like *Catcher in the Rye* or John Steinbeck. We just watched *Rebel without a Cause* too, which I'd already seen, but was cool to see in school. James Dean lived too fast and died too young.

I also got out of some classes here and there to see Mrs.

Clark, my guidance counselor at school. I've seen her on and off since my little "episode" freshman year that landed me in the hospital, but now it's pretty regular. Even though I deny using drugs and act like everything is fine, my school record tells a different story.

She's pretty nice and I can tell she means well. It's not helpful, but I like getting out of class. I don't give her much, only little bits of truth when I need to.

For example, I can't deny not being at school. So when she asks, "Chris, I see that you missed a few days and some classes here and there. What's going on?"

I lay it on.

"Sorry, you know with my mom and everything, it's just too much. Sometimes it's hard to concentrate on things like history or gym class."

I don't do that a lot, because it does feel a little icky using my mom as an excuse and I worry about making myself sound too emotionally unstable. I can't just tell Mrs. Clark that I think school is boring and would rather get high and see what's on HBO. I smiled accidentally the last time I was in her office thinking of that.

"Chris, you have a nice smile. You should smile more. It lights up your face."

Ugh, do they teach that in guidance counselor school?

"How are things at home?"

Oh you know, the usual. Sober. Drinking. Rehab. Sober. Rinse. Repeat.

"Do you ever feel like hurting yourself?"

"No. Never," I answer.

I mean it. That will always be a question I guess. I know she's asking partly because of what happened a few years ago, but also to gauge if I am suicidal in any way. As bad and sad as things get, I still have my friends. My cigarettes. Music. Drugs.

The bell rings and it's the last of the day. I'm free.

✳ ✳ ✳

"Maureen? Maureen Thomas? Are you sure?"

I was at my locker and my neighbor Mike had just given me some far-fetched news. Maureen, a girl I had an unrequited crush on in eighth grade, apparently has been talking about me. We talked sometimes in Lit class, but I never thought my flirtations would go anywhere. I did make her laugh though. That was always my secret weapon.

"For real, man. You guys should go out."

Next thing I know, it's Friday night and I'm in Maureen's car driving to the famous Ed Debevic's diner downtown. She doesn't let me smoke in the car, but I don't care. Maureen Thomas! I can't get over it. I spent countless periods just staring at her, daydreaming of walking around and holding her hand. She was pretty, but also smart and confident. She was also quiet, so you never knew what she was thinking.

At the diner, in between getting charmingly berated by the server in typical Ed Debevic's fashion, we share secrets.

"I had the biggest crush on you in middle school. You have no idea! It's crazy to sit here right now," I tell her with wide eyes.

"What? I had a crush on you during freshman year. But you were dating so many girls, I didn't think you'd have time for little old me."

She smiles and my insides drop. All this time. At least we're together now.

It's going fine. Well, until I meet her mother the next week. She's super strict. Loud. I get the sense that she doesn't want Maureen dating.

"You're not her boyfriend are you? She doesn't have time for all that with school and her job. I'm glad you guys are friends though."

I just smile. I'm not sure where Maureen's dad is and don't want to ask just yet. Some nights Maureen can't go out because her mom makes her stay home to do school work and study. I can barely talk to her on the phone. I don't tell her that my mom couldn't even name one class I was in, my teachers or anything.

On the weekend, Maureen tells me that her mom is working late at the Italian restaurant she manages. Maureen has to watch her little sister Jenny, but can

I maybe sneak in her window and hang out and sleepover?

Here we go again.

"Why can't I just come over in a normal kind of way? Then I can hide or something from your sister. Do I need to sneak in like a burglar?"

"I don't want to risk having Jenny see you at all. When my mom comes home, I can't give her the smallest chance of thinking something is up. What if she checks on Jenny and my sister says she saw you over here?"

"Okay, okay. I'll see you then."

We work out the details. I call Scott and let him know what's up. I leave a note at home saying I'm sleeping over at Scott's.

Scott doesn't live far from Maureen so he drops me off around the corner. He's excited for me. I'm excited for me too.

"You bring any condoms, man?"

"Dude! I don't kiss and tell."

I wink as I leave his car.

Damn, I didn't bring any. Could be like the cruise cabin all over again.

I wait in her backyard, sitting next to her shed. I want to smoke but can't risk any neighbors seeing some strange guy lighting up in the dark. At ten o'clock exactly, I see

Maureen's bedroom light flash on and off. Our signal. I duck and walk over to the window. Like the other two times I've snuck into a girl's window, this one was on the ground floor too. I smile at the strange synchronicity.

She closes the blinds and pulls me close. I notice a candle lit in the corner.

"Hey, you."

She smiles and kisses me. Her whole body is smooth.

"What is this?" I say rubbing her pajamas over the sides of her stomach.

"You like? I picked them up at Victoria's Secret. I think it's silk or close to it."

"It feels amazing. You feel amazing. Thanks for inviting me over."

She doesn't say anything and just takes me over to the bed. We kiss. She smells good too. I'm guessing it's also Victoria's Secret perfume. Maureen works at the mall, so it wouldn't surprise me.

The kissing intensifies and after I unbutton the front of her pajama top, I hear a door close upstairs. Walking.

"What's that? Oh no, is that your mom?"

"It's fine, just be quiet."

"Are you sure? Is your door locked?"

"Yes. Stop talking."

We keep kissing, but I'm nervous and have a hard time focusing. A few minutes later, there's a knock on the door.

"Maureen?"

The door handle jiggles. It just got real. I get up and put my shirt back on. Maureen is doing the same.

"What, Mom? I was almost asleep."

"Why is your door locked? I just brought home some lasagne from work. It didn't look like you guys ate much by the dishes in the kitchen that you didn't wash."

The door keeps jiggling. I'm already opening the window.

"Don't go," Maureen whispers.

I can tell by her eyes though that I should. And I do.

"Hold on, Mom. Let me get up. I must have locked it by accident."

I hear this as I'm running across her backyard.

Great. Now what? That didn't go as planned.

I'm in the middle of nowhere except for the silent houses in the dark. I can't go to Scott's. It's too late. I reach into my pants pocket for my cigarettes. Not there. My front shirt pocket. Not there either.

They're likely in Maureen's room or her backyard. Great. I still have a joint I rolled after school and my lighter though. I was planning on smoking it on the way home tomorrow, so it will be a consolation for the interrupted evening festivities.

I light it up and continue the slow walk home. I haven't walked home at night in a long time. I usually have my mom's car or a bike at least. This just sucks. What is usually a five or twenty minute ride is going to take much longer.

I inhale slowly and hold it in. I stop walking. Then I blow it out in one big puff. I laugh, thinking how this has become my morning routine, but in reverse. I usually light up and smoke on the way to school. Joints are good for walking through neighborhoods because it looks like a cigarette. Smoking a pipe or bowl is pretty suspicious. Plus, my walk to school is about fifteen minutes, which is a perfect time to smoke a joint then a cigarette or two before getting talked at all day.

It's made a lot of things easier I think. Avoiding my family makes things easier. But drugs and cigarettes makes it even easier. To escape. Feelings. Pain. Life.

I should smoke a little more if I ever make it home. What a night. I deserve it. I still have half a dime bag. Mental note to ask John at work for some more. I'm dizzy now.

So much weed. A dime bag here. A nickel bag there. I've even splurged and bought a quarter or half ounce of it sometimes. Then you don't have to worry about it.

Otherwise, I end up driving around all night, aimlessly looking for more. We've killed whole nights just knocking on doors turning out to be dead ends, because we heard so and so has some or might have some.

I stop at the gas station at 147th and Central to buy some more Camel cigarettes. When I get home, I notice my note about sleeping at Scott's still on the counter. I throw it away and see my brother asleep downstairs with the TV on.

I go upstairs and hear my mom snoring. I look in her room and she's asleep on top of the bed, comforter and all, wearing the same clothes I've seen her in the past two days. I close her door and go to my room. I smoke a little more weed in a bowl and put on a bootleg CD of Nirvana's *MTV Unplugged* show. "About a Girl" comes on and I think about Kurt Cobain and his suicide just last month. We've all been listening to Nirvana almost nonstop since then. My stomach hurts thinking about it, but I relax and just listen to every note. By the time "Come as You Are" is playing, I'm enveloped by the guitar sound. I think about listening to this song just two years ago when it came out. The world was so different then. I think of the video and Kurt swimming and swimming and swimming. I think about where Kurt is now and close my eyes.

❋ ❋ ❋

Mrs. Thompson takes my hall pass and directs me to the worn couch outside Mrs. Clark's office for our regular meeting. At least it's not one of our increasingly rare "group sessions" this time. I still don't share much in those, since I know the information would end up as gossip in the school locker rooms. Mrs. Clark has ground rules for "confidentiality," but c'mon, it's high school.

The door opens. Joe, who I remember from a history class last year, half smiles at me and walks out.

"Hey, Chris, come on in!" She says with a big smile.

I don't know how she does it.

I need a cigarette. I'm tired too from staying out too late with Scott at a diner, drinking coffee and talking, well, debating the movies *True Romance* and *Reservoir Dogs*. *True Romance* is obviously the best movie ever, but Scott is obsessed with the soundtrack to *Reservoir Dogs*.

Mrs. Clark grabs my file. I wonder what could possibly be in it.

"So, how are things going?" She smiles.

Ugh. Where to start. Do I tell her about Maureen? How she's grounded, mad and broken up with me? All because I dropped my cigarettes on her bedroom floor. We haven't even talked in a week. It was all over before it even started it feels like.

"It's alright, I guess. Same old sh--, um, stuff."

"It looks like you are still missing school, Chris. Is everything the same at home?"

I'm bored and half-awake, so for whatever reason, I decide to let loose some truth. Maybe it will help with the absences by getting a little pity?

"I don't know. It somehow gets worse and worse. My mom's sober for a week or two. Usually right out of rehab. Kind of herself. Talks to my girlfriends on the phone. They like her. She likes them. She tells me how sorry she is for everything.

"Then the next week, she's drunk all day, every day. Half drunk in the afternoon and fully drunk in the evening. Instead of telling me how sorry she is, she's surly and mean. 'CJ, who cut your hair? You need to get it fixed. It looks ugly. Makes you look ugly. You think you're gonna get a girlfriend with that haircut?' Then she laughs at me and tells me how hard it is to be a mom. Same old story. Every day she is a different person.

"And she keeps lying. She can't just ask me to get her cigarettes, she has to tell me a long story about how she went to the doctor and she isn't allowed to drive because of her nausea or some random illness of the day. She's perpetually sick. She used to just say she didn't feel well. Now she acts like she's dying."

"You know, not to defend her, but she might really be sick and in pain because of the alcohol withdrawal, but she doesn't say that. Or even know," Mrs. Clark chimes in.

"I get that. Either way, if I refuse her request, she makes me feel guilty by saying I don't love her and she raised me and she's done so much for me. And so on. Sometimes I go and get them. Sometimes I don't. It depends on how drunk she is and how much I can take.

"She makes up long stories about my stepdad that I know aren't true. She's done this before, but they're getting more crazy. Abuse. How mean he is. She'll say he tried to kill her the night before, yet he wasn't even home. It's not even lies I think, which is even more upsetting, but I think she's drinking so much that she literally is seeing things! Hallucinating. I heard her talking about how she saw her dad recently too. He's been dead for a few years.

"My stepdad. I feel bad for him. I don't even know if he sees her that that much anymore. I hear them yelling, but it's usually just him exasperated at her drinking. 'It's his fault I'm this way,' she'll say sometimes.

"Totally bizarre. My stepdad does seem to try if and when he's around. He loves her. Sometimes I'll take her to rehab, but he does too. And he goes for the counseling sessions. A few weeks ago, she was clearly on the path to her usual couple weeks of being drunk, but he had hid all the liquor in the kitchen. Did she buy more? No, she called the police instead to retaliate. Again.

"We used to be living the good life. I don't understand. My mom traded it all and is just a scarred mess now."

My eyes well up a little bit, but I stop and take a breath. I keep going because for some strange reason, I feel a little better already. Who else do I have to talk to? It's like a fire hose of reality I'm spraying on this poor woman though.

Mrs. Clark hands me a tissue. I'm embarrassed and wave it away.

"Now my tan, happy mom has turned into a pale, skinny shadow of herself. I don't know when and how she eats. Sometimes I'll save some of my food or whatever for her. Mostly, she seems to live on her liquid diet.

"Not only is she skinny, but she used to pride herself on her appearance, spending hours in the bathroom fixing her hair or make-up. Now, she'll put on make-up sometime before a binge and days later, she looks like a raccoon smoking away in our dining room. It's scary.

"She used to drink jugs of wine. Now it's just straight vodka. She's drunk more often and drunk faster. And a different kind of drunk. She didn't used to be so mean. Or aggressive. Or sad. It makes *me* sad, coming home finding her passed out with her bedroom door open, both pants and sheets wet. She either couldn't get up to go to the bathroom or didn't care."

I put my head down. The weight of it all.

"Most people my age are doing homework or having dinner with their parents. Instead, I'm in the laundry room washing my mom's urine-soaked clothes. Why? I just want to know why. Or what to do. It's not fair and I know nothing is fair, but it sucks. How can she say she loves me one minute, but ruin her life, no, *our* lives by just lifting a glass?"

Mrs. Clark is stunned. I don't even know if she took any notes. She stopped writing a while ago and looks like I just told her one of her cats died.

"Thank you for sharing that, Chris. I know it's not easy.

It sounds frustrating at home . . ."

I tune out at some point. What can she do or say really? Unless she can make my mom stop drinking, then it's all just words.

✳ ✳ ✳

"Hi, is this Jim? This is Christopher Stone, calling on behalf of the Illinois Fraternal Association of Police and Fire Chiefs. How are you doing tonight?"

Click.

I check Jim Nordrup off the list. Pick up the phone and call Rebecca North, who is next on the list. I hate this job. Well, some of it.

Telemarketing. I feel a little dirty doing it. Most people hate when you call. Because the name of the organization is very official, a few times a night, you actually do get a few people that say yes. I fill out the form and give it to Janet, who smiles while taking care of all the donation paperwork. I get an hourly rate, but even more money based on how much I raise.

I worry it's not entirely legitimate. Janet is married to the boss and they both live in Indiana. I do know that it pays okay. I also know that I can smoke at my desk and my friend AJ sits nearby. We try to make each other laugh by using different fake names and even accents sometimes. The early evening hours are nice too. It's usually when people are eating dinner I've come to find out.

AJ is on the phone now, trying not to look at me. He's a year older, but was in my gym class and we hit it off immediately. He has a similar family situation and lives with his mom and her boyfriend. I don't know if she drinks, but her boyfriend is a total dick to AJ. In addition to music, movies and life's deep unfairness, he's one of the few people I talk to about what's going on at home. He usually punctuates many conversations by putting out his unfiltered Camels and saying, "Man, I don't have all the answers, just more questions."

AJ also taught me the art of Zippo lighter maintenance, which upped my smoking game. I immediately bought a black one and lighter fluid, wicks and flints. There's something oddly satisfying about flicking the top of the case with its signature metal clinking, rubbing the flint wheel to light the flame, and closing the lid to extinguish the flame. I'm still a little afraid of getting high and leaving the lighter open and burning something down, but that hasn't happened yet.

AJ fits right in with Scott and Corey too, so it's all good. We first all bonded over watching Denis Leary's *No Cure for Cancer* at Scott's house. It's a no holds barred standup special we'd all seen separately and love, especially the "Asshole" song in the beginning. AJ and I just saw the movie *Clerks* and can't stop quoting, "This job would be great if it wasn't for the fucking customers."

The fake names at work were actually encouraged by Willy, a longstanding employee. He has long dark hair, mustache and looks like he should be riding in a

Camaro, drinking a cold beer. He says he uses a fake name because a lot of people know him in Oak Forest for a "whole bunch of shit you wouldn't believe." After a while, I gather from dropping him off a few times that he does drink a lot and probably just did something stupid to his neighbors in his apartment complex. At least I hope that's all he did.

I look around and aside from me, AJ and Willy, I don't recognize a lot of folks. The whole office churns out people. Someone starts and quits a week later. People of all ages, colors and both men and women. It's a weird place and it's only been a few months. At least it's a paycheck. If I have a bad night, I just circle a few people that hung up on me rudely and tell Janet that they said they were good for twenty-five dollars. AJ just shakes his head.

"You know they aren't gonna pay. You're just gonna get in trouble."

"What are they going to do? Fire me? C'mon, man. We have tenure now!"

I don't know if that's true, but it feels right. AJ is a good guy. Like me, people tell him he seems older than he is.

My arm starts to cramp from holding the phone, so I get up and walk outside for some air. I need to ask for a headset like Willy. We're in a little office area off of 147th Street, full of insurance offices and real estate agents. I pace around and smoke. It's been a nice change hanging out with AJ more. I'm starting to pull back from my old friend Jack. Again. I have to. The guy just doesn't quit.

We pierced our own ears. His idea. We gave ourselves tattoos! His idea. I gave myself a big mysterious "M" on my arm by dipping a needle into black India ink. Morris? Mom? MTV? He did a smiley face. Jack said someone told him this is how you do it, but it hurt like hell. I didn't think the tattoos would last either, but they did. My mom hasn't noticed it yet.

It got worse. I think about ditching school with Jack recently to go to Lincoln Park Zoo. We got high on the way in his little green car, a Geo Storm. The week before, we came to the zoo almost as a joke, but it turned out to be more fun than we thought. Watching monkeys jump around for an hour here or there, then try not getting paranoid while staring a tiger in the face. Brookfield Zoo is nice, but Lincoln Park is free and last time we went to Brookfield I got sneezed on by a walrus. Also, the gorillas at Lincoln Park Zoo are always mesmerizing.

We walked around the zoo, which was almost completely empty. It was surreal. It was also a Tuesday at about ten in the morning. After walking out of the reptile house, we walked past the outside exhibits where they feature African animals and others. The first one we saw looked completely empty. Just a little grassy area surrounded by rocks. There was a fence in front of us and I didn't see a closed sign or any sign really. I was also a little high. So was Jack apparently.

"Man, screw this, we came to see some wild animals."

Before I knew it, Jack is across the fence and even the

little moat area between the fence and exhibit.

"Dude, what are you doing? You're gonna get us in trouble!"

I looked around and didn't see a thing. Still though. He was making me nervous. As usual.

Jack was just standing there, looking at the rocks. Then he turned around at me with his arms up.

"Well, I bet no one has done this before! Haha, yeah! I flipped the script. Next thing you know, an animal is gonna walk by you and it will be like some sci-fi movie where *we* are on display."

He was shouting too loud. As I laughed and went to light a cigarette, I saw what looked like a dog lazily walk out of a hole I didn't notice before. Right behind Jack.

"Hey! Be cool, man. There is something in there."

"What?"

Jack turned and immediately ran towards me. Thankfully, by the time Jack was back to safety next to me, I finally saw that it was a wolf walking around sleepily. He was smelling the grass and then just looked at us.

"That was close, huh? Haha!" He smacked my back laughing hysterically.

That was too close. I swear. That guy. He stayed out of the animal enclosures after that at least.

Then a few days later, we were driving two girls home from school, Denise and Brandy, both a year younger than us. Plus, Denise is hot. They actually asked us for a ride on the way out to Jack's car, which I thought was interesting because it doesn't happen much.

We drove, passing a joint around and were driving through the suburban maze of houses between 151st and 159th when Jack slowed down past a little boy walking home. Jack glanced at us with a smile on his face then rolled down the window.

"Hey, kid, want some candy?"

The boy ran in the opposite direction and we drove off. The girls were laughing in an awkward "did that just happen?" kind of way. It was kind of funny, but stupid.

A few days later, I was at work, looking through the paper by the coffee machine and saw us in it. Not us specifically, but in the police blotter it mentioned how four people in a little green car asked a kid if he wanted candy. It said the boy didn't know these strangers and if anyone knew who they were, to contact police.

I got in the habit of checking the police blotter, since we would make it in there occasionally last year due to the antics on our bikes, water guns or whatever, but this was serious. Suddenly I remembered one of the girls in the back seat, Brandy, coming up to me in the hall before lunch yesterday.

"Hey, thanks for the ride the other day. I have to say though, that was kinda messed up what you guys did.

It was funny for a second and I know you were just joking, but I couldn't stop thinking about that poor kid's parents when he came home. You know?"

I just nodded. I didn't think that far. She was right.

I light another cigarette. My arm still hurts.

The last straw was Jack declaring a mock war on my old friends from freshman year - Dan, Andy and their new friend Jay, who I didn't know, but kind of rounded out their group after I started hanging out with Jack. I think Jack thought he was being funny, but it was just messed up. Dan and Andy and I were still cool, but now they were coming up to me asking, "What's up with Jack? He just ran into Jay in the hall. Like *ran* into him."

I didn't have any answers as usual. When I asked Jack, he just shrugged his shoulders and said, "To hell with that Jay dude, man. Thinks he's so smart. I don't have a problem with Dan or Andy, but Jay is going down."

Made no sense. A few days later, I heard from Dan that Jack jumped Jay out of the blue in front of Dan's house and just started beating on him until they pulled him off. Jack ran away once someone said they were calling the cops. The guy has issues. Since Jack's connected to me though, Dan and Andy now keep their distance.

AJ comes outside through my cloud of smoke.

"What have you been doing? Willy is asking about you."

"Yeah, my arm hurt. I need to get one of those headsets. You know, finally be legit," I say, exhaling smoke.

We go back inside and sit down. Willy just looks at me. He's on the phone but I move my arm in a dramatic fashion with a pained face to kind of mime to him that I wasn't just taking a spontaneous smoke break.

"Hi, is this Ed? This is Christopher Peters. I'm calling..."

* * *

It's May. Saturday. I'm getting ready. My ears are still ringing a little from a Matthew Sweet concert a few days ago at the Park West downtown. It was a school night and Scott had the bright idea to go up to the front row, standing right next to the stage. That night and the next day, I could only hear high pitched noises and I left school after my first period. Everyone sounded like chipmunks. It was worth it though.

I comb my hair. Sarah is coming by in a bit for lunch and a movie. I hope it's a date. We met at a party last week at Eric's house. I don't know him that well except chatting with him in science class here and there. Eric did the classic "my parents aren't home, let's invite everyone I know over" thing.

It was a strange night. Scott, Corey and I smoked a little beforehand and people were drinking beer inside. I haven't drank much since the cruise. I don't like how it makes me feel. I can feel myself losing control when I drink. With pot, even in my highest moments, I still feel a little conscious of what is happening. It feels somewhat manageable.

I was pretty buzzed though and it was dark in the house at the party. *The Crow* soundtrack was blasting. It's all everyone is listening to lately. I went on the back porch to smoke and it was only after a few puffs that I noticed someone in a wheelchair already on the deck.

"Hey, what's up?" I ask.

"How you doin', man? Cool party, huh?"

Oh my God. It was Chad. It was only a little over a year ago that he was in my face before I beat up his brother Lucas. What happened? I obviously had been missing too much school and gossip.

"Yeah, lots of people," I said, smoking a little faster.

"Totally. Hey, um, I know what happened last year was crazy, but we're all good now, right?"

What was happening? Why wouldn't it be? I looked at him and felt bad about everything just staring at him in his chair, watching the party from the outside.

"Chad, definitely. I was all caught up with that girl and sorry your brother got caught up in it too. It's all good. I'm going back in, you want anything?"

"No, thanks. See you later."

Whoa, that was heavy. I went inside and searched frantically for someone I knew. I saw Scott in the corner drinking a beer and talking to a girl I didn't know.

"Hey, man. Can I talk to you for a sec?" I said and looked

at the girl. "Sorry, it will only take a second."

"Do you want me to leave?"

She was blonde, tall, and cute. Who was that? I looked around and noticed a lot of people I didn't know.

Scott put his arm around her in a friendly way.

"No, no, it's fine. Stay here. What's up?"

I leaned in a little closer.

"Hey, what happened to Chad? I don't remember his last name, but I got in a fight with his brother Lucas last year. Now the guy is sitting in a wheelchair out back?"

The girl looked stunned. It was a lot of random information at once.

"Oh, yeah. It happened in March, I think. I'm surprised you didn't hear. It was all everyone was talking about for a few days. You were in MDP probably. Anyway, he was out riding his skateboard with friends and tried to do some sort of back flip off a ramp or something and hit his head or neck or whatever. Ended up paralyzed from the neck down."

"Damn. I had no idea. He wanted to make sure we were all good after everything that went down last year."

Scott just looked annoyed because I stalled things with the girl he was talking to.

"Alright, man. That's what's up. Let's talk later," Scott said with a look that said he had better things to do.

The information sunk in. My mind wandered to all the times Jack and I were high riding our bikes on busy roads. Then I remembered snowboarding a while ago, trying to do a jump off the ice and ending up in stitches. That could've been me.

I shuddered a bit and turned around. There was a pretty girl I didn't know talking to a tall guy that I recognized from school. As I got closer, it became clear that he was talking to her yet she didn't want any part of it, based on her body language and expressions.

"No, it's cool. Come on. I heard people are upstairs, just chilling," he said before noticing me. "Oh, hey."

I reached my arm around the girl and smiled at her. Thankfully, she smiled back.

"Hey, what's up? John, right? I see you met my girlfriend."

"Oh shit. Dude, I didn't know. We were just talking. Sarah is great You're lucky. I gotta get another beer. See you guys later."

And then he was off.

"Thank you," she said, looking up at me.

That's how I met Sarah. We talked for a bit and she seemed alright. I didn't get her number, because I smoked a little more weed in the bathroom with Corey later and kind of forgot about her. Not on purpose. However, she reached out to Eric, who gave me her number at her request in science class the Monday after.

Turns out she lives in Frankfort and goes to Lincoln High. We made plans and here we are.

When she pulls up to my house though, I get in and am almost sure that this isn't the right person. She's really tall. Short hair. Not particularly attractive. Not ugly per se, but just not how I remembered. I'm mad at myself almost instantly. And feel bad for wasting this poor girl's time.

"Hey. Good to see you, S-a-r-a-h," I say her name slowly, almost to make sure this is in fact the right person.

"Hey, yourself! Chris, it's nice to meet you."

She shakes my hand to mock me and laughs. How high was I at that party? And how dark was it exactly?

We end up at Aurelio's Pizza and I get the newspaper to see what movies are playing and when. We settle on *When a Man Loves a Woman*, which I think is probably too romantic sounding for a date that I'm already pretty sure will be our last one. Sarah insists her friend saw it yesterday and it was good. At this point, I'm just along for the ride.

Much like the date, I immediately regret the movie choice once it starts. Out of all the movies in theaters, we pick the one about an alcoholic mother causing chaos in her family's life? I squirm a little and am so distracted by the movie, it takes my mind off of Sarah, who is probably sitting there wondering why I'm not making a move on her. Alice, the alcoholic played by Meg Ryan, goes through a lot in the movie, but her husband does too and learns a lot about being married to an alcoholic. It's an intense movie. I feel like I'm going to have a panic attack multiple times during the movie.

In the end though, Alice is six months sober after rehab and makes up with her husband. I'm sure that happens sometimes in real life, but to me it feels like a bullshit Hollywood ending.

Sarah is crying as the credits roll.

"Wow, that was so good. Right? I'm sorry for crying."

"No, it's fine. It was good. Um, Meg Ryan was amazing. I'm not feeling well by the way. Do you mind just taking me home?"

It's a quiet drive. I really don't feel that great. I'm still a little off by being confronted with alcoholism for two hours that wasn't my mother's and having it wrap up so nicely at the end.

"I'll call you soon," I say to her when we pull in my driveway. I know I won't.

She leans in and I give her a hug.

"I don't want to get you sick," I lie, as an excuse not to kiss her. I'm terrible.

I walk in and see that my mom is in the kitchen. No Meg Ryan.

"Hey, you're home early. What you been up to?"

She seems sober. She's mom. I'm a bit shocked.

"I just had a date with a girl. Didn't go well."

"Oh no, what happened?"

I light a cigarette with her lighter on the counter.

"She was nice, I just thought she was someone else. I know that sounds weird, but I met her recently and she was so pretty. But when she showed up today, she looked completely different. I'm not sure what happened. Don't say anything. I know it's mean, but there are too many girls out there for me to just date anyone."

"No, I get it. I was in high school too once you know," she says, smirking at me. "What did you guys do?"

An idea comes to me.

"We ended up seeing this movie, *When a Man Loves a Woman*. Have you heard of it? Meg Ryan and Andy Garcia are in it. It's really good. You guys should go see it. As soon as you can. What are you doing tonight?"

"Nothing, your stepdad is out fishing with his brother now, but maybe we'll go tonight."

I give her a hug. I don't usually, but damn that stupid movie. I need her to know how important it is that she goes and sees it. I go upstairs and lie down for a while. I remember I'm meeting up with AJ later. Who knows where we'll end up and for how long.

The next day, I'm eating breakfast and I hear my mom come downstairs.

"Hey, CJ."

She looks . . . happy.

"You were right. That was a good movie. I know why you wanted me to see it now too. It's okay, I'm not mad. I'm glad you didn't say what it was about either because I'm not sure I would have."

"I know. So?"

As if her alcoholism can be cured forever thanks to Meg Ryan's extraordinary acting.

"Your stepdad and I talked after and I'm going to work on getting better. It's not easy, but I know it's best for all of us. I needed that. I love you all so much."

She comes over and hugs me. Holds me for awhile. Then lets me go.

"I want things to be the way they used to be. Before all this. Remember when we first moved in here? We used to have so much fun. We were even talking about going to the Wisconsin Dells again this summer. All of us. His girls too.

"I'm even going to look into some local AA meetings. Alcoholics Anonymous? I only went to a few in the hospital, but I think it could help."

Who is this? AA? Outside of rehab? Maybe Meg Ryan *is* that good.

"I'm sorry. I know it hasn't been easy for you and your

brother."

"I love you too, Mom. You know that. I'm here for you."

She cries softly and I go upstairs, hopeful and proud. Did I just change her life? I had lost hope before, but she looked genuinely remorseful.

It feels like having my old mom back when I hear her tell me that dinner is ready. She cooked? She asks me questions about my day. She laughs a sober laugh.

A couple days later, I open the door after a night of cold calling at work and immediately feel the difference. The house is black. Smoky. The air is different. She's drinking again.

I don't look for her. I can't talk to her. I go right up to my room and turn on the TV. I fill up a bowl with as much weed as I can fit. I usually smoke with a little empty toilet paper tube stuffed with fabric softener to mask the smell when I exhale, but tonight I fill up the room with as much smoke as I can.

I look up and the movie *Tron* is on the TV. Finally, something good. I loved this movie as a kid. Deeply. Jeff Bridges gets transported into the bright computer world and has to fight his way out to save himself and the programs.

I keep smoking. I think of a laser shooting at me from behind like in the movie, escaping into another world. Lasers. Computers. Light cycles . . .

The TV feels farther and farther away as I get higher and

higher until my mind seems to disintegrate. I lose the ability to think about anything or anyone. Especially Meg fucking Ryan.

❋ ❋ ❋

Scott, Corey and I are practically screaming the words to "Gold Soundz" by Pavement driving down the Dan Ryan Expressway. We are coming home from their show at the Metro downtown. I'm glad they are touring on *Crooked Rain, Crooked Rain,* which came out in February and we've been listening to it ever since. As soon as we heard they'd be here in May, we got tickets immediately.

It was awesome. I love shows at the Metro, because it's all ages, but almost everyone there is an adult. It's a crazy feeling standing by the staircase smoking when a grown-up asks, "Hey, you got a light?" We fit right in. Sort of.

I'm stretched out in the back seat. We smoked a little before the show and now we are passing around a joint. Corey is all about the joints. I think they're too much work if you have access to a pipe, but if he's rolling them, it's all good.

We hit the point where we are all just enjoying the music and settle into being high. I lost my cigarettes at the Metro somewhere.

"Corey, you got a cigarette? I don't know what happened to mine."

He smokes Marlboro, which is better than nothing. I'm

thankful that none of my friends smoke menthol like my mom and dad.

"Yeah, man. I got you," he says, while lighting one for me and passes it back.

"Scott, you good?" I ask, noticing how distracted he looks.

"Yeah, I'm fine. Just focused on driving."

He bobs his head to the music, trying to look serious at the same time.

"Thanks, dude."

These are my favorite moments. Outside of the suburbs and our day-to-day lives, driving with friends, good music and not a care in the world except for where we're going to stop and eat. Or get some more weed if we need it.

It's been fun lately. Sometimes scary, but in a good way. I've been hanging out with Scott and Corey almost non-stop. Sometimes AJ. Since my mom relapsed hard a few days ago, they've been my lifeline a bit. They don't know that, but I do.

If it's not a concert, it's mini-golf. Bowling. Late night diners and pizza places for coffee and conversation. The mall, but not as much anymore. We probably just drive around it more than anything.

Scott's dad has been traveling for work lately, so we've started hanging out at his townhouse on the weekends more. His older sister Laura is graduating in a few weeks and has a boyfriend. We don't see her that much, but she has friends over too, so we get to know some more people in the graduating class. Always a plus. They're all pretty cool. Ever since I got in a fight last year, I've realized the value of knowing as many people as I can in school, especially older kids.

Scott had a few parties too. Well, the first few were just a couple of us and some other guys from school hanging out in his basement. While Scott was talking to his sister upstairs, we called the "1-900" adult numbers on his phone, the ones where you had to pay by the minute. That was as crazy as it got. We were too high, so it was just us laughing and screaming "Balls!" at the women at the other end but it was funny. Until he got his phone bill. His dad was pissed. Scott had to pay his dad back. We picked up a few of his dinners and weed for the next week or two.

This happened after Scott being mad at me already for what happened at his older brother's apartment in Lincoln Park. Scott's brother invited us up for a party he was having and we hung out all night. I drank screwdrivers one after the other, even though I didn't really want to and blacked out in a bedroom. I woke up, the room was spinning and I vomited right on the floor. Then I panicked and tried covering it up with a *Chicago Tribune* newspaper nearby. Of course, Scott's brother saw it in the morning.

"What the hell is this?"

Scott was rightly upset and embarrassed too. We finally get invited to one of his brother's parties in the city and

I messed it up. I used to be shamed by wetting the bed at friend's houses sleeping over. Now I have to worry about drinking or smoking too much?

The next party Scott held at his place was awesome though. Mainly because it was Laura that put it together. There were seniors everywhere and then us, with some more guys we hung out with sometimes - Pat, Adam and Bryan. They went to middle school with Scott and Corey, so there was a connection there. The new guys didn't smoke, but there was beer and they drank all night.

Laura's friends weren't stuck up and treated us all like we belonged. I had brought some CDs and played some dance music in the kitchen, mostly remixes of "Get Off" by Prince. Laura and her friends made me play it over and over. One came over to me smiling and said, "You're cute."

Laura whispered, "Krista likes you. Don't get any ideas though. She has a boyfriend and he plays football. He's here too."

"Yeah, yeah, okay. I'm flattered."

I checked out Krista. She was cute. I did remember her talking to a big looking guy earlier who was passing out beers to everyone in the living room. No, thank you.

I went outside to smoke and came back in to find Pat walking up the stairs with a pitchfork.

"What's going on, man?"

"Oh, I found this in the garage. Crazy, right?"

"Um, yeah, what're you gonna do with it?"

"Watch me scare the hell out of Adam. *That's* what's gonna happen."

I then watched Pat hover over Adam lying on the sofa, half passed out with a pitchfork over his head. Adam woke up and screamed. Poor guy is always being made fun of.

Pat just laughed and walked away. Strange.

I needed to go to the bathroom. Small bladder and beer is a bad combination for me. The door was locked so I waited in the darkened hallway to Laura's bedroom. The door opened and Krista appeared.

"Hey, you waiting for me?" She asked.

Before I could say anything, she kissed me hard on the lips. I could taste the beer. It felt good, but the whole minute or two, my eyes were open, looking towards the living room, waiting for her boyfriend to appear and then slowly kill me.

"You're so cute. I want more," she said with a sly smile.

"Thanks. We can't though. You have a boyfriend. And he's here. I've seen him!"

"He's downstairs. It's fine."

She took my hand. The bathroom door opened and I

pulled my hand away hard. It was just another one of Laura's friends. Phew.

"I got to go to the bathroom," I said.

"Want me to come with you?"

"No, listen. We can't. I can't."

"Why? He doesn't have to know."

Jesus. Before I could say or do anything I probably would have regretted, I was never so happy to see Scott as he materialized from his sister's bedroom.

"Hey, what's up? You going to the bathroom? I gotta go," he said.

"Yeah, man. I was just talking to Krista. Be right out."

Krista frowned and turned around to leave.

The rest of the night was a blur. I tried my best to avoid her. I'm stupid, horny and single, but not that stupid. At some point, I found myself in Laura's room too, where people were smoking pot and doing other drugs too. I was so high and might have snorted something. I honestly don't remember if I did it or thought of doing it. I did pass out soon after on his floor downstairs, and slept until noon the next day until Scott nudged me to help him clean up.

Corey ended up getting grounded because of the party. He didn't tell his parents where he was going and stayed out way past his curfew. Grounded? Curfew? I felt bad for him. My home life was far from perfect, but in moments like these, I was glad to not have to live my life constricted to normal teenage rules. I could do whatever I wanted, and most of the time I did.

While Corey was grounded, Scott and I went out to Lockport to get some weed from someone he knew from work, someone named Rick. Scott was back working at the Charley Horse in Orland Park, which I miss a bit more than usual. Telemarketing was slowly draining even more life out of me.

We went to Rick's house, where he seemed to be having a party too. After smoking a bit of the weed we had just procured, we realized we were too high to drive back home.

Before I knew it, we were in some strange sedan driving down 159th Street. We seemed to be going way too fast. Rick's friend, Joe, was at the wheel. We had never met this guy before. He lit a joint and we all ended up sharing it. We were already pretty out of it, but the joint kicked in and all of the traffic lights and headlights blurred together. Joe turned the volume up.

"You guys like Nine Inch Nails? The new CD is insane."

The music started to fray all my senses. I only knew the CD a little bit, thanks to Corey, but it sounded different that night. The first song, "Mr. Self Destruct," was like lightning hitting my brain. Fast. Loud. Intense.

I looked over at Scott and Joe and I swore I could see their bones like I had x-ray eyes. By the time the song "Closer" came on, I was half asleep trying to direct Joe towards my house. I could barely talk.

I snap back to reality and see the Robert Taylor Homes in the distance on the highway. I tap Scott's shoulder.

"Hey, remember that time we got a ride home from that crazy Nine Inch Nails fan?"

He turns down Pavement from the stereo.

"Dude, yes! We should've just driven home! I'm so glad we didn't get killed, raped or in a horrible car accident. I can't remember ever being that high. My sister was so pissed having to leave for work early to take me to get my car. Oh, man. That was the last time I get weed from Rick. It was good, but not worth the hassle."

"I don't know, that weed lasted a week it was so strong. You should just give me his number. I can go and get it sometime."

Scott was so responsible. What did I have to lose anyway?

❊ ❊ ❊

It's the second to last day of junior year. Finally. I walk a different way to school, this time on Central. Since I don't have any pot, there's no need to take the side streets and this way is slightly faster.

I can't believe it's going to be summer soon, even though school seems more optional every day. Aside from the usual punishments of detention and MDP, surprisingly very few people reached out to me about missing class except Mrs. Clark. Ever since I gave her that big dose of truth about my mom, I think it scared her. I've been much more quiet at our meetings since then. I don't know if she can call someone to investigate what's happening at home. So I've kept my mouth shut or even ditched our meetings altogether. I don't need to make things worse than they already are.

The only other person who reached out was Mrs. Tidds, my geometry teacher from last year. She'd see me in the halls occasionally and stop me.

"Everything alright, Chris? I've been seeing you in MDP a lot lately."

"Um, yeah. Everything is fine."

"Okay, well, I'm here if you ever want to talk."

She must've had some special radar for the not-normal kids. What could I say? It was still nice of her though.

A car slows down in front of me as I walk on the shoulder of the road.

"Hey, you need a ride? Get in."

It's Bryan and his girlfriend. Jenny maybe? There are so many Jennys it's hard to remember. Plus, Bryan is more Scott's friend than mine.

I get in. Snoop Dogg is on the radio.

"Thanks, man. It's not that far, but I appreciate it."

"Dude, we were taking the scenic route anyway. About

to smoke a bit. You know Jenny, right?"

I was right. Jenny. Of course.

"Hey," she says, looking back smiling. Then she lights a joint.

"Good timing. Best ride ever," I say, laughing.

We smoke. We drive. We smoke some more. Barely any words are spoken. I forget where we are even going at some point or who I'm with.

We pull into the parking lot. My hands feel numb. I stare at the car door for what seems like forever.

"Shit's strong right?" Bryan says, looking in the rearview mirror. "Better be, it's laced with coke. Or crack cocaine. I can't remember. You've had that before right? Much more intense high."

"Yeah, yeah, yeah, it's cool, man," I say nodding my head probably too much.

I finally get the door open. COKE, WHAT THE HELL?!?

"Thanks for the, uh, ride, Bryan. See you later."

"Gonna be a good morning thanks to some good weed! Wake and bake!" Bryan says, seemingly unfazed.

I feel like my whole body is weightless and my mind is melting. I make it to my locker somehow and try number after number on my lock. I remember the first number – twenty-seven - but that's it. Shit.

I go to the main office. Be cool, be cool. My heart is practically beating outside of my chest.

"Hi, I go to school here," I say. OH MY GOD SHUT UP. "I, um, can't remember my locker combination. My name is Chris Morris."

I sound like a robot.

"Okay . . . how do you forget your combination at the end of the school year?" The woman behind the desk says. "You feeling okay?"

Get it together.

"Yeah, just tired. Really tired. I'm so sorry."

She looks at me, sighs and rummages through a cabinet, then hands me a piece of paper. I can feel the room vibrating.

"Write this down. Twenty-seven. Sixteen. Five. Got it?"

"Yes. Thanks. Sorry to bother you."

I hold the paper with two hands.

"Well, take care, son. Go to the nurse if you don't feel better."

Crisis averted. The bell rings. I'm already late for first period. I get my books for my history class and walk to the room.

I walk in, sit down and say, "Sorry, I forgot my locker combination."

Some people laugh. I wish I was joking. I feel so stupid. I turn around to see Adam.

"Heyyyyyy," I say. "What's up, man? You ... good?"

"I'm always good. Are you okay?"

I whisper, "Dude, I'm so high right now. Too high. I forgot my locker combination. I can barely feel my body right now."

"Yikes. Man, you know we've got finals today, right?"

I immediately feel sick. Sicker. I look around. Scantron bubble test sheets are being passed out. The teacher is saying something about pencils.

"Chris, you at least have a pencil?" Adam asks.

I shake my head. He puts one in my hand.

"Good luck, man. Just relax."

I forgot that Adam doesn't smoke. I'm trying to listen to the teacher but he seems so far away. I suddenly have a test booklet on my desk and the room goes silent. Eerily silent.

I fill out my name slowly on the test sheet. I open the booklet and I try to settle my eyes on the first question. I read it over and over. Something about the American government? It's familiar, but not. I try the next question. Vietnam War related. I don't know. I don't know. I want to just put my head down and sleep. I'm getting dizzy.

I finally just put down "C" for as many as my answers as I can and then randomly fill bubbles until the end of the form. I get up and walk over to the desk, papers in hand.

"Mr. Morris, you're done already?"

I nod. I don't want to try to speak in front of the teacher or the class, afraid of what might come out.

I impulsively decide to not return to my desk and just walk out of the classroom.

"I'm sorry, I have to go right now. I'm done."

That just came out of my mouth. I barely feel in control of myself.

"Mr. Morris, where are you going? You can't . . ."

I can't hear him anymore. I know he won't leave because everyone is taking a test. I'm walking to the nearest door. I don't look around at all, just walk calmly. Focus. Walk.

I'm outside. I head towards the side streets. The ones I didn't take this morning. I'm too scared I'll get hit by a car on the main street. I walk back home. I want to run, but I can't. I'm getting paranoid, thinking someone is going to see a teenager walking during school and call the cops. I walk faster.

I get home and open the door. The house is quiet. Where's my mom? I just want to close my eyes. I turn to go up to my room, but the stairs seem insurmountable. I crumble down to the first step, put my head in my hands on the carpeted steps in front of me and fall asleep.

SUBMERGE

September 1994

My pager beeps and I pull it out of my pocket. The number is eight, one, five . . . oh, it's Annie! We've only been dating since July, but it's been amazing. She's my longest girlfriend since Kim when I was a sophomore. I've been faithful too, which is surprisingly easy. She's so hot and she's smoking. Literally. Just pot though. Her friends are now friends with my friends. Corey is even dating her friend Julie. Annie likes the same music as I do. It's pretty perfect.

I go downstairs and don't hear a thing. My stepdad's factory closed and he's got a new job in Cincinnati, which means he is now gone for weeks at a time. It also means my mom has been drinking more and sober less. I haven't seen my brother in days.

"You rang?" I ask Annie on the phone.

"Hey! You got back to me fast! Can you still hang out tonight?"

"Of course, can YOU still hang out tonight? I'm always free."

"Yes, yes. I already asked. Let's go see *Natural Born*

Killers. It's the one that Tarantino wrote but I think Oliver Stone directed? It looks awesome."

"You had me at Tarantino. I want to see that too. The soundtrack is so good. I'll bring it. AJ just saw *Killing Zoe* and said it was amazing. Similar thing where Tarantino was involved but didn't direct. It's got that *True Romance* magic. He's such a good storyteller. I can't wait for *Pulp Fiction* next month. Anyway, I'll pick you up at five?"

"Yay! I can't wait. I'll find the times and we can pick out the show when you get here. Orland Park, okay?"

"Of course. Maybe we can hit Papa Joe's for pizza before?"

"Totally. See you then. Love you."

"I love you too."

I hang up smiling like a goofball. Annie told me she loved me in our first few weeks together and it seemed odd, but I grew to love her almost immediately. We met in a parking lot, where Scott, Corey and I were meeting up with Sarah and her friends. Even though the movie date didn't work out with Sarah a few months ago, at least it led me to Annie, and Corey to Julie. Annie was part of the group that night and I could hear her laughing as soon as we got out of the car. She was loud and so funny. I was drawn to her right away. Especially after I saw her. Long brown hair, dimples, blue eyes and a perfect body. She had the "girl next door" look, but elevated.

She was different too. She lived in Frankfort in a nicer suburb. Her parents owned a restaurant, which she helped out at occasionally. Her parents didn't like me, but I was used to that. I smelled like cigarettes. I cut my own hair, long on top now, shaved on the sides. Sometimes it was black. Sometimes it was auburn. I wore thrift-store clothes. They put up with me, but I hated the way they looked at me and could only imagine what they said to Annie when I wasn't there.

I can't wait to see her. I hesitate, then take my mom's keys and head out. She's not going anywhere. I grab my *Siamese Dream* cassette and put it in the minivan stereo. I find my way onto Harlem Avenue, which is almost a straight shot to her house, driving past Tinley Park where I think about how long it's been since I saw Nana Dody. My birthday? I don't even remember.

"Today" comes on and I turn it up. I always said I disliked the Smashing Pumpkins, even after repeated attempts by Scott and Corey, but in truth, I never really listened to them. They're so popular because they're from Chicago and I think I just said I didn't like them to be a music snob or something. Annie listens to *Gish*, their first album, and this one constantly. I locked in pretty quick. Same thing happened with Pearl Jam. The Pumpkins though? Damn. I love how melodic, loud and sonically beautiful all their songs are.

I blast the music and sing along all the way to Annie's house.

"I wanted more, than life could ever grant me. Bored by

the chore, of saving face . . ."

As soon as I ring the doorbell, I can hear her massive dogs barking on the other side. I don't know what kind they are, but they're huge.

Annie opens the door. She's wearing jeans and a Grateful Dead shirt. She hasn't gotten me into that band yet but is trying.

"Hey, Chris!"

"Hi."

I go to kiss her and quickly stop myself. I know her dad is probably right behind.

Yep, there he is.

"Chris," he says, nodding at me with mock sincerity. "Annie, don't forget. Eleven o'clock. No later."

Clearly they are finishing a conversation that started before I got there.

"Yes, Dad. See you tomorrow. Or tonight. I'm sure you'll be up."

He just looks at me with no expression and closes the door.

"It's good to see you," she says, as we get in the van. "What've you been doing today?"

I pull out onto the street towards Orland Square Mall.

"Not much. Just read a little. Smoked a little this

morning. You?"

"Homework. I've got so much. Senior year is going to kill me."

I just shake my head.

"I don't have that problem. With the way things are going, I'll probably have to go another year to graduate."

"That sucks. You just need to go to school more! I don't get how someone as smart as you would have to repeat senior year."

"It's more about attendance. I didn't go to school a lot last year and didn't pass a few classes. The ones I did pass were just by the skin of my teeth. I'm still in a few honors classes, which still mystifies me. When I'm actually there, I can still play the game. Your man isn't as dumb as he looks!"

"I know you like MDP and detention, but don't your parents get mad? My dad would kill me."

"No, they don't even know half the time. I used to intercept the mail so they wouldn't see the letters from the dean about it. Now with my stepdad not home during the week and my mom being, um, sick, it doesn't even matter."

"I'm sorry."

She doesn't know what to say. How would she? She looks at the radio instead.

"Ooh, were you listening to the Pumpkins? Haha, that

makes me so happy."

We talk all through dinner. At the movie, we hold hands. The movie is really great and very violent. Not in a bad way.

"Wow," Annie says. "That was so good! I know it was intense, but that could happen right? So crazy. It's one thing to have a couple with childhood problems going on a killing spree, but the media making them stars? Genius. Tarantino, I tell ya."

In the car, I put on the soundtrack and we listen to "Sweet Jane" by the Cowboy Junkies over and over. We end up stopping at one of our secret spots in the woods past the railroad tracks at the end of Long Avenue and 163rd Street in Oak Forest. I found this place years ago with Kim, since she lived nearby, and then used it later to smoke with friends. Judging by the empty beer cans, it's a pretty regular teenage tradition. I lay out a blanket and we make out under the stars until we hear a rowdy group coming.

I drive her home and we kiss for a few minutes in the driveway. Her dad is probably peeking, but I don't care. It's worth it.

❋ ❋ ❋

The thirty-minute drive home seems like nothing when you are in love. I'm smiling and smoking cigarette after cigarette the whole way, listening to the Natural Born Killers soundtrack, thinking about Annie. Only when I hit Oak Forest, do I start to think about what is waiting for me at home. Suddenly, I'm anxious and mad. Why, when I finally find some happiness in one part of my life, things somehow get worse at home?

I'm glad my stepdad bounced back after his old factory closed, but being gone for so long created more chances for my mom to get into trouble. He at least kept some order in the house and there were more periods of sobriety. I bet he actively looked for a job that kept him away from all this madness. I wouldn't blame him.

It's predictably unpredictable now. Especially at night. Last week, a guy was in the kitchen when I came home, while my mom sat in the dining room, drink in one hand, cigarette in the other. A guy I've never seen before.

"Um, who are you?" I asked, looking bewildered.

"Oh, hey. What's up? I'm Don."

He looked like he was younger than my mom, but hard to tell. He was wearing a White Sox baseball hat, tee-shirt and jeans. Don was probably a construction worker if I had to guess.

"CJ, it's okay. I called him. He was just dropping off some things for me," my mom said, waving me away.

I looked on the counter. Booze. Cigarettes. Ah, okay.

"Just go upstairs. It's fine."

I don't know if they did anything, and I don't want to know. My brother was home too and he just shrugged his shoulders when I opened his door and asked about Don.

"Mom's new delivery service?"

He was a freshman in high school now and we talked a bit more since I also passed him in the hallways at school. A few nights later, I came home and thought I saw Don and him hanging out downstairs. It was odd to see them in the same room where my stepdad relaxed after work watching TV. It reminded me of when my mom was newly divorced years ago and entertaining potential boyfriends in our Chicago Ridge apartment by getting me to dance or whatever. Bizarre.

The worst development though in my mind was the return of Maria Mueller, my mom's friend. The same Maria who still lives in Palos Hills and hopefully isn't stealing from children anymore. In some ways, I'm not surprised. My mom used to have a lot of friends, but over the last few years, they've all been burned, used and lied to too many times. But I suspect that when my mom called, Maria saw an opportunity and showed up to see what she could exploit. I hope Maria was at the end of her long list of friends. At least Maria had the decency to not bring her kids. There's already too many involved.

It's one thing for this stranger Don to come in and enable my mom's drinking, but Maria? I don't get it. The first time I saw her, I was too shocked to say anything, but she laid into me anyway.

"Hi, Chris, your mom called me. Said she needed some

things."

"Oh? Let me guess. A liquor store run?"

"Yes, but that's not your business. Your mom is an adult and can do what she wants. Don't you have homework to do?"

"No, I don't and it *is* my business. She's my mother. You haven't seen her in years."

"Well, we've been friends for a long time and she needs me."

I didn't like her tone. I'd bet that a lot of those clothes bought on a sober shopping spree, now piled up unworn in my mom's room will be gone soon. Not all at once, but a few at a time as to not arouse suspicion.

I'm thinking about all that and what else Maria can steal when I turn onto our street. I see Maria's car parked under the streetlight by our mailbox. Great.

After pulling into the garage, I light a cigarette, take a deep breath and open the front door. Again, Maria is standing in the kitchen finishing a plate of food, while my mom is slowly eating at the counter. Well, she's pathetically holding a fork anyway.

I mock a smile.

"Hi, Mom. Hi, Maria."

"Hi, Chris," Maria says. "Lynn, did you know your son smoked? Aren't you seventeen?"

"Yes, she knows and it's fine. I've been smoking for awhile. It's not the worst thing happening in this house."

"What's that supposed to mean? Your mom is sick! She has a disease."

Oh, here we go. Now instead of arguing with my mom, I have to argue with a surrogate. I walk into the kitchen and lean against the cabinets while folding my arms.

"Yeah, I know. Welcome to the present day. A lot has changed since we all hung out back in Charleston. I'm glad you noticed. Don't you remember what my mom was like back then? Why aren't you helping her? God knows we've all tried."

"What do you think I'm doing? She wouldn't eat if I wasn't here."

"Yeah, but bringing her more alcohol isn't exactly helping. I –"

She cuts me off and starts pointing at me.

"Chris, I've told you before. She's an adult. She can do what she wants. And so can I. She's sick and I'm just trying to help."

"Okay, okay. I'm just saying, if you were a friend and you wanted to help, you'd take her to an AA meeting or something, not the opposite. Not this."

"Don't tell me what to do!" Maria shouts at me.

She's practically shaking. What a nasty person.

She keeps yelling something, but I just go upstairs and slam my door. It's not worth it. If I can't argue my mom out of drinking, I won't argue her friend out of enabling her drinking either. She'll find a way to get her addiction fed. I flick my Zippo lighter top open and closed.

Clink, clink, clink...

I lie down and find my stash underneath the bed. I grab the hollowed out history textbook containing my weed, rolling papers and pipe. I light up and breathe in. I think for a second about playing with Max in Charleston as a little boy, with Maria and my mom in the kitchen watching us. How long ago that seems.

I exhale. I feel better almost instantly. I still feel sick though.

I think about smoking more. I need to. School sucks. It's my fault for missing so much and not doing the work. I probably am passed the point of no return. I still have been ditching too much At this point, it really doesn't matter.

I haven't smoked as much thanks to Annie. Even though she smokes pot too, I like being with her and don't need it as much. She's been a slightly healthier filter and escape.

Not that I haven't got pretty messed up at times. I think about last week. Corey, Scott and I went to see the Rolling Stones at Soldier Field. Corey's dad went too. He's a big Stones fan and was the one who bought the tickets. Plus, he volunteered to drive and pay for parking. I'm not a huge fan, but Lenny Kravitz was opening and I'd never seen him live before.

We all smoked a little pot before we left, hiding behind Corey's house. Then before the show, I was going to the bathroom and the guy next to me wanted to know if I wanted to buy some acid.

"Sure, how much?" I said, just trying to be nice.

"Fifteen bucks a cube"

"A cube?"

Is that normal? A cube?

"Oh yeah, it's good. It's liquid LSD dropped onto sugar cubes."

Why not? I looked around. No one else was in the bathroom. I gave him twenty dollars. He gave me the cube in a little bag and a five-dollar bill.

"Just put it in your mouth and let it slowly dissolve. It will last for awhile. Enjoy the show!" He said, winking at me.

I thought for a minute how strange it was to be taking acid for the first time at a Rolling Stones show. This show of all the ones we've seen. We had just seen Weezer at the Metro days before. I guess I don't remember anyone ever selling acid at other concerts. Weed, yes, but not LSD.

I went back to our seats in the stadium and just quietly sat there waiting for it to kick in.

"What's up, man? You okay? Lenny is almost on! I bet you're stoked!" Corey said.

"Dude, I just bought some acid in the bathroom," I said quietly, so his dad couldn't hear.

"For real? Man, just don't think of anything dark. Don't get paranoid. That's the trick."

Wait . . . oh, no. I thought of a few days ago where the three of us found an abandoned house in Tinley Park. Someone told someone who told someone who told us about it. It was a regular looking suburban house, off by itself, past a row or two of houses. No one knew why it was empty and why it wasn't sold or why the back door was open.

We thought it would be cool just to hang out there and get high. It was eerie though. You never knew if someone was hiding out or if there were animals or ghosts. I just remembered going upstairs to the master bedroom facing the street and finding a huge pentagram on the floor in white paint. We sat down, smoked and hardly said anything.

I thought of the pentagram. The devil in Tinley Park. Spirits. Bachelor's Grove Cemetery. All the lights in the stadium made me dizzy. I had to fight away thoughts of my mom, but then Lenny Kravitz took the stage. It changed my whole mood and mindset. The music sounded amazing. I felt high, but not anything too crazy. For a moment. It ebbed and flowed.

The rest of the night I could tell things were different, like being buzzed from weed, but on a very different level. It was like all my senses were heightened. I had a hard time talking or finding the right words. I would be super scared to near tears one moment, and blissfully happy the next. The whole ride home I was just worried that Corey's dad would notice. He didn't.

Maria was talking loudly downstairs so I put on some music. The Violent Femmes hushed the noises in the kitchen.

I wonder what would happen if my stepdad came home right now? I don't think he ever met Maria, but he'd kick her out immediately. She's bad news. He'd see that. Anyone can tell. It's all bad news, I guess. I look in my wallet for a picture of Annie. I find her school picture and fall asleep with it in my hands.

❊ ❊ ❊

The house is quiet as usual. I haven't seen Don in a while, but some other guy whose name I can't remember was here a few nights ago filling the same role. It's sometime before Halloween and I'm in my room again waiting for Annie to page me. I just smoked a bowl and eating a half cold chicken patty I forgot to heat up long enough in the microwave.

I think about the little fight Annie and I had last night. I don't know if it was a fight really, but Annie and I were having the typical talk about past boyfriends and girlfriends, sharing stories, numbers, and all that. She's had about three ex-boyfriends. I told her I had too many to count. Or just couldn't remember. Freshman year was a blur, just trying to make up for that lost time with girls. Even though nothing happened with any of them and I'm still a virgin, she was upset, barely talking the rest of the night and didn't kiss me goodbye. I don't get it.

Just the week before, we went with all of our friends to the Lincoln Way High School homecoming dance. It was so much fun. I wore a white suit I found at the mall, with just a black tee-shirt and an oversized, shiny cross necklace as kind of a tie. I thought it looked cool, but I could tell the parents were not impressed, which was partly the point.

The dance was fun, even if I found myself too self-conscious to bust out my old eighth grade moves. We partied all night afterwards, smoking pot and ending up at the Olympic Star restaurant for coffee. We laughed for another hour or two, until everyone left. Annie told her parents she was sleeping over at a friend's house and we just spent the night in her car, parked somewhere in the outskirts of Frankfort.

How do I make this right with Annie? I can't lose her. I thought of the new hostess at the Charley Horse, who has been seriously flirting with me when I went to see Scott at work. She's pretty, funny and lives in Tinley Park. But for the first time, I'm not even considering the idea. I want to be with Annie.

It's confusing. Does she think I still care for all the girls I dated before? I can't erase them from my mind, but I can erase the traces. I suddenly get a wild, partially stoned idea. I find the shoebox under my bed filled with notes I've kept from a lot of my ex-girlfriends. Aside from a handful of pictures, it's mostly notebook paper filled with flowery lettering, hearts and how cute I am, how boring such and such class is, and on and on. I'm not sure why I have this collection, except maybe as some sort of weird proof that I'm not a dork anymore.

I shake the contents of the box all over the middle of my room. I grab my lighter and light a note on fire and throw it into the pile. Slowly it burns, a collage of cursive writing, puppy love tributes and memories. I get up to open my window and when I sit back down, I realize the carpet is starting to catch on fire!

Of course the fire wouldn't contain itself to the paper. Shit, shit, shit. The room is filling up with smoke and I run out and turn off the smoke detector in the hallway, then grab a towel from the bathroom. When I return to my room, there's just a black hole in the center, slowly getting wider. I smother the hole, coughing until it's finally out. I get a fan out of my closet and place it to blow the smoke out the window. I light some incense to mask the smell of my room on fire.

After about two cigarettes to subside my panic, I realize that I'll have to explain this to my stepdad at some point. Or do I? I decide to do some spur of the moment room redecorating. I move my bed from against the wall lengthwise to stick out from the middle of my room, so the end hides the burnt carpet. With the shadows and all the crap I stuff underneath, you would never know. After surveying my work, I move the desk a little too, so it looks like I changed more than just my bed.

I sit down, exasperated yet proud. I've got almost too good at covering things up, literally and figuratively.

* * *

It's Sunday afternoon and I'm sitting in Annie's bedroom. Her door is open as usual, per her dad's request, but we still sneak kisses here and there. I told her about the ceremonious burning of my lovelorn past a few weeks ago and she laughed about the hasty firefighting aftermath.

"What were you thinking? I mean, I'm glad you did it, but of course, duh, your room is gonna catch on fire! Why didn't you go in the backyard, get some foil, or put it on the stove . . . I don't know."

"I guess I didn't think that far. I just wanted to make you happy."

It's been fine ever since. Better even. We've started to hang out even more outside of our friends, but still make time for them too. It's finally felt good for a change.

I sense a vibration in my pocket. It's my pager. Everyone knows I'm here, so who could it be? I look and just stare.

"What? Who is it?" Annie asks.

"It's my house," I answer.

It can't be my mom. She's out of it. I wonder if it's my stepdad? Or my brother perhaps, but I doubt it.

"Oh no, that's odd. What if something happened?"

I'm so not ready for this. I call home. My stepdad answers on the first ring.

"Chris, where are you?"

"I'm at Annie's just hanging out. What's going on? Everything alright? Is Mom okay?"

My voice shakes a little. Annie is motionless.

"Here's the deal," he says, then pauses. I hear him take a deep breath. "You need to find somewhere else to sleep tonight. I can't do this anymore. I - "

"Wait, is everything alright? You can't do what anymore?"

"It's just everything. Everything that's happened. I'm done. Your mom is in the hospital. I took her this morning. Back in rehab. Then I changed the locks on the door. Your mom can't stay here anymore. You and your brother too, unfortunately. I'm sorry, I really am. It's over. We'll figure the details out later."

I don't know what to say.

I'm shocked, but there's nothing I can do. It's his house. His life. My mom pushed him this far. Too far.

"Okay, can I just come home in a bit and grab some things? I'll find a place to stay for a while until, well, I don't know."

"Of course. I'll be here. Again, I'm sorry, Chris, this has nothing to do with you or your brother. I hate that it's come to this. For all of us."

"Me too. I'll see you soon."

I hang up and just sit there with the phone in my hand.

"What? What happened?"

I tell her.

"Oh, I'm so sorry, what are you going to do?" She says, pulling close to sit next to me with her arm around my waist. "It's so sudden. I wish you could stay here."

"I'll call Scott. His dad is usually traveling. I'm sure I can crash there for a bit. He lives right by school too, which is good I guess."

As I thought, Scott is very accommodating. He's a tad confused, but I'll fill him in later. It is all a little bewildering, even for me.

Annie drives me home. Since my stepdad was home earlier, I didn't take the car. Up to this point, Annie has only met my mom a few times and they got along great. I fill her in a bit more on the last few years. Like most people, she just thought my mom was sick. When she's sober now, she certainly looked sick, thanks to the withdrawal symptoms - nausea, sweating and pain - so

I've been ashamed either way to have Annie or anyone else see her.

When we get to my house, she offers to sit outside and wait.

"I won't be long. My stepdad isn't much of a talker. Especially now I would imagine."

I go up to the door and take out my keys. Was he bluffing about the locks? It's something my mom would say. I try to unlock the door and it doesn't work. Damn, this is actually happening.

I take a deep breath and ring the doorbell of my own house. I hear footsteps and my stepdad opens the door.

"Hey, Chris. Is that Annie? Does she want to come in too?"

"No, it's fine. I just want to grab some clothes and stuff. I'll be quick. Where's my brother?"

"He's staying at a friend's house so he doesn't miss school. I think he'll probably end up with your dad in Chicago pretty soon. What about you?"

I haven't thought that far. My dad has only one extra bedroom and I don't want to leave Annie and all my friends behind, living in the city.

"I'm staying at my friend's house tonight. I'll figure the rest out later. What about my mom?"

He shakes his head, looking confused and tired.

"I don't know. I really don't. She'll have to figure it out. Being sober is step one though."

"True, true. See you in a bit."

I run up to my room and grab what I can. Some jeans. A few shirts. Cigarettes. Weed. I close my door and grab some stuff from the bathroom to fill up my duffel bag. I pass my mom and stepdad's bedroom, half expecting to see my mom snoring on the bed. Where is she going to go when she gets out? I'll worry about that later.

When I get downstairs, my stepdad is just standing in the kitchen.

"Hey, Chris, so when you get settled, just call and you can grab your stuff and everything," he says, almost too nonchalantly.

I leave and we drive to Scott's. After a tearful goodbye with Annie, I tell him what's happening. He is a great host, but there isn't much room except for a couch. It will do for a night or two.

At Scott's, I hardly sleep and we walk to school together. I don't even smoke any weed. I'm almost too stunned still by everything. I finally get an idea about where to stay for a while and call my Nana Madge from a payphone. I offer to take her to dinner tonight at El Dorado, her favorite restaurant nearby on Cicero Avenue. The whole school day goes by so slow. I'm like a zombie, physically sitting in my classes, but not there mentally. It all seems so trivial. Even more than usual.

Scott agrees to drop me off at El Dorado with the notion that my Nana will drive me later. She's already there in a booth and gets up to hug me. I instantly feel bad that I haven't seen her since my birthday in April. She lives so close too.

After we order and catch up on small talk, I tell her the latest highlights and lowlights. My mom. The last few months. The last year. My stepdad's decision yesterday.

"So, what are you going to do?"

"Nana, remember how you always said that your patio door is open if things get too out of control at home? Well, I'm actually at that point. I'm wondering if I could stay in your extra bedroom a little while? I promise I'll contribute and help out anyway I can. I don't know what else to do."

She doesn't hesitate at all.

"Of course you can. I meant what I said. You can come in anytime. Just give me a few days to clean it up a little. I need to move some things out of there from the bed to the closet. What about your brother?"

"He's going to go up with my dad probably. Makes sense. He has less of a choice than I do, being younger. I'll be eighteen before you know it."

"Right. Have you talked to your dad about any of this? I'll call him tonight."

"No, not yet. Thanks for doing that."

After dinner and her usual tradition of taking everything, including the bread, in a bag home, she drives me to Scott's. I call Annie and let her know what's happening. I remind her that my Nana only lives five minutes away, so it's not the end of the world. Then I get a hold of my stepdad and see if I can come by this weekend to move my stuff to my grandmother's. My plan is to box up some stuff and move on Sunday. He agrees. I call Nana. I think about calling my mom, but it's too soon. I can't deal with that right now. I'm exhausted by all of the logistics I'm dealing with. I call work and just say that I'm moving suddenly for "unexpected personal reasons" and need to take some time off, which is all true. They're fine with it.

Scott and I take a walk and smoke a bowl. My dad pages me. Nana must have called him. We talk and he offers to take me in too if I want. He means well, but I know I can't leave my life behind here.

"I understand, but your Nana isn't the easiest person to live with either," he says. "Just be careful. I know you will. I'm sorry this is all happening."

"Me too, Dad. Me too."

* * *

Clothes, books, CDs, tapes . . . all into boxes. Sigh. It's taking me longer than I thought to get my stuff together. Yesterday, Nana gave me a set of keys to her condo, since she would be at work all day. My stepdad is helping me fill up his truck and we drive over together.

It's quiet, then he clears his throat and says, "Chris, I hope you know this isn't what I wanted. I mean, I've spent over a hundred thousand dollars or something in medical bills to help your mother. Nothing has worked. I have nothing to show for it. She's not the same person I met and fell in love with. I still love you and your brother like sons. I want you to know that."

It sounds rehearsed, but it doesn't matter. I feel bad for him. He did and does love my mom.

"I know. I don't blame you. It sucks. Thanks for everything."

What else can you say really?

We get to Nana's and I prop open all the doors in the hallway. When we open up the door to her condo, my stepdad is taken aback.

"Whoa! What's that smell? It's like a cat shit somewhere in here."

I suddenly remember that he's never been over here before. My grandmother is very loving, funny, and amazing in many ways, but her two-bedroom condo isn't the cleanest with a puppy and three cats. One of the cats, a little black cat named Jewel, has some problem where she doesn't poop in the litter box and Nana hasn't got around to taking her to the vet yet. E.T. and Elliott, the other two cats, are mostly fine, even though Elliott hates me. I'm so used to the condo's usual state that it didn't occur to me to warn him. He looks a little disgusted.

"It's fine," I say. "I'm pretty sure one of her cats is sick."

"Pretty sure?"

I suddenly see the place through his eyes. It's dark. Smoky. Blinds closed. The furniture is antique, old and a little too big for the condo, remnants of my great-grandparent's house in south Chicago that Nana sold five years ago. She has a hard time letting things go and doesn't clean much. Man, it does smell. I hope this is just temporary.

We load up everything into my new room wordlessly. The walls are ironically covered in rainbows, including the blinds. It used to be a nursery before Nana moved in and she never updated it. I plan to quickly cover as much as I can with posters from my old room. Smashing Pumpkins, Lenny Kravitz, Nirvana, and so on.

My stepdad leaves and lets me know I can call anytime to get something or to just come by the house. I almost hug him, but we don't do that, so I shake his hand awkwardly.

Later that night, Nana and I eat dinner together. It's nice. She smokes too, so is ok with me smoking in her condo, even though I can tell she's less approving than my mom.

"I wish you hadn't started that. It's such a bad habit."

"I know, I know. C'mon, you all smoke! It was bound to

happen."

I go in my room and lay on the queen bed. It's so big it covers the majority of the room, which is a mess. I light a cigarette and try to work up the nerve to call my mom. I flick my Zippo lighter open and closed. It's the first time I've talked to her since everything went sideways.

"Palos Hospital, can I help you?"

After five minutes of transferring and hunting down my mom, I finally hear her voice. They put me through to the pay phone out by the main office. I remember it well.

"CJ, hey, how are you doing? Everything good? Your stepdad was just here and said you and your brother are out of the house. I can't believe he did that. Don't worry, when I get home, I'll fix everything. I promise."

I almost laugh. I think of my stepdad talking to me in the truck on the way over here. I've never seen him so stoic. She's a week sober and sounds good. Shaky and nervous, but good. I know that's the alcohol leaving her system.

"I don't know, Mom. I'll probably stay here. Nana doesn't live too far away. It's fine. I'm going to be eighteen soon anyway. It's not his -"

"No, no, no. It's not right. Moving your brother up to Chicago and all that. And you going to your grandmother's? What about me? Don't I get a say in any of this? I think he's coming in for a counseling session soon and we'll talk about it."

She's living in a different world. I take a big drag of my cigarette and don't know how to answer. No matter what happens, the damage has been done.

"Okay, Mom. We'll talk soon. I love you. Good luck with everything there. I'll be fine. I can take care of myself. I have been for a while you know."

I can hear her sniffling now. There is a lady yelling in the background.

"I know. I know. I'm sorry, CJ. I love you too. I- I gotta go. Someone else needs to use the phone. Bye."

* * *

Weeks go by. Life is the same, but very different. I still go out with Annie. See friends. Sometimes I go to school or instead I just hang out at Nana's during the day, getting high and watching TV. It doesn't feel like my place and I wonder if it will. My brother moved to Chicago with my dad and I haven't talked to either of them almost at all.

When it's time for my mom to get out of rehab, something amazing happens. She goes back home. I don't know what she said to my stepdad, but whatever it was, it worked. I don't know if it's permanent, temporary or a delusion, but I'm completely surprised. My stepdad seemed pretty final. But my mom has a way of getting what she wants.

"CJ, it's all good. I'm so much better. You should come back home."

My whole body gets sick at the idea. I just can't. I've heard and seen her swear she'd never drink again so many times. Now I've moved. Upended my life. My brother isn't coming back either, since he's already in a new high school in Chicago. We've both started over in our own way.

I take a breath.

"It's too late," I tell her. "I do need your help though. I'll come by this week. I have some papers for you to sign."

A few days later, I walk over to our old house from Nana's. It's a Tuesday around lunchtime.

I ring the doorbell, which still feels odd. My mom opens the door.

"Hey, CJ, come in."

She gives me a hug.

We go into the kitchen. I get right to it. Besides, it's too weird being here.

"Mom, I've decided to drop out of high school. I'd rather get a full-time job and start being a proper adult or whatever. It's pretty cheap at Nana's, so I'll have more money for other things. I just need you to sign this, since I'm not eighteen yet. It's from the school."

She takes the paper and looks at it.

"I don't know. Are you sure about this?"

I'm not, but I don't know what else to do. My grades suck. I've missed too much and would likely have to repeat senior year. And if I am at school, I'm sitting in class bored and desperately trying to make some connection to my life with whatever the teacher is talking about. I don't see the point anymore. Might as well work more and make some money.

"With my situation now, this seems like the best option. Please? I don't ask for much."

"If this is what you want, I'm not going to fight with you on it. I know you'll figure out a way to do it anyway."

"It is. You know I'm smart. I'll figure something out. I can always get my GED at some point if I need to. I'm already looking at jobs."

It's true. Now that I don't have access to a car, my options are limited, but there are a ton of stores on Cal Sag Road and Cicero Avenue, within walking distance from Nana's. Aside from the dollar store I used to work at, there's Best Buy, Target, a movie theater and Menards. I have an application from Menards at the moment since they were the only one advertising.

"Oh, that's good. I know you'll be okay. I just wish you didn't have to drop out of school. I wish I could do things over."

I stop her.

"Mom, don't start. We can't go back. We can't. It is what it is. It's too late for any of that."

She nods and signs the form. I hug her goodbye and decide to walk my old route to high school for the last time. I've got nothing better to do.

* * *

A few nights later, Annie is over at Nana's. She's gotten used to the smell and strangeness of my new dwelling. It took her a few times though, as it was for my friends too.

Annie and I go in my room. Nana is a bit old fashioned and insistent on us keeping the door open, but with her asleep, it's fine.

I put on *Definitely Maybe* by Oasis. The song "Live Forever" has been playing pretty much nonstop and we love it. Annie kisses me and we fall onto the bed.

Before I know it, we're both naked. This is new.

Then it happens. Finally. Awkward. Amazing. Honestly, more awkward than amazing.

Afterwards, we lay in bed, smoking cigarettes. She usually doesn't smoke, but this is a special occasion.

She has her curfew, so she kisses me and goes home.

I fall asleep immediately. Smiling.

When I wake up, Nana is already gone for work and the phone rings. It's Menards. I got the job!

Apparently, I'll be working full-time in their millwork department. Doors, windows, countertops, moulding and much more. That's what the manager said on the phone. I'm nervous because I don't know anything about any of that really, but happy I got hired. I left my high school graduation date blank on the application and when it came up in the interview, I was careful to say, "I finished a year early." Which wasn't untrue. I'll figure it out. I've already worked for five years and am a fast learner. I start Monday.

I light a cigarette and sit down in the recliner in Nana's living room. My living room? E.T., the white cat, jumps onto my lap. I'm confused, scared and slightly hopeful, yet wondering how I got here, how it came to this and how things will get more messed up.

BOTTOM

April 1995

Eighteen years old. I'm officially an adult. Legally, anyway. I feel like I've already passed that threshold a while back. Probably when the tables turned with my mother.

Shit, work! I get up and quickly get dressed. Khakis, dress shirt and tie. Everything is wrinkled and too big on me. Did I lose more weight again? I slick back my hair, which is getting longer on top, still shaved on the sides.

"Hey, Nana," I mumble as I look for my shoes in the dining room.

She's in the kitchen making coffee with little Chiquita, her dog, at her side. I know she's leaving soon too. What does she do again? A secretary, I think. Some type of administrative work. I know she misses teaching music to elementary school kids, but she doesn't anymore for some reason. I make a mental note to ask her about work later.

"Good moooorning," she says with a sing-song voice. "Are you leaving already?"

"Yeah, I'm running late. It's fine though. I'll get coffee at work."

I don't usually eat breakfast. Just some coffee at work and cigarettes. Breakfast of champions. I probably should though? I don't know. Probably should be brushing my teeth and showering more, but whatever.

"See you later, Nana. Love you."

"Love you too. Hope it's a good one."

"Me too."

I find my car in the condo parking lot. My eighty-four Chevy Celebrity. Brown. Big dent on the front-left side, as if the previous owner smashed into something and couldn't bear to keep the car anymore. It's slightly broken, which is fitting.

I still can't believe I have a car of my own. It's only been a month since I ran into my ex-girlfriend Kim at Mickey's restaurant by the bowling alley. She was with her boyfriend, but asked about how things were going. I told her the quick version and her eyes fell. We met up that night and coincidentally, I was already going to meet someone who advertised a car for five hundred dollars in the paper.

"Let me come with you. You know I know cars."

She did. Her dad was a big car guy. I am definitely not.

She drove and we met this guy in the Brementowne Mall parking lot. The car was older looking than I thought.

But it ran. That's all that matters. Kim talked him down to only four hundred before I could even say anything.

"Thanks. You didn't have to do that."

She smiled.

"It sounds like you could use the money. Hope things turn around for you."

She kissed me on the cheek and left. I sat there, stunned, feeling like a stray dog.

I put the keys in and let it warm up. It's strangely cold.

I needed the car. There weren't any good jobs within walking distance. I pull out of the parking spot and turn slowly onto Midlothian Turnpike. I need to wake up. Smoked too much last night. Annie was busy with homework. My friends too. I forget they're all still in high school sometimes.

I just sat in my room playing X-Men on Sega Genesis, taking breaks for a bowl here and there. Lame. I couldn't even afford a Super Nintendo, which was old too, but newer than Genesis. It's what my friends played. Nana bought the Genesis when it came out for when my brother and I visited on Saturdays sometimes. It's all I got.

My mom called last night too. I couldn't tell if she was drunk or not, but I just remember her asking if I could get her some cigarettes, she didn't have any money and so on.

"What am I gonna do?" She kept asking.

Hell if I know. I just need to make it through the day myself.

I stop at the Speedway gas station on Cicero for cigarettes. This is a new place for me to buy since turning eighteen. They rarely ask for ID anyway. I get back in my car and light a cigarette before pulling out.

I wonder what kind of day it will be. You never know with this job.

It will be a long one. I don't get paid by the hour, just by what I sell. It's only been a month and I can already tell it's a place where people work a week, a day or don't even turn up again after their second interview. It's like telemarketing all over again! I'm still there though. I'm not proud of it and just tell people I'm in sales, which is true. Very true. It was one of the only options available after Menards. It's not perfect, it's demoralizing hard work, but getting paid in cash every day is pretty nice.

I drive down Cicero. I turn off into the industrial parking lot by McDonald's and park in front of the nondescript brown building. "Direct Pioneer Marketing Solutions" is just one of the names on the door. I walk upstairs, putting my name badge on my shirt pocket. I can hear the high energy music is already on inside.

"What up, Chris? You ready for today? Gonna make some money!"

Paul. Boss man.

"Juice by dat!"

That was the answer for everything. A secret word we used as confirmation, exclamation and explanation.

I grab some coffee and wait for others. Nick comes in. Anita. Derek. Jim. As more people come in, we clap. A new face. Looks like he's in his thirties.

This whole place just gets a little shadier the longer I'm here. I saw the ad in the paper for a sales position with "opportunity for advancement." I called for information, talked to someone about my work history and next thing I knew, I was meeting with Paul for an interview.

He asked about my work experience. Am I comfortable talking to people? Do I want to succeed? Do I have the drive to succeed? What would I think about a job that pays you cash daily? It all sounded great. Even though I wasn't exactly sure what I'd be doing.

He didn't even ask about the gap in my work history either. I was worried about Menards. I hadn't mentioned them in case they called for a reference. I'm still bummed they fired me. They had a right to I guess. I never fit in there anyway with my dyed hair, earrings and surface level knowledge of windows, doors, cabinets and just about everything else they sold.

After calling in sick too many times to hang out with Annie, they had enough. What hurt the most is the very last day I called off, it was a legitimate excuse as my stepdad called me to take my mom to rehab. I didn't want to, but I didn't know what would happen otherwise. She'd already been kicked out once, so the ice was thin. I picked my mom up and went through the whole process again. She refused. She yelled. She cried. She relented.

The next day, I showed up for work and the store manager called me up to the front of the store and let me go. Too many absences. It was one thing to ditch school, but apparently you can't ditch work in the same way. Noted. I've had a job since I was in middle school and it made me feel like I failed.

After "making it" to the next interview after meeting with Paul, it meant I rode along with Andy the next day. I watched him go from door to door at businesses all along Devon Avenue in Chicago. It didn't matter if it said "no soliciting" on it, he told me. Half the time, they bought stuff anyway.

In his bag and trunk were three different wholesale items. They varied almost every day, with one or two staying the same until something new arrived back at the warehouse under our offices in Crestwood. Today was a flashlight, a collection of board books for kids and a small tool set.

By the time the day was done, I learned the script and tactics by observation. It was like telemarketing in this way too, but even more direct and a little scary. After walking in, you find the first and most friendly person working.

"Hey, how you doin'? I got some new items that you'll love. You won't believe it!"

And if they don't say no or kick you out immediately,

you go into, "Alright, we got a couple things. First, this tool set for your car, office, home . . . all the basics are here. It retails for thirty-five dollars at Sears, but we're selling it for only ten! How many do you want?"

The item you start with depends on how you read the person you encounter or whatever is the best item of the day. That day it was the tool set clearly. I honestly don't know if any of these things even sell in stores, but people liked to think they were getting a deal. It seemed like they were.

By the end of the day, minus the cost of each item - ranging from two to four dollars each - Andy was set to make about seventy-five dollars. Cash. As we rode back to the office on I-57, Andy talked about how long he was working there, how much he likes it, his son, ex-wife and the whole system. First you sell, then you move up to trainer and take people on interviews. Then you become assistant manager and then, possibly your own office. Next, the topic turned to how much Andy thinks I'd like it there.

"If you want, I'll put in a good word with Paul."

"Really? Thanks. That would be great."

I didn't realize that was just the signal to Paul that I was fresh meat.

Seems like yesterday. I drive. I sleepwalk through work, picking a street at random on the North Side of Chicago, trying to not drop cheap knives out of their box set. I figure I made about a hundred and ten dollars, which isn't bad. On my worst day, I only made forty dollars.

I walk downstairs, unload the unsold merchandise from my Celebrity and settle up with Paul. I put the cash in my pocket and drive home.

When I get inside, Nana is already in her room. I hear the TV on. It smells like red wine in the hallway.

I quietly go in my room. I've learned the hard way that she's fine and nice in the morning, but the evenings are unpredictable. Which wasn't all bad. Some nights she's super sweet and wants to watch an old movie like "Arsenic and Old Lace." Or she's playing piano and singing. Or she's in her room all night silently, like tonight.

AJ comes by from Chicago sometimes, spending the night to get high and listen to music in my room. He's living with his grandma too on the South Side after his mom and boyfriend had a bad break-up. Nana didn't smell the weed usually. Incense helped.

Other nights though were different.

"Hey, what do you have a pager for anyway? Only drug dealers have them. It was on the news! Are you selling drugs too?"

"What did you do with your hair? Oh no. No, no, no. You need to cut it short."

"Hey! If Annie is in there, you keep that door open. When I was your age, we barely could hold hands, I know what you're up to. If you stay here, you abide by my rules."

Before I got my car, she let me take her car to see Annie and then was waiting up for me when I got back. I forgot my pager that night too, which was a mistake.

"Where have you been? Who said you could take my car? No more. Mm-mm. Driving all over. Not returning my pages. You are this close . . ."

It didn't matter that she let me use it. She forgot. That's around the time I bought my own car.

Until I lived with her, I didn't realize that Nana drank too. It was different than my mom though. She was functional for the most part. Got up, went to work, rinse and repeat. From the outside, she seemed okay.

I found this all out only after I moved in. It was almost funny knowing alcoholism fell from so many branches of my family tree, but it was depressing because Nana was one of my favorite people before everything with my mom. When she was drunk and erratic with me, I just nodded and pacified her the best I could. I couldn't risk losing my room.

* * *

"That's it, CJ. It's over. Officially. I'm moving this weekend."

My mom. I called to check-in. She was out of the house now for the second time. My stepdad filed for divorce and it was weeks away from being final. I can't tell yet if she's drinking. I just finished a shrimp basket for dinner, celebrating after breaking a hundred dollars in sales today.

"Well, look on the bright side, Mom. At least he let you stay in the house until everything was final."

I didn't know what else to say, but it was true. The guy was too kind.

"Yeah, I don't know about that. I know that I'm keeping my minivan, which I had to fight for."

I think for a second that technically he bought that too, but don't say anything.

"Okay. What are you going to do for money? Are you still working?"

I knew she wasn't anymore but played dumb. When my stepdad let her back in the second time, he had some conditions and one was getting a job. She ended up working at a thrift store on 159th Street in Markham. I'd come in sometimes to say hi and buy some vintage shirts. I think it only lasted a month or two. It was impressive though, being my mom's first paid job in almost ten years.

"No, working was getting too hard. Dealing with the divorce and, well, everything."

Yep, she's been drinking. I can tell by her pauses. I hate that I can tell, even on the phone.

"Uh-huh."

We both know the real reason, but it's better unsaid.

She's of a clearer mind now.

"I'm going to get a settlement too, which should, um, last a little while. I'm going to stay at a motel for a bit on Cicero until I figure things out."

"What about our stuff? I mean, your stuff?"

I think of all our pictures, Christmas ornaments. Years and years of sentimental treasures. I also wonder if my stepdad ever found the burnt part of carpet under my old bed in my old room.

"I'll bring most of it with me. In the van. It's fine. You can come by and get anything. You know that. I'm going to miss the house. And the girls."

I had forgotten about my stepsisters. They were almost never over, especially as teenagers. My stepdad likely kept them away from the chaos at the house.

"Just a shame. It was nice having them around sometimes. I always wanted another child. You know?"

"What? What do you mean? We barely got by with just the two of us."

"Yeah, I never told you this, but you could've had another brother or sister."

"What are you -"

"I was pregnant again after you were born and, um, lost that baby. Then, well, again after your brother was born. It was so sad. Just awful. Two babies."

"Okay . . ."

This was news to me. I feel like something this big I would've heard before. Classic drinking mom move. Another lie to garner sympathy?

What if though? Jesus.

I try and ignore it and give her an update on work, Annie and Nana. Regardless of the lies, I hang up worried. My mom alone. Homeless. It could be a wakeup call, but with some money from a settlement possibly coming in too, it could be a recipe for more disaster.

❊ ❊ ❊

Another day, almost the end of May. Driving home from a long day selling this and that, I realize that I've been working full-time about six months now. The "sales" job is the same. Unsurprisingly, almost the whole office has turned over except for Paul, Andy and me. I start to know what streets are good downtown such as Irving Park, Devon or west Belmont, and hit them every time we get new products. I like being able to eat out every day for lunch. I love having cash all the time. I still don't have insurance for my car, but I'm a good driver.

Last week was Prom. After dropping out late last year and working so much, it was odd to go to such a stereotypical school activity. But Annie wanted to go and I can't blame her. I knew she'd look amazing! I rented a tuxedo from the mall and cut my own hair that day at Nana's so it was newly shaved on the sides and back.

We rented a limo with another couple from her school, Jason and Amanda. We took the pictures at her house. Corsages, garter, the whole thing.

Her parents still looked at me disapprovingly. Even in a tuxedo, you can't hide my homemade haircut and yellow teeth, which were starting to get brown spots near the top too. I know it's my fault for forgetting to brush them, along with smoking and drinking coffee. I've started brushing again, but it's too late. I can't remember the last time I went to the dentist. Middle school? I didn't smile much for the pictures.

We slow danced. Snuck kisses. More photos. We took the limo up to Michigan Avenue downtown and then a carriage ride on the street. More kisses. Good night.

The next day, the four of us drove to Starved Rock State Park for hiking and hanging out. I was the only one smoking, so it felt awkward. As we sat on top of one of the higher rocks, we took a break and started to talk. Jason and Amanda were fun to hang out with, but pretty normal. The Cubs, finals, blah blah blah. I don't even think they had part-time jobs. Sometimes I forget there is this whole other different teenage universe. The normal one.

Annie knew I was feeling a little left out, but there wasn't much she can do. I put out a cigarette and listened to them talk about colleges. Illinois State vs. University of Illinois vs. Indiana University. Scott and Corey were talking about this recently too. Even AJ mentioned going to Columbia downtown part-time. Fall seems so far away to me. I realize listening to them that I rarely think farther than a week ahead. Sometimes even tomorrow.

"Chris, what school are you thinking of?"

Ugh, they didn't know. How would they? Annie has had me keep up the charade of still being a high school student, especially with her parents. I shrug.

"Um, I don't know yet. I've got a job lined up so I'm going to focus on that for a while."

They nodded politely. I could tell they were thinking, "Who doesn't go to college after high school?"

Up until that moment, I hadn't thought about it. I'd need a GED at the very least. For what? Community college? Still tens of thousands of dollars. Seems outrageous. Sales isn't forever, but I'm sure I can find something else someday. I don't want to think about it.

I looked out over the river and tried to seem interested in their ivory futures. After dropping them all off later, I headed home with a heavy heart, finally dawning on me that there will be a day that Annie will leave for college. She's already been accepted to Illinois State.

I'm thrust into the present, almost home from work and I'm still thinking about that. She graduates from high school next week. I'm not going, but will be at the party afterwards. Surrounded by her family. I think about my dad who I haven't seen since my birthday last month. I talk to him a tad more now that I live with Nana, his mom.

I think about my mom. I've put off going to see her, but I should. It's been a few weeks since she moved into the motel, which is only about ten minutes away. She's called almost every other day, asking for cigarettes or just for me to visit. It's like when we were home and she'd yell upstairs. Now she just picks up the phone. Sometimes I change the subject and she forgets why she called me.

She knows better to ask for booze. I think she has someone already bringing that over as far as I can tell. Otherwise, she wouldn't need me to bring over anything. She has a car! She's called a few times after midnight too, which Nana hasn't been happy about. As usual, my mom is in her own time zone. So is Nana too, which is why most nights she doesn't even hear the phone.

My mom talks of friends stopping by. Some guys. The only name I recognize is Maria, which I'm surprised by. I think she's met other people staying in the motel too, which can't be good. I get to Nana's and the phone is ringing when I walk in.

"Hey, Mom, it's me. Yes, tonight. I know. I'll bring dinner too."

I stop by Nicky's Carryout on Cicero and grab dinner before heading over to the motel where my mom is staying. It's predictably run-down and rents by the hour, night and week. I see her minivan, the same one I used to have so many adventures in, parked by the street.

The motel is two floors, about a dozen rooms on each, all facing Cicero and flanked by strip malls. I notice a liquor store in one. Hmm, how convenient.

I knock on her door, in the middle of the second floor. My mom answers.

We hug. She smells of wine. Not vodka at least. She seems okay enough though. I've certainly seen worse.

"Hi, Mom. How are you? I got you a hamburger. Shrimp basket for me."

"That's great. Thanks for bringing food, CJ. I only have a microwave here."

I scan the room quickly. There is indeed a microwave on the counter as part of the bathroom with a mini-fridge underneath. Otherwise, there's a TV on the dresser opposite the queen bed along with a small table and chair by the window next to the door. Next to the microwave there is a plastic bag of ramen noodles and other food I don't recognize. I see a few boxes and a suitcase on the other side of the bed. It's dingy, brown and outdated.

"Where's all your stuff?"

I look around some more. The room feels sad.

"It's here. Don't worry. Some stuff is in the van. Some stuff I've sold. I don't need so many clothes right? I've traded this and that for stuff with other people here. I told you on the phone there are some good folks.

Everyone is helping each other out."

"Uh-huh."

I decide not to press further. I'd rather not know.

"How's Annie? Work? Nana?"

"Annie's great. Graduating soon, which is, um, good. I'm happy for her. I-"

"I wish you'd bring her over here. It would be nice to see her . . ."

I pretend not to hear.

"Work is you know, work. Every day is different, but it's not something I'll do forever. It's okay. For now. Nana is good. Speaking of, you can't call too late though, she has to get up for work. There's been a few times when you've called, I had to make excuses. I don't want her to kick me out."

"I'm sorry, CJ. I didn't think of that. Did you bring any Benson and Hedges Menthol? I don't know if you heard, but I only have half a pack left," she says, laughing awkwardly.

"No, but you can have a few of mine. They're Camels though. Maybe next time," I lie.

We eat. I sit at her small table while she's on her bed. She updates me on my brother. Her mom, my Nana Dody. They've all talked on the phone a few times. They seem so distant talking about them in this strange hotel room. We talk more and I gather that she did get some money from the divorce or my stepdad, but it's not clear how much. More is coming though apparently.

"What are you going to do then, Mom? What's the plan?"

"I don't know. I'll figure out something. 'One day at a time' as they say," she says laughing. "You have your own trials and tribulations. Just promise me you'll visit me."

I get up to leave. I have to drive forty minutes to Frankfort from here just to see Annie for an hour.

"I will, Mom. Just be careful. I love you."

"I love you too. Don't worry."

I do worry. But what can I really do? We're both just trying to survive at this point. I know this. I think I do.

❉ ❉ ❉

"I can't find my stuff. Someone stole it."

My mom. She's been calling every day. I shoo the cats away from the hallway to get into my room at Nana's and step over what looks like a new shit stain outside my door. Thanks, Jewel. She's gotten worse and Nana won't take her to the vet because she knows she'll be put down.

"CJ, please, can you . . . honey, I'm your mother, you have to help me . . ."

I shudder. She's playing the mom card a lot lately, but I'm a bit wiser now to her manipulative moves. I'm pretty sure that's why she hardly has any friends anymore. You can only use people so much before they realize the relationship is woefully unbalanced.

I did give her a few bucks here and there, which probably was for cigarettes, but you never know. Sometimes I'd rather give her five dollars than have an all out argument or hear how "I don't love her." I should check in on her though.

It's been two weeks since I was last over there. Annie is out with her family today, so my afternoon is open.

"Mom, calm down. I'll be over in a little bit."

I get dressed, clean the poop out of the carpet quickly and leave. It's hot out. I smoke a little bowl in the car just to calm my nerves a little bit. To prepare.

When I get to the motel, I park and stare. During the day it somehow looks even more run-down. I pass a guy on the stairs that looks homeless. Everyone I've seen around here gives me the impression that they've been through something heavy. I think that most "residents" are like my mom biding their time, in between some intense life event and whatever is about to happen next.

My mom opens the door before I can open it. She was waiting for me.

I take a deep breath.

"Come inside, CJ. You won't believe what happened."

I sit in the same chair as before. No food this time. The room looks emptier. Dirtier. Don't they come in every day and clean? Doesn't seem like it or my mom keeps the "do not disturb" sign on all the time. I light a cigarette and offer one to my mom.

"No, thanks, I just got some from Ty down the hall," my mom says, waving it away. "So anyway, I wake up this morning and all my jewelry is gone. Earrings, rings, necklaces . . . everything."

"Is that it? It looks like more is gone."

"No, I've just been making deals. I told you I know what I'm doing."

I raise my eyebrows, but don't say anything.

"So what happened, Mom? Jewelry doesn't just disappear. Not in a room this empty."

"Well, this couple who stay right below me came up last night to watch TV and talk. It was fun. Too much fun."

She laughs.

"Okay, that sounds promising. Then what? Before you went to bed I mean. What are their names?"

"Well, that's it. We were hanging out and when I woke up this morning, my jewelry was gone. I don't even remember going to sleep honestly. I think the guy's name is Jim? It's very blurry."

"Did you check yesterday? How do you know it was

taken last night?"

"I don't know. I just know. It's not there."

I run through all the scenarios. This Jim and mystery woman have cased out my mom by this point, brought over some liquor and easily took stuff from my mom's room. She could've traded or sold it one night and forgot. Someone else could've taken it. She might never have had it at all or it's still at our old house. I shake my head. Why did I come over here again?

"I don't know, Mom. I would just ask Jim or maybe the hotel front desk."

"You're right, you're right. I will. The people at the hotel aren't much help. As long as they get their money, they pretty much leave you alone otherwise."

"Seems that way. You've got to be careful, Mom. You're not gonna have much left soon. I thought you were getting some more money?"

"I . . . I did."

She pauses. Looks embarrassed.

"You know how it is. I've got to pay for the hotel room, food and all that stuff. Plus, with my health problems, it hurts to walk around too much, so I've got to pay my neighbors to get all that for me. Everything is expensive."

Ugh. I hate that she has got herself in this situation, but even more so, these predators in the hotel, skimming off whatever they can from a helpless woman. My mom for chrissakes.

I think about how she used to happily shop for all of the things she's slowly parting with, trading each for another chance. Another day, another sip. And health problems? More like being drunk or not drunk enough or hungover. I'm both sad and angry at the same time.

I take a breath.

"I know. It'll be alright, Mom," I say, hoping.

I go over and put my arm around her. She hugs me. We sit like that for a while. I don't know what else to say or do, but this feels good. My own mom, so undone. It's so frustrating and so upsetting, but she'll always be my mom, which is what hurts the most in all ways.

* * *

Al turns down the radio where "Scream" by Michael Jackson is playing.

"I can't believe it's August already. Been the hottest summer I've seen in years too. You picked a hell of a summer to do landscaping, huh? I'm just kidding. You know we're glad to have you."

Al is driving me back from the worksite in Oak Brook. He likes to talk. For the past few weeks, we've been mostly just putting in a brick driveway. The record heat wave last month put a big dent in our progress. It was so hot that Al said to stay home and we did. If there is heavy rain, we don't work, but heat? Thank God though. People died it was so hot.

The main office is only a mile away from Nana's, so Al has been driving me home here and there on the days that Mike can't do it. Mike is in college and working at Al's landscaping company, Magretti's, for the summer. There's me, Mike, Randy, Larry and Tom the foreman on the project. Mike lives the closest in Orland Park. He plays guitar too, so we've also gotten together a few times to show each other some songs we've figured out. I've only recently started playing, two years after my dad bought me a guitar. I know the basic chords and my fingers don't hurt. So there's that.

"Hey, Chris, forty cents."

Shit. The highway tolls. It's the least I can do. I hand Al a dollar for the next two.

"I need to get a new car. Thanks again for driving me home."

"Yeah, you need to buy a newer one or if you get an older one, just take care of the damn thing. You have to do more than put gas in it. Mike and I can't keep driving you. That kid isn't as nice as I am."

Al's near retirement and has a sweet gig himself. Does some sales, buys materials, manages projects and drives around to check in on them, occasionally giving a sad sack like me without a vehicle a ride home.

"I know. I'm going to start looking soon."

He's already heard the story. I think back to last month when my car completely broke down. Still hurts. I'm so stupid! I had the car for barely four months, but drove it all around Chicago and back for my sales job going door to door. I put a lot of miles on that ugly thing. Too many miles. Apparently, you have to change the oil every so often? And it died. On my anniversary of course.

Annie and I had the whole day planned. Go to Starved Rock State Park during the day. Romantic hike and then get a hotel room for the night. We were about ten miles away from the park on I-80 when a few lights I've never seen before lit up the dashboard. Before I could even tell Annie, smoke started coming out from the hood and it stopped accelerating. I slowly turned on to the side of the road, while the engine just went up in smoke as I raised the hood.

We eventually got a ride from a nice guy in a truck to the nearest gas station, where Annie called her dad. Since he owns a restaurant, he knows a guy that owns a service station. He offered to send someone to tow the car and pick us up. I left out the part about not having insurance. Annie just asked him. This was embarrassing enough. With Annie of course, but her dad too. I was never good enough. And this didn't help my case.

At the service station, they said they'd look at the car and let me know. A few days later, Annie said that the station called her dad and said they'd have to replace the entire engine or junk it for a hundred dollars. The car wasn't worth that much, so I told Annie to just junk it and give the money to her dad. I still owed him another fifty for the towing.

I almost got busted in another way too, after taking Nana's car when she was sleeping and then deciding to light up on the way home from Annie's house. It was an off night and I had a pocketful of dope, which was stronger than I thought. I could barely drive. I kept stopping ten to twenty feet in front of all the red lights. I almost just pulled over to sleep it off for a bit. I was so thankful that the streets were nearly empty and I drove slowly back to Nana's. Dodged another bullet there.

Al pays another toll. In some ways it's nice not to drive.

As a group, we did a lot of driving this summer. Before and after my car bit the dust. Either just Annie and I or with Scott and Corey with their girlfriends. Some different configuration each time. We'd go to Six Flags Great America, the Indiana Dunes beach, or just miniature golfing around the suburbs. We all took turns getting weed these days, which was nice. By now, we all had our special friends we could call up for more, as opposed to the old days driving around in circles hoping that so and so might have some.

With work, I haven't been to as many shows during the week like before, but we still managed some big ones this summer: Pearl Jam, Lollapalooza, and even the Grateful Dead, which just happened to be their last show ever. Jerry Garcia died days ago. Overdose. Regardless, I remember the parking lot more than the actual concert. So many people immersed in a world of drugs and music. I could relate, but these were vagabonds, getting high and following a totally different rhythm. I did pass by one woman with a sign that said only "I need a miracle," which stopped me cold. Should I have a sign too? Does she know something I don't?

"Do you have an extra ticket? Just one?" She asked.

Oh, that kind of miracle.

We've also got tickets to see REM, with Radiohead opening, in Tinley Park and the Flaming Lips at the Metro downtown next month, which I can't wait for. A few bright lights.

Now that AJ wasn't in the burbs anymore, I'd either drive up or take the Metra train and then the Red Line to see him. Or he'd do the same to stay in my room. Stay up late, smoking, getting high and talking about movie ideas, movies, philosophy, music and just make each other laugh. Another bright spot.

I start to nod off a bit in Al's truck. Between the heat and the work, it's draining. I had a solid tan though. The best I've ever had. So much so that there were freckles appearing on my shoulders. That was new.

"Have you thought about what you're gonna do when the summer's over?" Al says, waking me up a bit.

I swear this guy loves to talk and give life lessons.

"Not yet. Still have a few weeks left, don't I?"

"Yeah, but you gotta start looking now so you have your pick. You have enough wide experiences - retail, restaurant, sales - you should have some solid choices. When I was your age…"

I zone out. Shit, I don't know where my next job will be. I'll figure it out when the time comes. Something will turn up.

I still can't believe what landed me in this truck. It was just any other day in June, walking along north Sheridan Avenue with a bag filled with teddy bears, flashlights, and a couple nice black briefcase-like bags. Something for everyone.

I walked into a diner. It was empty, except for one guy at the counter. As I walked up to the waitresses gathered in a booth, they quickly raised up their hands.

"No, we're all good. Thanks for stopping -"

"Whoa, ladies, you didn't even see what I've got."

I smiled. And pulled out a few things quickly.

"All new stuff too! I'm sure you have kids, or at least know kids? This bear sells for twenty-five dollars at Toys-R-Us, I'm selling it today for only five! What about flashlights? This one is probably better than any one you have here or at home. Sells for thirty dollars at K-Mart, but I can give one to you for only ten dollars. How many do you want?"

Soon the ladies were giving me a bunch of singles and buying a little bit of everything.

"Hey, hold on there, young man."

The guy at the counter stopped me. Bob Gunther. Turned out he owned a building supply/design/ construction-type company. Gave me his card.

"You should call me sometime. I think you could make some real money."

"Thanks, but to be honest, I don't know much about building supplies or selling siding, that sort of thing."

"Yeah, but you can sell. That's the hard part. I saw what you just did there with the wait staff. We can teach you the other stuff."

After a short phone call soon after, he wanted me to start the next week. It was hardly an interview. A formality really. I was nervous, but excited. It seemed like a real job. One that I wasn't as embarrassed about. No more cash daily, but no more days making fifty dollars or getting yelled at by angry barbers to get the hell out of their business once and for all.

I told Paul it was over. He tried to talk me out of it. Then Andy did. It was no use though. I was a long way away from having my own office there. What a joke. With the turnover I'd seen, I saw how much of a ruse that was. No one stayed for long. I felt a little bad for them. On my last day, Paul was just cold to me.

On the first day of my new job, I was intimidated immediately. It was a nice building with a showroom on the first floor. Bathrooms. Windows. Interior things, exterior things, etc. All very nice. All very foreign. Bob led the orientation. It was me and a few other new salespeople. They were all at least thirty or forty years old. I felt extremely out of my league. This was Menards times a hundred.

I learned over the next few hours what my job would be. When the company had a new lead or customer, I would go to their house and present them with all the options. New roof? Here are the choices. New siding? What type of vinyl? I thought back to my times at Menards when customers would ask about different storm doors, windows, or something else I didn't know anything about. I was seventeen and just read the little descriptions along with them. If they ever had a question I didn't know the answer to, which was often, I usually just got another salesperson or my manager. I couldn't do that in this job. It sounded absolutely terrifying. On a bathroom break, one of the guys looked at me and said in a condescending way, "So, young man, where did you work before this?"

"I did door-to-door sales and before that I worked at Menards."

"Oh, Menards, huh? You must know everything then about all this," he said, laughing.

What a dick.

"John, I've seen him in action. He can sell," Bob said, winking at me.

I almost wish he hadn't said that. I knew that I could only let him down.

As the hours went on and Bob showed us all the

different things they sold, pricing, availability, and on and on, my mind went completely blank. I couldn't do this. There was no way.

We broke for lunch. I went to my car and just drove home. Bob called once and left a confused message, but I didn't need to explain.

I lied and told Nana and Annie that there was some miscommunication where I was just there for an interview and didn't get the job. It was humiliating anyway you look at it.

A few days later, I saw an ad for a landscaping job nearby and here I am. Sounded different. No selling, just solid work. It reminded me too of Papa, that everyone tells me I look like now, when he worked at that local garden supply store.

". . . a car will definitely help though. Get that straightened out too. Just put a little money away here and there. Hasn't anyone told you how to save and stuff?" Al was still talking.

"I know, I know. I appreciate the advice. I need to save more. It's hard though with a steady girlfriend and all. We go out all the time."

"How long you been together?"

"Last month was our one year anniversary."

"Jesus, why? That's another thing. Listen, I'm about to tell you some advice my dad taught me. At your age, you don't go around dating girls for a year! That's crazy.

What you need to do is date as many girls as you can. Then in your twenties or whenever, you settle down with the right girl."

"How do you know then who's the right girl? I mean Annie's pretty cool."

"Let me finish. See the whole point is you date around because then you figure out what you like and don't like. Women are amazing, but very different creatures. Different bodies, personalities, moods . . . different all around. So then, by the time you are deciding whether to get married, you'll be damn sure she's the one. You got me?"

"No, I get it. I kind of did that my freshman and junior year a little, but Annie's cool."

"Yeah, but what about next month. She's going off to college ain't she? You're not. So what then?"

He's got me there. I don't say anything.

"Sorry, I don't want to sound mean, but it's just life. If it doesn't work out, there will always be another Annie. Don't worry."

We turn into the condo parking lot.

"See you tomorrow, Al. Thanks again."

He waves and drives off.

I light a cigarette immediately since Al doesn't smoke. I check the mail and forget that you can't smoke in the hallway.

It should be fine. With the smell coming from Nana's unit already, I doubt the condo association is going to fine us for this. Even after Jewel was finally and sadly put down last week, there is still some deep cleaning to do. But with the other two cats and dog, I don't know if it will help much.

Nana still isn't home yet. There are two messages on the machine. One from Bill, Nana's "friend", who comes over on the weekend to watch movies with her and the dog. I can't tell if he likes the dog more than my Nana, but she enjoys the company. He's fifteen years older, but always quick with a joke and can break out in song at any moment.

The last message is from my mom.

"Hi, CJ, it's Mom. I just wanted to call and see how you're doing. I miss you. I have some exciting news too. I just moved into a new part here and wanted to give you my address. It's in one of the little houses off of Arbor Drive in Tinley . . ."

She sounds alright. She's been there for over a month or so now. Two months? I couldn't remember. I just know one day she was in the motel hanging on to her last few possessions and the next she was suddenly in rehab. A new rehab at Tinley Park Mental Health Center. I don't know how she got there. I suspect it was her mom, my other Nana, but I didn't ask.

After she sold the minivan - it disappeared so I really hope she sold it - I knew she was past the point of no return. I'm still a little upset too that I didn't think to grab some of our possessions. Christmas ornaments my brother and I made as kids, mementos, and all the pictures. I hardly have any childhood pictures now except for what's in my baby book. It's all gone.

The rehab is good though. Different than Palos Hospital. I visited her once already and forgot that I used to play soccer out in front on their big lawns when I was little. Eerie to come back ten years later under such different circumstances. Now she is in this type of halfway house situation where she lives with a few other people on the hospital property. In a literal house. She moved into a new one. It's a good sign, I think. A step in the right direction.

I don't know where she's going to go from there. Hell, neither do I. As always. Thanks Al for reminding me.

I call the new number she gave me. As it rings, I picture the pay phone in the Palos Hospital ringing and ringing loudly throughout the whole common area. Seems like ages ago that -

"Hello?" Definitely wasn't my mom.

"Yeah, hi, this is Chris, Linda's son. Is she there?"

"Hold on, sweetie."

This strange woman sounds pleasant. I hear her hand the phone to my mom, who must've been right next to her. Do they have a shared phone in the kitchen? I couldn't remember what the deal was.

"Hey, CJ. How are you? I'm glad you called. I know you're

busy."

"No, it's fine. You sound good. Congrats on the new place. Do you like it?"

"Oh yeah, it's great. I have two roommates, Sheila and Kathy. They're both here for the same thing as me, but one - Kathy who isn't here right now – had kind of a problem with cocaine too, but she's doing so much better lately. We got a lot in common. Sheila's got a kid your age. The staff is nice. They come by once or twice a day and there's programming to do and other stuff. We have all these rules about the house and everyone on the street just hangs out in front. We talk a lot. A lot of stories. Some happy. Some sad."

"Huh. That sounds, um, nice? I'm glad you are getting better at least, Mom. On your feet I mean."

I never know what to say. Encouraging, but not too much so she doesn't feel bad or guilty or sad about what's happened or what's going to happen.

"And the best part! I said I had some exciting news. I -"

"Oh, I just thought that it was the new place?"

"No, no, no, CJ. You'll never believe it. I met someone."

* * *

I don't know how things could get worse, but they did. They almost always do. I think this to myself or maybe I even say it out loud as I walk to work at four forty-five in the morning. It's a twenty-minute dark journey through the backstreets to the McDonald's on Cicero and 137th Street. It was the only place hiring within walking distance. I knew the landscaping thing wouldn't last once the seasons changed, but I'm so damn tired of changing jobs every few months.

I walk fast as I've already been late a few times. My old alarm clock from Papa's old house is a little unreliable and certainly better than Marge, the morning manager, as my wake-up call.

I shake off the nightmare I had this morning too. Another one where I'm in the open ocean, naked and trying not to drown. I wake up only when I've inhaled too much water. Sometimes in these dreams, I hold my breath and try to see through the water. Most of the time I wake up coughing, holding my throat.

I feel like I'm sleepwalking. In high school, I used to joke about working at the Golden Arches as if it's the last place I'd be. Now look at me. I'm jogging, half awake and running to a place I don't want to be.

This is my daily routine. Work from five in the morning to one in the afternoon, Monday through Friday. Breakfast and lunch. Black pants. McDonald's polo shirt and hat. The only good thing is that it's usually just me and Ron in the morning doing breakfast prep, with Marge setting up everything else. Ron and I are both "cooks," but everything is pre-made, frozen, timed and basically produced to not be made incorrectly. Anyone can do this job and judging by the caliber of the lunchtime staff, anyone does.

I get to work and Ron has just punched in. We nod. Already, we have an agreement not to talk to each other until we open at six, unless it's necessary. He's crabbier than I am in the morning and I learned in my first week that he needs an hour or two to wake up.

Ron is in his mid-twenties from Robbins nearby, which is predominantly black. In any other situation, we probably wouldn't even talk, coming from such different worlds in such a segregated city. But here we're equals. Friends even. We spend a lot of time together talking all morning until other people come in at six o'clock and then during any slow periods before the lunch transition. He gets me back into rap music too, listening to 107.5/WGCI on the radio all morning while we work silently. One of us will do all the work for McMuffins such as cooking sausage and Canadian bacon, cracking eggs and cooking them in the round metal egg rings for McMuffins, toasting the English muffins and putting them together. The other makes hotcake batter, breakfast burritos and hash browns. If we have time, we'll do some lunch prep, getting some salads ready.

It was monotonous, dull work, but I found a little comfort in the order. The routine and defined tasks. For those eight hours, I knew exactly what to do. For the other sixteen hours in the day, I was lost. I just wish it wasn't at McDonald's. So conflicting.

I never got to see any customers, hiding in the kitchen, which was fine with me. Not that I didn't want to chat, but I was embarrassed. I longed for the days I would talk to people all day at any of the jobs I've had before. Even when I was a salesman. Now I was flipping burgers, not with skill, only when the timer went off and the grill cover popped up to tell me it was time to flip them.

I get a short break in the mid-morning and I usually just grabbed some coffee and smoked in the break room. I try to time it after Marge. Marge is maybe forty or so, heavyset with unkempt short hair. She looks exactly like I would picture a McDonald's manager named Marge. The first week I was here, I was trying to be nice so I'd take lunch with her, but she would have a burger in one hand and a cigarette in the other, alternating hand to mouth. It wasn't a pretty sight. Now leaving work at one, I grab my free lunch - chicken nuggets with fries and a chocolate shake - on the way out, devouring it on the way home.

I've worked there barely a month, but it feels like forever. It's already affecting my mood. What happened to the honors student? The jobs I excelled at? Oh, the drugs. My mom. My car smoking on the edge of the highway. I get it. What else do I have?

It doesn't help that Annie left. Gone. I visited her once, taking the Metra train to Bloomington-Normal. We hung out at her dorm with her roommate Tina. It was different. Too different. Everyone was partying, drinking and walking to the next party to drink more. I felt like an outcast too, not going to her school. It was a totally other world and I was just some random boyfriend who works at "a restaurant." At one of the parties, she barely talked to me, far more concerned with some drinking game. I was looking forward to just going back to her dorm and getting some quiet time together. But she was too drunk. I could tell I already lost her.

The morning I left, I was moping around and I started to tell her how I didn't want to leave because all I had was McDonald's and barely anything else. I didn't exactly want to stay in her dorm either, so it was odd. She gave me a half hug.

"It's okay. I'm sure you'll find something better soon."

Ouch. It was a long train ride back to Nana's condo in Crestwood.

I'm sitting in my room now, smoking. I hear E.T pawing at the door, so I let him in. He rolls around the bed next to me. I smell like fast food. I put on Radiohead's *The Bends* CD, which has been in constant rotation since early summer. "Fake Plastic Trees" comes on and I immediately think of driving around with Annie. Happy. How foolish I was to think that could last.

I just lie there and cry. I used to get high and relax. Now I'm sad more often. I don't know. If I'm not at work lately, I'm high. I think it helps. Numbs a little. Smoking used to be a great way to escape, but as I think about the last few years, my parachute seems to have gotten smaller.

The phone rings.

In the afternoon, it's probably Bill calling to check up on Chiquita. Nana doesn't usually call from work.

"Hey, CJ, how are you?"

It's my mom. I lie back down and wait for it. After the pleasantries, inevitably . . .

"Are you free later? I've asked our neighbors and no one can help. Can you stop and get us a pack of Benson and Hedges Menthol? Or Newports even. Whatever is easiest. I'm not feeling too hot so I can't walk down the few blocks to the gas station. My stomach is killing me. I love you and -"

"Mom, I can't. I've got plans."

It was only half true. I was gonna call AJ and see if he wanted to stay over since it was Friday.

"Oh. I'm not sure what we are gonna do then. Aaron isn't feeling well either. Are you sure?"

"Yes, I'm sure. I can't."

After all these years, it still made me cringe to tell my mom I couldn't help her, even if it was for something I knew that wasn't helpful.

"Okay, just call me or stop by if you change your mind. I love you, CJ."

"I know. I love you too, Mom."

Sigh. She sounded okay enough. Why couldn't Aaron go out and get smokes?

I should have found out more about this guy, but it

all happened so fast. She met Aaron in rehab in Tinley and next thing you know, they are both out and living together in a small apartment in Markham. My mom seemed to like him, but only relayed parts of his story, which I take with many grains of salt. He used to have two kids but they died in a house fire. He told them to hide in the bathtub and couldn't get back fast enough. He lost everything. Moved from Tennessee because he has family here. I wasn't sure if he had a drug or alcohol problem. Maybe a bit of both? One time I think she casually mentioned he had been in jail, but it was a misunderstanding.

I was worried about her. More than usual. She didn't seem to be drinking lately. It was hard to tell. I wasn't around, so I don't know. But she seemed lucid on the phone when she called, which was a lot. She complained about being sick a lot more. It could just be that her version of sober now is different than what I was used to a couple years ago. She seemed to have a hard time coming to grips with her new reality too.

I could tell that her relationship with Aaron wasn't all roses, but they understood each other. They fought sometimes too, which is inevitable when two addicts share space. I stopped over a few times, almost out of curiosity as much as I wanted to make sure she was alright, and Aaron was very protective of her.

"Your mom is doing well. Really good," Aaron said last time I was there.

I had brought over McDonald's.

"Thanks, CJ."

It was a little better than cigarettes or alcohol. I did help her get back on food stamps though too. Every now and then I did relent, in my weaker moments, to give my mom a few bucks here and there. It's still hard not to. She would say it's for groceries and I should know better, but it's just a few bucks. If she wasn't my mom it would be so much easier to say no all the time.

Besides, I didn't have much money to give, making minimum wage at McDonald's, barely five dollars an hour. Every paycheck went to eating out most of the time, movies, cigarettes and weed. I'd give Nana some money here and there for food, a utility bill when she asked or I'd surprise her with sweets. We'd fallen into an okay rhythm, but I wasn't sure how long it would last. Like my mom, she is predictably unpredictable.

Later that day, AJ comes over, taking the Metra train from his house. I pick him up at the station. Nana likes AJ, so she doesn't mind me taking her car.

"What's up? How you been, man?" I say as he gets in.

"Alright. My grandma's health hasn't been great and her boyfriend has been stressed about it, taking it out on all of us. Just an odd time. It's good to leave for a bit. Work is about as fun as it gets at a manufacturing plant. Whatever. How's your job?"

AJ is one of the few friends that know I'm working at McDonald's. I've managed to somehow keep it a secret with everyone else, which I know won't last.

"Probably same as yours. Every day is the same, but hey, at least I get free Happy Meal toys?" I shrug, slightly embarrassed.

"I just found a bunch of leftover Batman ones and strangely, some music. You have to hear it. Apparently, we're giving away some cassettes soon for the kids. One is just a bunch of scary sounds. Yeah, that's what brings me joy these days."

We decide on going to Barrel of Laughs Comedy Club in Oak Lawn, a place we ended up by accident once, just driving around. They let you in if you are eighteen and we found that seeing live comedy when you're a little high is pretty amazing. And it feels good to laugh these days.

On the way back to my place, we stop at McDonald's for food and then the grocery store to buy half a dozen cans of whipped cream. Some chips too, as to not look suspicious.

Nana's already asleep, so we lay out the whipped cream on the bed and close my door. I light some incense and put the TV on, while AJ rolls a joint. After we smoke, we take turns doing "whip-its," where you turn the plastic end of the can slightly so you only inhale the air that comes out. The nitrous oxide.

We got into nitrous a few weeks ago when we visited AJ's friend, Brad, who also lives in Bridgeport. Brad was a total stoner and had just come from buying a bunch of canisters at some head shop.

"Have you guys done nitrous before?"

We shook our heads.

"It only lasts a few minutes and it's the best, like smoking pot on steroids."

Well, that doesn't sound too bad. He had a little tank where we filled balloons up with the nitrous. We each inhaled about two-thirds of the balloon and for a few minutes, the world completely shattered. It was like the hours-long effects of acid condensed into two minutes. I was hooked. Brad did caution us that it could maybe kinda kill brain cells, so you have to not do too much at once.

Hence, only a few cans of whipped cream tonight. We figured out if you do it when you are already a little high, it just brought things up to a whole other level. After taking a few turns on the whipped cream, we tried to play video games, but I couldn't even figure out how to work the Sega Genesis, fumbling around. AJ passed out and was snoring almost immediately. I woke up the next morning to find the TV on and a cigarette fully burnt out. Not smoked at all. I must have lit one and forgot about it. I'm grateful it stayed in the ashtray.

* * *

It's Tuesday. Worked this morning, then smoked and watched Comedy Central almost all afternoon, running back to McDonald's for some dinner. Nana and I watched two Hitchcock movies before she went to bed.

I'm in bed now reading *Zen and the art of Motorcycle Maintenance,* that either AJ or my dad got me. I can't remember. This one is good though, digging into life even more explicitly than Vonnegut.

Eventually, I start to read the same paragraph over and over and fall asleep. It's two a.m. now and I'm wide awake. My stomach is on fire. What the hell?

It's like I'm being stabbed by an invisible knife. I get up and walk around and it doesn't go away. It throbs. Burns. I start to get dizzy.

I knock on Nana's door, not knowing what else to do.

"Nana! I'm sorry to wake you up, but I'm sick."

I hear shuffling and the door opens. I'm standing bent over. It helps a little.

"Oh no, what's wrong?"

"I don't know. My stomach just hurts so bad. Not nausea, but stinging pain. Something's not right."

"Let's go to the emergency room. It could be bad. Just hold on a second."

"Thanks, Nana. I'm sorry."

Within a few minutes, we drive. I fall asleep here and there. Then the burning wakes me up.

We're finally in the ER. I'm in a gown with Nana sitting beside me. I'm so dazed and tired. The pain has subsided a lot, but after describing it and answering a lot of questions, they tell me it's probably a stomach ulcer.

Unhealthy diet? Check. Smoker? Check. Stress? Check.

They give me some antibiotics and instructions to come back for more tests. Nana steps out so I can get dressed.

It's only as I'm putting my shoes on that I realize we're at Palos Hospital. I can never seem to escape this place. How many times have I sat right where Nana was, watching my mom twisting and turning on these very beds? I think of the teenagers and moms, a few floors up in the psychiatric ward, sleeping or trying to. Waiting for release.

✳ ✳ ✳

It's five fifteen in the morning. I'm at work, tired after another sleepless night trying to stay afloat in a nightmare. I'm looking in the stock room for more sleeves for the hash browns. Ron walks in the back door. This time he's the one late. Marge has been pacing around angrily.

"What's up, Ron?"

He laughs and shakes his head.

"Oh, you know, another day in paradise."

Right. I find the sleeves and go into the kitchen to start yet another dull day.

Ron has given me a ride home a few times in the rain and I wonder if we'll ever hang out outside of work. It's mid-morning and we're shifting to the lunch menu. I bump into Max getting the beef patties out of the freezer. He just smiles at me. Awkwardly. I can't believe he works here. At least he works the lunch to dinner shift - I think - but still. Will this family edge their way into my life forever? What's next? Max's mom, Maria Mueller, will start working the register? Or move next door to Nana's condo? I feel like my life rhymes sometimes.

Maria does say hi to me if she comes in to get food after dropping Max off. I'm thankful for the registers and kitchen wall that separates us. We don't have to talk about my mom. I'm pretty sure that since my mom has been out of rehab and living with Aaron, she's kept a distance. Maybe my mom figured out that Maria was just a predator. An enabler. Or Aaron did. Maybe Maria realized she couldn't mooch off of her now that my mom's got someone else around. I'll never know and hate that I have to see Maria, reminding me of those nights in my old house yelling at each other.

A few years ago, I hardly saw Max at school, as he was sectioned off in the special education classes. Now, here he was, smiling and rocking side to side on his feet while waiting for the burgers to cook and the grill lid to automatically pop up when done. He's pretty quiet and has burnt the tops of his hands so much on the lid that they are always dark red. You'd think he'd learn or that Marge would move him to a different station.

Unlike me though, Max graduated high school in the spring and this was one of his only options to work afterwards. Somehow, in our own ways, after all these years, our paths landed us here in the same boat.

I think about this a lot while assembling rows of burgers. Quarter Pounders. Big Macs. Over and over. I picture myself at Menards, not getting fired, but becoming a department head. Or I'm smiling, stuffing a handful of cash in my pocket after selling all the cheap items in my bag at a store downtown. Sometimes, I even see myself sitting in someone's kitchen going over choices to remodel their house, driving back to my nice apartment in a company car. Nope. Never happened because I'm so stupid. I used to think this was a dead-end job, but maybe I'm the dead-end.

It makes me sick inside. And I'm already sick. Literally. I've been back to the doctor for a crazy kind of x-ray or scan where I had to drink dye so they could check out my stomach. I've got some medication and my list of things to not eat or do. All I've been able to do is cut out spicy foods. I'm still smoking, drinking coffee and eating the same as before. That's life now apparently, always sick to my stomach.

After work, I walk to Nana's, milkshake in one hand, cigarette in the other. Tiff comes over at two to pick me up. I smell like onions.

"How was work?" She laughs.

We all know it's a joke.

"Very funny," I answer. "What do you want to do? Bowl? Movie? Pool hall? Sit and make out?"

I put my hand behind her long blonde hair and pull her close.

She smiles.

"How about we make out for a few minutes and then go bowling? I have to work at five so I don't have a ton of time."

I don't say anything and just close my bedroom door to keep out the cat. It's okay. Nana isn't home.

After bumping into Tiff at the diner where she works a few weeks ago, we've been inseparable ever since. I was with Rob, a friend of Scott's that I've been hanging out with more, and she asked what we were up to since she was getting off soon. We hung out that night with her and her friend Amy, getting high and seeing the movie *Empire Records*, about a group of people around our age working at record store. I sat next to Tiff and looked at her in a different way.

I knew Tiff in high school, but we were never that close. She wasn't in honors classes, but she was around. She was always on the periphery, at parties or here and there. Tiff lived down the street from my ex-girlfriend Kim coincidentally.

The night after the movie, she called me.

"Want to get some food? I'm off and I can get us some free pancakes?"

How do you say no to that? Better than free McDonald's too. We started out as friends and grew on each other. One night she dropped me off and before I knew it, we kissed. She tasted like Marlboro cigarettes, which I usually didn't care for.

I didn't tell her about Annie, except that we broke up when she went to school. Which is kind of true, but I still talked to her occasionally and have visited her a few times since then. I saw Annie last weekend and told Tiff I was going to see my dad. I don't know how to let it go.

I liked Tiff. A lot. But I love Annie, even though deep in my heart I knew it wasn't going anywhere. The visits were mostly disappointing, with dysfunctional sex, since she was usually wasted or trying to get wasted. I just wanted her to love me for a little while, even for a moment.

I feel bad about both of them, but I don't know what to do. Was I hurting anyone? Like everything in life right now, I'm just taking whatever I can get, wherever I can get it.

We leave. We go bowling. Her friend Amy stopped by the bowling alley. Amy also works at the diner and I've quickly learned that on top of smoking weed, she is kind of a coke head. But she's Tiff's friend, so I roll with it. She's pretty, but Tiff is better looking.

"I don't work tonight. You want me to drop you off and then take Chris home?" Amy says to Tiff.

"Yes! Then we can have a little more time together," she

says, smiling, looking at me.

I was looking at my shoes, remembering a time bowling with Annie when she thought it would be funny to just keep them on and left wearing bowling shoes.

After we say goodbye to Tiff, Amy drives me home and stops at the gas station. She digs in her purse.

"You want a bump?" She says, pulling out a little baggie.

"No, I'm good. That's not really my thing."

"C'mon. You look like you need a little bit."

She puts it on her finger and then it's in her nose before I could answer again.

I take a little - a very little bit - as to not be rude. She could flip out and leave me here. I don't trust her.

Almost immediately, I feel my heart and whole body tingle. I want to jump out of the car and just run around.

"Are you alright?" She asks.

"I'm fine. I usually just smoke. I forget how intense this shit is."

"You're so funny. Let's go."

She gets on the road to Nana's.

I look out the window. We pass Bachelor's Grove Cemetery and I swear I see something in the woods. Whoa. I focus intently on the music in the car. Amy's got on Mazzy Star. I love Mazzy Star. The singer's voice is divine.

She stops in front of the condo entrance. Amy looks at me. I swear she seems like she's going to lean in and kiss me at any moment. That could be the drugs. Or her. Or both.

"You want to hang out a little more or do you got plans?"

Well, this is interesting. I consider it. For a moment. Sure, it could be fun. Intense. Do I want to complicate things even more though? Annie, Tiff and now Tiff's friend? No, no, no. I can't navigate this. Not now.

"Thanks for the ride home. I have plans with my grandma."

A lie. For protection. Mine and hers.

"Aw, you're sweet. Tiff is a lucky girl. See you soon."

* * *

I walk inside and get the mail. Nana isn't home yet. There's a letter from AJ. Oh no. I start to feel sick. He hasn't called lately. I open it up and just scan it. The first page just says, "A Letter to Chris Morris." It's formal and I already know what's coming.

I read the letter:

Dear Chris,
I've decided that I don't want you and I to get an apartment together. I've also decided, which hurts the

most, not to be your friend. Period. I have done this because I feel that you hate me. Why? Must you ask . . . A) "I'm not going to talk to her, see her or anything," said by Chris Morris after you wanted to see Annie at school but "you couldn't visit her anyway." B) You CALLED Bryan and asked him to drive you down to her school, so Bryan's girlfriend, Jenny, could see him. That means you used him so you could see Annie. C) You lied to me again (and Bryan)!

I loved you like a brother. But does a brother do these things to another one? No. But you have continually used me as a friend. When Annie wasn't around, you'd call me. ME. I actually thought you liked me as a friend. I was looking through a cloud of smoke.

Some people were saying to forget about you. That you weren't worth my time, but I just pushed that out of my mind. I could see that Scott and Corey had a lot of sense to stay away. But I didn't. I'm not even mad at you, I'm mad at myself for not seeing your lies and deceit. I thought you'd change, but you haven't. I've just wasted a Saturday sitting outside Wrigley Field with your dad. I saw your dad, but no Chris. I went home and found out that you went down to see Annie. Just like a sneak.

I have found some new friends. Friends that treat me with respect and like a human being. The most important thing is they don't use me. You did. I liked you a lot. I liked you so much that I even asked my brother to send you an invitation to his wedding, but thank God he didn't send it out yet because I called him and told him not to do it. I hold no malice or ill feelings toward you. I still like you as an acquaintance - that's it, nothing more. If you call and I have time, I'll talk. If not, I won't.

At one time, we had a lot of fun and saw some pretty good things. Saw some good movies, listened to good music, did some fun stuff. But you changed. Friendship is a two-way street. But not to you. I wish I saw the light earlier, but I didn't. You will never know the pain I'm feeling right now inside. This pain is very strong and deep. But I will get over it in time. I hope you understand the magnitude of your actions. Like I said, I don't hate you or anything. If you find the time, give me a call for an explanation. Here's a quote, "You never know how much you've had, 'til it's gone." Good luck. Tell Annie good luck. Tell Tiff good luck (I think that's her name? Tiff, right?). Tell Nana and your dad and mom good luck. I'll miss them. Most of all, I'll miss your company and friendship. But I didn't make this decision - you did. I'm just reacting and responding. As the sun sets slowly in the west, I bid you a fine farewell.

Good luck,
AJ Hanson
October 23, 1995

I lay the letter down on my bed and think about the last few weeks. I thought my white lies were innocuous, but now they are ruining my only true friendship with AJ. Seems that way. Up until the last month or so, things were fine I thought.

No, I'm such an asshole. I don't know what else to do though. I blew him off for Annie. Tiff too, but he doesn't know that. He hardly knows about her. And for what? He's a good friend. I should reach out to him. Break up with Tiff and Annie. Hang out with AJ and figure things out. I know I can't though.

Nana will be home soon. I call Rob and he picks me up almost immediately. He was always just a mutual friend, but in Scott's absence and well, a lot of my friends' absences, he's filled the void. He lives close by, has a car, doesn't ask a lot of questions, laughs at my jokes and just likes to get high. I don't know much about him and don't ask.

I get the feeling I'm more his friend than he is mine. I only hang out with him when Tiff is busy or at work.

"What's up, man?" Rob asks. "I've been trying to get some weed all day."

"Oh, cool, cool."

I was still a little buzzed thanks to Amy. Rob and I spent a lot of time driving around looking for weed and listening to music.

"And, dude, I've hit the jackpot," Rob says, sounding excited. "My friend Tony said his friend could hook us up. A quarter ounce!"

"Whoa. That's great. We gonna split it? How much is it? I've bought one for like seventy or eighty dollars before."

"I don't know. I think like a hundred though? So fifty dollars each. You good for that?"

I still have some money – about a hundred and ten

dollars - from Friday's paycheck. After cashing it at a currency exchange, I just keep it in my wallet until it runs out. I usually have enough to get by to the next paycheck. This will set me back, but it's an investment.

"Yeah, I'm good. Where do we have to go?"

"Man, somewhere in Markham. It's - "

"Since when do we go to Markham? You know we don't know that area. And to buy drugs? C'mon, man."

"Dude, it'll be fine. Trust me."

Trust him? I barely knew him.

Later, we pull up to some unassuming brown house. There's three cars in the driveway.

"I don't know, Rob. I got a bad feeling about this."

A guy with a bad buzz cut answers the door. Big guy.

"Can I help you?"

"Hey, how are you?" Rob is talking fast. "My friend Tony called. Said you could, you know, help us out?"

Rob looks like he's gonna pee his pants.

"Yeah, yeah, come on in."

He opens the door. We walk past and stand in the entryway. I hear bass thumping and shouting coming from underneath us somewhere. Awesome.

"Follow me."

We go down some stairs and another door. We walk in and everyone stops. The basement room is suddenly quiet except for 2Pac rapping from the speakers in the ceiling. There must be about seven guys, not including us. Some black. Some white. Playing pool, cards and who knows what in a deep, dark cloud of smoke. I feel sick to my stomach. This all feels wrong. And scary.

A guy stands up from a couch. Tall. Short, dark hair. Beard. Lots of gold chains.

"Who are these motherfuckers?"

He's holding his cigarette like he's about to stab someone with it.

"Hey, hey, it's cool. These guys are just here to buy some weed. These are new friends. What are your names?"

I wait for Rob to talk. I don't want to say anything if I don't have to. All I need is someone here to take something the wrong way and we end up bruised, beaten or worse.

"I'm Rob, this is Chris. You guys know Tony? He's a friend of ours."

Gold Chain Guy doesn't look convinced. I try not to look at him and swear I see a gun sticking out of his pocket. I don't look again.

"Tony? Who the hell is Tony? Man, we can't be bringing just anybody down here. We don't need any heat on us. You know what I'm saying?"

Buzz Cut Guy is opening up what looks like a safe hidden in a nightstand. He stops and nods at Gold Chain Guy.

"Jesus, it's fine. Look at these guys. They ain't gonna do anything or tell anyone. It's all good. They're cool. Right, guys?"

Be cool. I open my mouth.

"Yeah, it's all good. We just want to get some weed and be outta here."

Truer words have never been spoken.

"See? Relax, Ryan."

Ryan shakes his head and sits down. Buzz Cut Guy pulls out a big bag from the safe.

"Anyway, you guys can get a quarter ounce. That's a hundred even."

We had already got the money ready in the car, so we wouldn't be digging in our wallets in front of whoever. I learned that a long time ago. Don't count out bills in front of drug dealers, homeless people or my mom.

Rob hands him the cash. Buzz Cut Guy takes it, counts it and puts it in a shoebox. He smiles. I want to get out of here. The other guys go back to what they were doing, but still watching us.

"Alright, alright. Before you go, we do have a tradition at this house. First time buyers got to give us a gesture of goodwill."

And here we go. What do they want? Money? Blood? Who knows what these guys are into? I start to imagine getting tied up in chair and beat up like in *Reservoir Dogs,* but Rob speaks up.

"Totally, man. We'll do whatever."

I shoot him a look. Uh, no, I won't do "whatever."

Buzz Cut Guy smiles.

"Hey, our new friends here are gonna share with us! Anyone who wants in, gather round."

A few of the men in the room come over, laugh and pull up a chair or sit in the couch next to the safe. I can't decide if I want to sit down or run. I feel like I'm going to fall over.

Buzz Cut Guy opens up the quarter ounce and takes out about a dime bags worth. I immediately realize that he is talking about just sharing the weed. Duh. I exhale probably too loudly. Chill out, man. We'll just give them some of the dope and leave. Immediately.

He pulls out some papers and rolls a joint. Then another. It only takes about two minutes, but it feels like two hours. I don't know when we can leave, but I'm pretty sure it's when Buzz Cut Guy walks us out.

"Holla if you hear me, yeah!" A couple of the guys yell out in unison with 2Pac.

"To Rob and Chris. New customers. New friends."

Everyone cheers. Ryan still has a menacing look in his eye. The joints get passed around. I smoke, but not as much as I would usually. I don't hold it in my lungs until I can't anymore, until I almost cough. Nope, just short, polite puffs. I was already a little high before and I'm still too scared. I try to not to make eye contact with anyone. Just nod my head to the music.

Finally, Buzz Cut Guy hands us what is left of our ounce and gets up. We follow him towards the front door. No one else says anything.

"Thanks for coming over, guys. It was fun. Let Tony know if you ever need any more. Don't just stop over, we . . . we aren't quite there yet. And remember, you said we could trust you, right?"

"Of course. Of course," Rob says.

His face has gone pale. Like a ghost.

"Alright. I knew we could. See you around."

He closes the door. We walk fast to the car and get inside. I light a cigarette and take a long, deep breath. I look at Rob.

"Well, on one hand, we got some weed. On the other, that was terrifying."

In the car, on the way back to Nana's, we scream to Nirvana's "I Hate Myself and Want to Die" and I chuckle silently to myself. Kurt Cobain has a sense of humor alright.

* * *

When I get to Nana's condo, I have a headache from everything. Work, Tiff, Amy, drugs, the letter, lies, the basement drug deal . . . I realize I need to wake up in five hours for another day and more of this. What is my life?

I open the door and Nana is awake, pacing around the living room. All the lights are on.

"There you are! Where were you? I've been waiting for you. No note or call or anything. I was worried."

She was almost yelling. She was wavering too, balancing a cigarette in her hand. Drinking. I don't know what to do. She's usually sleeping, but it's another one of these nights instead.

"Shhh, it's late," I say, worried about the neighbors since it was almost midnight. "Sorry, I left in a hurry. I was out with Rob. Why didn't you just page me? Then I'd call you and let you know everything is fine. It's –"

"Page you? I don't know how to do that and you shouldn't have that thing anyway. I've seen the news, I know what pagers are really for. Selling drugs. Are you selling drugs too? Out with Rob?"

"What? No, no, no. We've talked about this before. Nana, the pager is just so you and others can get a hold of me. It's fine. I'm sorry. Come here."

I walk over and give her a hug. She was probably

worried for real. Some days we hardly see each other and it's fine. Other nights, it's still like this with all eyes on me.

"Okay, I'm going to bed," Nana says, looking down. "I just don't want anything to happen to you. I know it's a lot. And there's everything with your mom too. You seem so sad lately. So quiet. Lost. I..."

She stops midsentence, turns off the light and closes her bedroom door. I feel bad. The last year I haven't been the best houseguest, roommate or grandson. Taking her car without asking, disappearing, getting high in my room or worse, having Annie - or Tiff - in my room with the door closed sometimes. It's hard to adjust when you are used to having no boundaries or accountability at home and then to come here with rules only some of the time. We've fought more and more. Well, just Nana yelling at me and me apologizing.

It's confusing. I've learned more about her habits. I thought she started drinking at night after work, but one night when I took the car, I moved her travel mug and didn't smell coffee. It was half full of red wine. Huh.

I find some cold pizza in the fridge and go in my room. I lie down and light a cigarette. Head still hurts. Nana said I seemed lost?

I am, I think. Sick all the time. I don't know if my stomach aches because of the ulcer or just profound sadness. Feels like I'm sleepwalking more and more through life. One day to the next. Drowning in sleep and in life. What am I doing? Why? And what's the point of it all?

I think about Tiff. Annie. Amy. Rob. Scott. Corey. AJ. Nana. My dad. Mom. Who do I have to talk to? I'm not close with anyone and pushing those close to me away. Any happiness lately has been superficial or fleeting. The last few months it's gotten worse. I can feel myself getting more sad. More lonely. More sick.

And my mom. I don't know what to do about her. She might be the only one I know slightly worse off than me. She's been calling more. She's gotten more desperate. She seems lost too. More than usual.

Ever since she was in the motel, she'd call for cigarettes or money, and I'd usually change the subject, bring food or something else. Now, I've learned I just have to say no. Period.

"No."

Definitely shouldn't be this hard. I never thought I'd be upset with my mom begging me for anything. I'm not her parent! It's so messed up. At first, it was a weak "no" after she told me how much she loved me, missed me and so on, but now I'm used to it. Sadly.

I'm worried about her. She's barely hanging on it seems like. She's close to being kicked out of the apartment based on what she said in her calls. Sometimes I get the impression it's because things aren't going well with Aaron. Sometimes it's the landlord. Sometimes she says she just talked to my stepdad and she is simply going to move back there as if nothing ever happened. Sometimes she just cries - it's hard to tell if the tears are real over the phone - about her life, mistakes, starting over and how she ever can possibly go on like this?

The phone rings. It's my mom. As if I summoned her with my thoughts.

"Hey, Mom."

"CJ, how did you know it was me? Nana doesn't have caller ID does she?"

"No one else calls this late. What's up? I need to go to sleep. I work tomorrow. Or in a few hours? Whatever."

"Oh, I'm sorry, I know. Listen. I need a favor. Don't say no. I -"

"Mom, I told you, I can't -"

"No, no, no. It's not like that. We just need forty dollars to tide us over until next week. Aaron hasn't had steady work and you know I can't work right now, so . . ."

I stand up. My body aches.

"Mom, no. Why can't you work? I know you don't feel well, but there's got to be a job where you answer phones or don't move around much? Or -"

"CJ, I don't even know where to start. No one will hire me right now. I look terrible. Listen, fine, even twenty or thirty dollars could help. We have nothing. No food or cigarettes . . ."

There it is. Cigarettes. I know they have food stamps. Unless they sold them. Again. I make a mental note to pick up some food this weekend for them.

My mom starts to cry. I find myself listening more for legitimacy than out of love. I hate that.

"If you don't give me some money, I'll kill myself. I have no choice."

Not this again. She's said this a few times before and it's a mean lie. She wouldn't. No, she wouldn't. I think.

"CJ, I'm not joking. I've got nothing left. I'm taking this phone cord right now."

I heard choking sounds, then gasps, as if she was strangling herself.

"CJ, I -HRRKkkkkkkkkkkkkkk -"

"Mom, c'mon. Don't. Listen, I'll call tomorrow and try to stop by tomorrow night or Saturday."

God, she needs some help.

"Aghk, Ukk . . . CJ . . ." Click.

She hung up.

I sigh and shake my head. Did that just happen? Was it real? I doubt it, but she's never gone this far before.

I call my mom back. It rings and rings. I hang up. Do I call the police? No, that will probably complicate things and I don't want to get her in trouble at her apartment.

Damn it.

I call again. It rings once and picks up.

"CJ, sorry, I'm okay. That was close," she says through coughs.

"Jesus, Mom. Listen, go to sleep. I'll call you tomorrow, okay?"

"Okay, yes, I hope you can stop by too." More coughs.

Are those even real? I can't handle this.

"Let's talk about it tomorrow. Goodnight, Mom."

"Goodnight, CJ," she says, coughing even more. "I love you."

How do I go to sleep now?

*　*　*

After a morning at work, where I swear I was half asleep, queuing up breakfast burritos and egg sandwiches like a robot, I come home and pass out until four. Tiff picks me up for a quick dinner at Nicky's Carryout and here we are, driving around for a little bit, aimlessly looking at the suburbs through smoky windows.

"Are you okay? You're so quiet."

"Sorry, just tired."

That was true. I also couldn't stop thinking about my

mom. AJ. Buzz Cut Guy. Nana. I wonder if Tiff knows Amy wanted to hang out yesterday night?

"I don't know how you do it. I can't imagine waking up so early. I'd just die. I'll take you home so you can catch up on sleep. I've got an early shift tomorrow at the diner anyway."

I get inside and know what I have to do. I can't though, so I sit in the living room, smoking a cigarette and petting E.T. I smoke another one. Play with my lighter. Then another cigarette. I pick up the phone.

I listen as it rings and rings.

"Hello?"

"Mom, it's me. How are you?"

"I'm fine. I'm glad you called. Listen, we got a check from a neighbor. Can you take me on a couple errands? Just the currency exchange and a few other places. I promise it won't take that long."

It's like nothing ever happened last night. Different day, different mom. I think for a minute.

"Mom, I'm really tired. It was a long night last night and work this morning didn't help. What about tomorrow? I'll ask Nana if I can take the car for a little bit. She might let me if I say it's for you."

"That's fine. If not, maybe Tiff could take you over again? She has a car right? She seems so nice, CJ. I'm happy for you. I like her."

"Uh-huh. I'll call and let you know."

Before I know it, it's the next day and out of pity or love or both, I'm in Nana's car, driving to my mom's apartment. Nana was concerned about my mother so she actually let me use the car "for as long as I need it." I plan to take my mom out for a bit and then meet Tiff at the diner. Then who knows what.

I drive her to the currency exchange. The dollar store. My mom is quiet most of the ride. After the last stop – to get cigarettes instead of the groceries she told me she needed – we sit in the parking lot. I see wine in her paper bags too. Really? I've had enough. I crumple my face.

"I'm taking you back now, Mom, I told Tiff I would be there at five. Looks like you got everything, you, uh, needed."

"Oh, don't do that. You know what? Fine. I get it. Your girlfriend is more important. I thought you loved your mother, but whatever, I'll just get another ride. Or end it all. No one seems to care anyway."

What? She grabs her bags aggressively and opens the door. I shake my head driving away after she slams the car door and walks down the street out of sight. She wasn't that far from her apartment, but still. I'm mad for enabling her and sad that almost every time we talk it has to end so abruptly. So angrily. So violently.

* * *

"A truck hit her . . . bad shape . . . driver not arrested . . ."

It's nine thirty at night. Darker than usual. I stand at a payphone outside of a Wendy's restaurant in Tinley Park, answering two pages in a row from Nana with a Frosty in one hand.

My mom was in the hospital.

"Chris, it was an accident. I'm sorry. They say she's okay, but in critical condition."

I call Aaron, but he doesn't answer. I try my other Nana - Nana Dody - who tells me more about what happened. Apparently, my mom was crossing the street and a truck hit her. This was right after I saw her.

"She stepped out at the wrong time," my nana cries.

Hmm.

"The light was green though," Nana says sadly when I ask her.

I hang up the phone and lean against the wall. I feel heavy. This wasn't an accident. I have no doubt my mother stepped in front of that car. An act of suicide. For real this time. What was going through her poisoned mind?

My worst instincts take over. Did she do it just to make me feel bad for not driving her more earlier? I want to throw up. I shake it off and go back inside to get Tiff.

I take Tiff home. She tries to comfort me, but I don't

want to talk about it. She just thinks I'm sad about my poor mom in an accident, but I feel guilty too. What could I have done differently? I know it's not my fault, but I feel like I have blood on my hands and I hate it. That's what my mom probably wants too. I sigh, remembering her calling me the other night and faking her death. Even if I took her home, would she just have done something similar at home that night?

I can't stop picturing her slamming the door and walking away from me. Over and over.

"No one seems to care anyway."

Slam.

"No one seems to care anyway."

Slam.

Slam.

Slam.

THE BENDS

November 1995

The accident was a little over a week ago. It's been a blur. My mom is still in the hospital. I worked all week at McDonald's. Saw Tiff a few times. Mostly stayed home, smoking, getting high and watching nothing on TV.

My stomach hurts and I haven't been sleeping much either, thanks to the damn nightmares. I miss just trying to not sink under the water. I got used to that. But now there's shark fins. Even my dreams are getting worse.

It's Tuesday night. Rob picked me up a few hours ago and here we are. Again. Driving wordlessly, listening to "Bullet with Butterfly Wings" by the Smashing Pumpkins and looking for more weed.

The world is a vampire indeed.

This time we're driving back from Lockport, where I haven't been in years. I finished my eighth of weed this morning and Rob sold his a few days ago. Rob's lead in Lockport didn't pan out. He's embarrassed, but we're gonna try one more spot before calling it quits.

I didn't tell him about the accident. I brush off his

questions with an "I'm tired," which works since I am actually tired. He knows I work the morning shift. He doesn't know anything about my mom or my family. And vice versa. I look at him and wonder even how I ended up in this seat. Scott was my friend. My *friend* friend. Rob was an acquaintance, but now I saw him more than anyone else. I don't even think I like him.

I light a cigarette and stare out at the strip malls as we pass them by on 159th Street. I can't shake the image of my mom lying in her hospital bed, head partly shaved, stitched and ragged looking. The machines. The beeping while she sleeps. The monitors and tubes. I spent so much time with my mom in the hospital before - especially the ER - but not like this. It was jarring.

It's made me numb to everything all week, with emotions coursing through me at different times. Anger. Resentment. Fear. Shame. Sadness.

I mean what's going to happen to my mom when she gets out of the hospital? Attempt suicide again, real or not? More painful phone calls late at night? She narrowly avoided death.

I also keep replaying a conversation that I had with Nana Dody in the hospital, who was there when I stopped by to visit. I could tell she was struggling. We talked about my mom drinking, which Nana didn't usually mention much, but it was unavoidable. It was right in front of us.

This led into a discussion about my mom and this event and that event, what we could've, should've done, and so on. I mentioned how when we moved in with her for a year when I was little, it saved us in a way. Turns out, it truly did.

"Do you know why you moved in with us back then?" Nana said, glassy eyed.

"I don't know. I just assumed it was because my mom couldn't afford the trailer or take care of my brother and me on her own."

"I wish that was the case and probably part of it. No, your mom had started drinking heavily. Much more. She used to be able to manage it okay when you and your brother were little. But this was very different."

Nana paused and took a deep breath. I grabbed her hand.

"She called one night and said that she couldn't take it anymore. She was going to kill herself and take you guys with her. We talked for a long time and I told her she could come up and stay with me for awhile. I knew she was in trouble and did what I could. I wish I could have done more . . ."

We hugged and I didn't know what to say. I was shocked. I had no idea it went that far back. The alcoholism was just waiting for the right environment to take over and devour her it seems.

I look at Rob and out the window behind him into the darkness. What was in store for me? Where was I going? My mom was forty-two and here I am, not even half her age, driving down the same road in some ways at twice the speed.

I need a change. I need to escape. I have to. I think of my mom and my mind turns to suicide again. The idea had always seemed so outside the realm of possibilities. But now . . . it's popped up the past few days here and there. I hate who I am and what I've become. I hate my life. I've pushed everyone and everything away that matters. I have nothing to look forward to anymore either. How long has it been since I was truly happy?

But suicide. When I think about it, it's just a black hole. It's an escape. But a final one. The most final one. I don't even think I could go through with it. I think about Angie and others in the psych ward freshman year. That wasn't me. It just isn't.

God, it would kill my dad. My two Nanas. My little brother. They don't deserve that.

So what then? I'm eighteen. A high school dropout. I work at McDonald's with no desire to work up the ladder there. My only hobbies are getting high, watching TV, occasionally reading about other people's interesting ideas and lives, eating diner food or driving around looking for more outlets to get high. How can I not only completely change my mediocre life, but also be far away from the deep, dark hole I was in? I need a plan. I need possibilities.

Where do I even start? It feels hopeless. Been feeling like that for a long time now.

We are in Orland Park and pass by another strip mall. Suddenly, I see the stars.

"Rob, just take me home. It's fine. I got stuff to do tomorrow."

I smile a small smile. I think I know now how I can leave this all behind.

* * *

The next day, as soon as I get home from work, I grab the phone book. It sits in my lap while I stare at the phone. Is this the right choice? I was suddenly getting cold feet. Think, think. If I ever thought about the future at all, it was me acting on a soap opera or hosting a game show, but both were probably just byproducts of watching daytime TV while ditching school.

"What do I have to lose?" I think, which has become a sad mantra of sorts.

I dial the nearest Army recruiter. All morning, while assembling breakfasts and then all the parts of lunch, I weighed the merits of all the armed forces and remembered the conversations with the Marines back in high school. Unfortunately, the Marines seem like they have the most intense training and is more hardcore than I want to go through. I don't need to go full-on "Full Metal Jacket." I'm not a fan of boats or the open water like my nightmares, so the Navy is out. I don't know much about the Air Force, so that's a potential back-up. The Army seems like it has a little bit of everything, with all the benefits of the other branches but also the most basic. That's all I need.

I call and whoever answered could tell I was serious. Serious enough that they come and pick me up right away to take me to the recruitment center in the same strip mall Rob and I passed. I expected a Jeep, Humvee or a tank. Nope, just the soldier's own personal Honda Accord.

"Come in," he says.

He's a tall, built guy.

"Hey, nice to meet you. I'm Chris."

At the recruitment center, he tells me everything I want to hear. I swear he has the right answer for any question. I hear about how it's not just all the action and adventure you see on the TV commercials, but I can also get almost every type of job imaginable.

"I just want a change," I tell him. "All the G.I. Joe stuff sounds cool, but I just want to put on a uniform and march away honestly. I like having options for college too. Speaking of, what's the deal with the GI Bill? Does it pay for everything? There's got to be a catch right?"

"Oh, man. No catch. Once you pick your classes and everything, you'll get a check every month while you are in school. All good. *And* Illinois has separate grants for veterans which will pay your tuition directly. So you can use your GI Bill check for books, cost of living, whatever you need to get through school or life. Do you know what you want to study?"

He talks and talks, but I'm only half listening. I feel

overwhelmed as I haven't thought through any of this, not to mention a world that involves me going to college, much less what I want to be when I grow up.

It sounds like I just show up on my first day and they take care of the rest. Twelve weeks of basic training or boot camp. Then I go to specialized training for whatever job I pick. Afterwards, I get my assignment and go to wherever I'm stationed, which could be anywhere in the world, even Hawaii! Then when my time is up, I can re-enlist or go home and go to college. It all sounds too good to be true. I know a good salesman when I see one.

I want to leave tomorrow, but it's not that easy.

"Here's the thing. Before you can do anything, you need to get your GED, since you dropped out of high school. After that, you have to take the ASVAB, which is like the SAT but for military service. The better you do on the ASVAB, the more job options you'll have. Next, you have a physical exam and finally, meet with someone to go over everything, pick your job and sign all the papers. That's it! Then you leave shortly after."

Seeing the wide-eyed look on my face, the sergeant grabs a business card from his desk and gives it to me.

"Here. Call me if you have any questions at all. About anything. I know it's a lot and I'm here to help."

I hold the card in my hands.

Sergeant Christopher Moore.

I snicker.

"What?"

"Christopher Moore. I'm Christopher Morris. Just a funny coincidence."

"Is it though?" He smiles. "I think it's a sign you're in the right place."

I get home and even though I have a lot of work to do, I feel different. Everything is pretty much the same, but for once I'm looking forward to more than the next fleeting event of the next day or two. I put on "Tonight, Tonight" by The Smashing Pumpkins.

The impossible *is* possible tonight.

I try not to think about how hard it will be or scary or just the myriad unknowns. I focus on how things will finally change and how it will be worth it. A fresh start. A roadmap of sorts for the first time in a long time. A lifeboat.

❊ ❊ ❊

I don't tell anyone about any of this.

I'll tell Tiff soon and everyone else, but I want to at least get my GED first. As bad as things are, I don't want to disrupt it all without making sure this will actually happen. I could easily fail the GED test. The ASVAB. A drug test . . .

At work today, I put a mental plan together to take the GED test. I remembered seeing information at the library on GED testing sites by the table that I'd pick up my tax forms every year. After work, I walk the thirty minutes down Cicero to the Midlothian library. The older librarian is very helpful. Either that or she wants this young, greasy smelling man out of the library as soon as possible. At any rate, thanks to her, I'm walking back to Nana's with some pamphlets on testing sites and dates, along with a fat GED study guide.

I plop the book down on the coffee table and change out of my McDonald's uniform. I sit down and read through the pamphlets. There is a test in ten days and looks like it's about a hundred dollars. I call and register immediately. I decide to just take the whole test in one day, as opposed to breaking it up. It will be seven hours total.

I pick up the GED study guide and realize maybe I should've looked at this first before registering so fast. It's a lot. The test is mainly reading, writing, math, science and social studies. Hmm . . . I was in all honors classes up until I stopped going to school here and there after sophomore year. It must be all in my head somewhere. I can do this. Right? Reading and writing should be no problem, but I resolve to focus in on science and social studies, with a little math here and there as a refresher every day.

The phone rings.

"Hey, CJ. It's me."

And so it begins again.

"Mom, um, how are you? Where are you?"

"I'm in a lot of pain. The headaches are awful and I look terrible. I can't go outside because my hair hasn't grown back yet with the stitches and everything. That's the worst of it. You know I hit my head mostly on the pavement and just bruised everywhere else. I'm on pain medication too, which helps. A little."

I shudder, thinking of my mom potentially taking on a new addiction or drinking on top of whatever drugs they gave her. I shake it off.

"Where are you though? Back at your apartment?"

"No, Aaron decided it was best for us to move in with his sister and mother in Markham. It's not too far away, just another five or ten minutes east on 159th. They're good people. Aaron said you visited me in the hospital right after it happened. I don't remember, but I'm glad you did."

I think of her in the bed again, bandaged and helpless. I think of her leaving the car angrily. Slam. Me driving away. Slam.

"Of course, Mom. I'm glad you are okay. Well, not *okay* okay, but you know what I mean. You're doing better and out of the hospital, which is good. Mom, I have to ask, what happened though, really?"

I stop myself before asking if she wanted to kill herself. She'd likely deny it anyway or it's always possible she doesn't remember.

"Oh, CJ, it was terrible. I was just crossing the street and a truck came out of nowhere and hit me. Knocked me right off my feet and I smashed my head on the curb. We're trying to figure out now if we should sue."

I think about this poor truck driver who unwittingly entered into my mother's web.

"Out of nowhere? Mom, I heard the light was green."

"Green? Oh sure, that's what they said. Yeah, right. I was at the wrong place at the wrong time."

I don't know what to say. Not surprised. I look down at the GED book and wonder how much longer I'll stand here in moments like this, answering phone calls in my grandmother's house, shaking my head.

"Uh-huh. So, what's up? You don't usually call unless you need something. No offense."

"Oh, don't say that. You know I love you. I just wanted to let you know where I am and my phone number."

I take down the number, even though I won't need it. She usually calls me. Well, I'll have to call her soon and let her know about my plans.

But not yet. I need to wait until the last possible opportunity. I'm one of the few people she has left. My stomach sinks into sadness. Because right now, I just want to leave her.

❋ ❋ ❋

I load up the CD changer with both discs of *Mellon Collie and the Infinite Sadness*, my constant soundtrack lately, and decide to take the practice tests for math, science and social studies.

Tiff is at work and so is Nana, so I get some coffee and retreat to my bedroom. I'm already tired of the GED study guide, but I feel a lot better about everything. So much of it I vaguely remember. It's just a matter of refreshing my memory. I forgot how much I used to like math too.

Hours pass and I hardly break for anything. Some questions are easy, some I take educated guesses and others I don't know at all. I calculate my score. I didn't pass.

But my score is close enough that I'm not discouraged. I have a little more time. I have to do this. I have no other options.

I hear a buzzing. Someone is here.

I hit the intercom button. "Who is it?"

"It's me. Tiff! What are you doing?"

"Hold on. Come in and I'll show you."

Tiff comes in. The cats disperse. We kiss. She smells like pancakes. The diner.

"Follow me."

I take her into the room where my GED information,

study guide and notebook paper is spread out all over my bed.

"What's this? Are you gonna get your GED?"

I tell her all about it. I feel bad for keeping it a secret, but she is less worried about that and more concerned about me leaving.

"What about us?"

I hadn't thought about it.

"I don't know. Why don't you join too? Your brother is in the Army, I'm sure he'd be happy about it. Maybe we could all be stationed together."

"Is that what you want?"

Shit, I don't really know. I just know I want to leave. If Tiff comes, at least I'll know someone. I regret even asking, but it seemed like the easiest thing to do or say. I'm so stupid. Doing it again.

"It would be good. For you. Think about that. We both get away for awhile and come back and start over. No more diners. College maybe. No more restaurants for either of us."

"I'll think about it. Now come on, let's go over to Amy's. We can go downtown later."

I look at Tiff again and I feel bad.

I picture my mom in the hospital, sleeping. Head shaved and stitches visible. The tubes. Beeping.

I'd leave tomorrow if I could.

* * *

I'm at my dad and Nancy's apartment in Chicago. My brother is there too, along with a few of my dad's friends I've known since childhood.

Streamers and balloons decorate the living room. I'm sitting on the couch trying to recall the last time I was here. Too long.

"Congratulations to you, congratulations to you, con-grat-ulations, Christopher, congratulations to you!"

Suddenly there is a cake in front of me and I tuck my ever-growing hair behind my ears to blow out the candles.

"We're so proud of you, Chris."

Nancy sits next to me. Everyone is happy. I am too. I was shocked I passed, proving that desperation is a damn good motivator. As soon as I got my GED test results back, I called my dad to surprise him. And now I'm here. The graduation party I never had.

I called my mom too.

"She's asleep," Aaron's mother said.

Yeah, asleep. It was six o'clock at night. She's called me a few times here and there, but not as much. I think she's mostly been drinking non-stop again now that she has another safe haven.

The GED certificate should arrive in a few days. I still can't believe it. I look around. I should probably tell them what I got this for. Now that I have my GED, the ASVAB should be a piece of cake.

I think of it the whole night, but I feel like I'd be popping a big balloon. Plus, I know my dad. If he was born ten years earlier, he'd be on the front lines of the peace movement in the sixties.

The next day, I call him. He's in a good mood.

"Dad, it's Chris."

"Hey, it was good seeing you yesterday. We're so happy for you. That's a big deal. A lot of places don't care whether you have a diploma or a GED."

"I know, Dad. Thanks for the party yesterday. That was really nice of you and Nancy. I actually wanted to talk about something. I already have a job I'm going to apply for."

"Oh? That's great! What are you thinking of?"

"Well, it's . . . um, the Army. I know, I know. Just wait. I've already met with the recruiter and I have a whole plan in place."

There is silence.

"Hmm. Honestly, I wasn't expecting that. Listen, there are benefits I'm sure, but have you seen the news lately? Everything that's happening in Bosnia? That could be you fighting over there soon."

"Dad, I'm not going to Bosnia. I mean, I have months and months of training before I'm even ready for anything like that. It will be fine."

"I still think you should maybe look around. Why do you want to join? It doesn't seem like you."

"Dad, look at my life. Even with a GED, I still don't know what to do. All of my friends are at school."

"You can take student loans or -"

"No, I don't want to do that. I don't know anything about that. I can have school paid off entirely this way. I need to get away for awhile too. Nana could use a break and I need a break from Mom and everything else. Not you, know that. I love you. It's just . . . it's just this life I created. I need to hit the reset button on almost everything. This is the most I've thought about my life I think ever. Please trust me."

It goes on like that for awhile. In the end, I'm an adult though and he'll support me with whatever I do. I feel bad for hurting him and worry about him worrying about me the next three years.

I call my other Nana, Nana Dody. It's been too long and after getting caught up, which isn't much on my end except for getting my GED, I tell her about my Army plans. I tell her about wanting to do something different. I tell her about my mom. I tell her I need to leave.

"It sounds like you made up your mind. You know your grandfather was in the Army. Or the Air Force . . . I can't remember. I think they were the same thing back then. It was good for him. He used the GI Bill too."

"I know. I still miss him. I miss you too actually and I want to visit you soon. I promise to come for Christmas sometime."

"Oh, that would be great! I can't wait. I still have that picture that lights up that used to be in your bedroom when you lived with us way back when."

I laugh. Even though I'm older, I do get a kick out of seeing that. I miss falling asleep to that picture, nestled in bed in Nana's house. So long ago. Before all this.

I know she worries about my mom too. It's her only daughter.

"I'm glad we could help you back then. I wish we could do more for your mother now. I've called a few times and she hasn't got back to me. It's just too bad."

I hang up the phone and sigh. She doesn't know the half of it and that's probably for the best.

✳ ✳ ✳

Today, I feel hopeful. Again. It's still a new feeling.

I got a seventy-eight on the ASVAB. Seventy-eight!

"That's pretty good and above average from what I've

seen," Sergeant Moore says.

Before hanging up, we make plans to talk soon about jobs and next steps.

After the GED, I actually wasn't too worried. The ASVAB was only three hours in comparison, covering a lot of the same things on the GED test, but also practical things like auto, mechanical and electronic knowledge. Plus, you only need a thirty-one on the ASVAB to be eligible for the Army. I still wanted to do better though to have a better menu of jobs available to me.

The next day, Tiff picks me up from McDonald's and I can tell right away something is wrong. Mainly because she's crying into napkins.

"What's wrong? Did something happen?"

"I'm sorry, I signed up for the ASVAB test but then canceled. It feels so wrong. Nothing about it seems right..."

I tune out. Silently relieved but I feel awful. I don't know what to say. I just hug her a little too long.

"It's alright. The Army's just not your thing. You have a lot more opportunities than I do anyway."

We drive off and the rest of the day is awkward. I could sense a shift and we both don't know what to do about it.

A few days later, I decide to pick up some more pieces of my life and put them back together a little before I get on a plane to basic training someday. I start with AJ. He was my best friend and only true friend over the last six months or so. And I was an asshole. We talked yesterday morning. I first invited him over, but realized I'd done that before and then wasn't home, so instead I took the train and spent the night at his house. I called in sick to McDonald's.

We stayed up late last night talking into the night and now I'm up early-ish, smoking quietly in his bedroom. I can hear his grandmother scuffling in the kitchen getting ready for work.

After countless apologies and letting him know how much I hate my job, my situation and everything else, I tell AJ about my plan.

"I'm going to miss hanging out with you. Stuff like this. Hell, I've missed it lately," he says.

"I know, AJ. I know. What about you? What are you doing? Why don't you join with me? We could do this together."

I say it without thinking about it. Something is really wrong with me. He paused though. I could tell he was thinking about it.

"You know, I could see that. But not now. I'm not sacrificing three years of my life so you won't do it alone. I don't trust you that much. You hurt me, man."

I did. I hurt him and others. Clearly just coming up for one night and trying to make amends isn't enough to repair all I'd done. Still though, at least we're talking. It's a start.

When he wakes up, we make plans to hang out again soon. On the train, I think about Annie, Tiff, friends, my dad, and Nana. My mom. What will they do after I leave? What will they be like when I come back? *If* I come back?

I shouldn't have asked Tiff or AJ to join me anyway. I hate that I'm broken enough to not stand the thought of being alone or that I don't know how to be a good friend or boyfriend. Nobody prepared me for this.

＊ ＊ ＊

Annie. I finally saw her this weekend. I took the train down to her school Friday night. She forgot I was coming or was too drunk or high to get to the station and I had to walk to her dorm. Not a great start. On Saturday, we walked around and I met a lot of people I'll probably never see again. I finally told her about the GED, the ASVAB and my Army plans. She was happy for me. Or seemed so. Probably just to end whatever it was that we were doing. She was preoccupied. It felt like I was just following her around.

I tried to get her to stay in Saturday night so we could just be alone, but she insisted on going to a party. By the time we got back to her dorm, she passed out almost immediately.

I don't even know why I went down. The only highlight was seeing the movie *Mallrats* in the afternoon. We used to see so many movies, but it's different now. She's so familiar yet so distant. She used to be a light in the darkness. But I forget about the new Annie until I'm in front of it. This college version of her is a caricature of sorts.

When I got back to the train station in Oak Forest, I saw Amy, Tiff's friend on the platform.

She just stared at me as I got off and walked home.

Tiff called me last night. Sunday. It was over. I had told her I was going up to see my dad and couldn't hang out. Amy saw me at the train station and must have told her. What could I say?

I deserved it. She didn't. I hate myself and the hurt I can cause. What a bad weekend. It's all coming to an end I hope.

I'm thinking about all this in Sergeant Moore's car on the way to the recruitment office in the strip mall. Soon we're in the office, going over what my visit will look like a few weeks from now at the Chicago MEPS facility. He tells me MEPS stands for Military Entrance Processing Station after I ask. I'll spend most of the day there. I'll have a full physical examination, including urine and blood tests.

"They're also going to do drug and alcohol tests. I know you're too young to drink, but have you ever tried any drugs such as smoking pot?"

"Like in general? Or just today?"

I wait. Blank stare. Note to self: don't joke about drug

use with the military.

"I'm just kidding. No, I don't do anything like that."

Another note to self, stop smoking pot. Soon.

Sergeant Moore just moves on. Surely, I'm not the first wiseass to join the Army.

"As long as everything checks out, you'll meet with a service liaison counselor who will talk through your MOS choices. Sorry, MOS means military occupational specialty. The job you'll do in the Army. Then, you'll finalize that as well as all the necessary paperwork. Have you thought of a MOS yet? I know they are giving signing bonuses for some too."

I want something easy and also useful for when I get out. I need to remember I was joining not for noble purposes or to become a career military officer. I just want something to keep me alive and out of harm's way so I can go to college after three years. The listing of jobs he gave me before were mostly ones that didn't interest me at all.

"I'm thinking of being a cook. Sorry, a 'food service specialist.'"

"A cook? You sure? With your scores, you could be a combat engineer and make ten thousand dollars right away."

"Yeah, but what's that job do? I'm not doing this for the money."

"Well, they build bridges, do other things to get soldiers

over obstacles, construct fighting positions . . ."

"Sounds dangerous," I say, thinking of my dad.

"Let me guess, are they in Bosnia right now?"

"Well, yes, but that's because there are a lot of mines over there and one of their many jobs is to detect mines and protect everyone."

"Yeah, I'm not here for all that."

Eventually, Sergeant Moore stops pushing other jobs and assures me that I'll almost never go out in the field as a cook - field training, meaning camping without any of the fun - and work basic hours during weekdays.

"With this job, Chris, why you can probably have your associate degree by the time you get out!"

The thought is bewildering still. The idea of going to college in any form.

I get home and smoke what I know is the last joint for a while. Well, at least until after the drug test.

* * *

Today is just another Monday, but it doesn't feel like it. It's MEPS eve. Tomorrow it all happens. January ninth.

I already have the day off work and only told Ron the real reason. He just shook his head. He totally understands why I'd want to leave this monotonous low wage work existence, but in the mornings, Ron and

Chris run the kitchen like Batman and Robin. Whoever is Batman depends on the day and our mood of course.

I leave work as usual with the shake in my hand and a bag full of chicken nuggets. Walking home I try not to think about tomorrow and what will happen. Will I pass the physical? What's in the physical exactly? What if they make me sign up for a job I don't want? Will I fail the drug test even though I've been incredibly good about not smoking pot except that one little time on New Year's Eve?

New Year's Eve was my own fault. I got caught up in the moment. AJ and I saw *Four Rooms* at the theater and then I spent the night at his house after a long conversation about the movie at the diner near his place. Just like old times. A few weeks earlier we did the same thing after seeing *Heat*, which blew our minds. Before bed, in celebration of a great evening and a new year filled with new possibilities, we got high. I don't regret it. Okay, maybe a little.

The last few weeks have been strange and surreal. Being totally clean has been interesting. I'm fine most of the day, but in the evening, I just get antsy. I can see now how I've been getting high for so long just out of boredom and to help me sleep. I've been distracting myself with reading, games and smoking twice as many cigarettes.

Christmas felt different too. It took on a different meaning. Will this be my last Christmas with family for years? I spent a little more money than usual and actually saw every single family member. It was bittersweet. Sad, but good.

On a whim, I even stopped by my old house the other day. I was out with Nana's car, knocking things off my Army checklist. I set up my first bank account and bought some things I needed like shower shoes. I just wanted to see my old street and spottted my old stepdad bringing in groceries. I caught him up on everything and leaving for the Army.

"That's good. Good for you. How is your, um, mom?" He said, looking at the backyard. He never was one for eye contact.

"The same. Well, a bit worse. It's hopeless. She's one of the reasons I'm leaving. It's sad."

"It is sad. Well, I wish you the best. You're always welcome here if you want to stop by and say hello."

"Thanks. Thanks for everything."

I've been hanging out with Scott a little here and there, in addition to AJ. Just driving around, talking and getting good food. They make fun of me for going to "military rehab." Corey's doing well. Going to school for marketing and already off to a good start. I'm jealous but happy for him. I keep on putting off Rob, even though he still calls. A lot. I still can't believe I met up with my old friends from freshman year Dan and Andy too. I just popped into their work at Circuit City and we caught up as best we could.

Then there's Tiff. Slowly rebuilding our relationship. Not romantically, but I called her just to come clean and apologize. A few days later, we talked. Then we hung out. I guess we're friends now?

I think of Annie and shake my head. I talked to her yesterday, which was awkward. It's been on and off since she started school, but it feels off now. She apparently hooked up with someone around Christmas. Some guy on her floor in the dorms.

"It was just after a party and one thing led to another . . . Remember though you're my first love. My first everything."

I hate that it's true. I was jealous too though, which surprised me and then I was angry at myself for being jealous. I had no right. I tried to pretend like it was fine. She had found out about Tiff from a mutual friend too, so what could I say?

"I know, I know," I tell her. "You mean so much to me. We have so much history. I've got to leave though. Promise you'll write? Send pictures?"

I don't know why I said that, but I suddenly had a thought of pictures of her on my locker or wall or whatever I'll have in basic training. I think about her beauty and know other soldiers would be jealous.

I hang up, wondering if and when I'll see her again.

It's all been so weird. Out of the blue, Kim called me Friday. My first real girlfriend. The one I literally fought for a few years ago. My first true love. I get the feeling she's on a break from her boyfriend and feeling lonely. I gave her the short version of my life – things are bad, so leaving it all for the Army - then she picked me up for dinner at New Horizon Diner, the old standby. She told me about being a senior and updates on this friend or that friend or her big move to Orland Park. After dinner, she asked if I want to see her new house and say hi to her mom and dad. I said yes, because like Dan's family, they were always good to me. More than good.

It was like a family reunion. Her sister was there too. It felt like nothing had changed in some ways, even though three years had passed. At a certain point, I realized how late it was. Kim just said I should stay the night and she'd drive me home in the morning. I was intrigued. And tired.

She laid out an air mattress in the living room. After a smoke outside, I came in and laid down. The house got quiet and her dogs kept licking my face, but they eventually went downstairs. After a half hour or so, Kim came downstairs, stroked my face and kissed me on the lips.

"It's going to be okay."

I was a bit shocked, so I didn't say or do anything. A part of me wanted to kiss her back. Another part of me was still hurt after she rebounded so quickly three years ago. But she seemed so tender and genuine in that little moment.

It was the right move not to respond. Now is not the time to start or re-start a new relationship. Maybe I really am changing for the better? I went home in the morning just a bit more confused.

Thinking about it now, it still feels like a dream. I take a breath and call my mom. She seems to be doing better. Well, physically at least, after the accident. Instead of being sad about it, now she acts mad. She's going to use the accident to her advantage like anything else.

"CJ, Aaron and I got a plan. We're either going to sue that driver for as much as possible, or at the very least, get disability benefits since I can't work. I've already applied."

Yes, the accident is why she can't work. Okay.

I tell her about my MEPS appointment in a few days and she's quiet. I think she's still in denial or disbelief about this "whole Army thing." It is a lot to take in, for anyone in my family, but for her, I just don't know. We've been through a lot. To put it mildly.

* * *

Today has been a good day. I quit working at McDonald's and gave them my notice that my last day would be in mid-February. It was immensely satisfying to tell Marge during a shared lunch break. It's been a few weeks since my MEPS visit, so I figured it was safe. I didn't want to do it right away as I was still nervous about that drug test, but they must've done random samples. Dodged another bullet.

I think about calling Tiff last night, who was friendly, yet didn't want to see me. She has a new boyfriend already, which surprised me. I was mad, but I get it. I didn't even want to see her. But I did. Ugh. If I'm being honest with myself, I miss Annie too. Scott and Rob sensed my frustration and took me to a strip club in Indiana instead, treating the night like a bachelor party. Every day has been different for a change.

I sit on my bed and look at all the paperwork. It's really happening. I'm technically in the Army right now! I can't believe I took the oath and everything. I have about a month as a sort-of civilian. With the Delayed Entry Program, I start on February twentieth, which will be my first official day as a soldier.

I pick up some papers. It looks like I'll be going to Fort Jackson in South Carolina for basic training based on my MOS as a Food Service Specialist. That training is in Fort Lee, Virginia. Eight weeks in South Carolina and then another eight in Virginia learning to cook. How to cook in dining facilities and in the woods.

Of course, just like at the recruiter's office, the counselor at the MEPS office tried to talk me into a variety of jobs all with a nice list of bonuses. I held my ground. He was a little confused as to why I would pick that MOS with such a good ASVAB score. They don't understand.

I filled out a ton of paperwork after all the tests. The counselor was confused again because I didn't seem to know my mom's address. I just listed it as unknown.

At some point in the afternoon, after signing away the rights to the next three years of my life, I stood in a line of strangers and held up my right hand.

"I, Chris Morris, do solemnly swear that I will support

and defend the Constitution of the United States against all enemies, foreign and domestic; that I will bear true faith and allegiance to the same; and that I will obey the orders of the President of the United States and the orders of the officers appointed over me, according to regulations and the Uniform Code of Military Justice. So help me God."

I went from working for Marge and McDonald's to serving the President and our country. From blowing up mailboxes to throwing grenades. Could be worse? I look at the pamphlet and try to picture myself dressed in camouflage, rifle on one shoulder, marching to wherever soldiers march, doing whatever soldiers do.

The other guys at MEPs talked about the drill sergeants and how mean they can be. I've been through so much with my own mom. And all the training? I've dodged so many metaphorical bullets. Car accidents, all the stupid things with Jack, drug deals and on and on. This is just a different kind of crazy. I'm not scared. It reminds me that I haven't thought much about what the Army will actually be like.

I can't though, because it's just so unbelievably far outside the limits of my thinking.

I just know I must get out of here. Somehow, some way. And somehow this is the way. I laugh at how wild this all is. I keep laughing, thinking about how my salvation started in a little strip mall.

✳ ✳ ✳

I light a cigarette and let Nana's car warm up. I can't wait to leave the cold.

It feels like a long, slow parade of goodbyes lately. Solemn for everyone, but inside I'm itching to go. I've been so isolated from my family anyway, I don't know if they can miss me any more than they already do. I know they're going to worry about me. I feel bad about that.

Yesterday was the last time I'll see my dad, Nancy and my brother. We went out for pizza with Nana and tried to pretend it was just like any other time. It was good though to see my brother living in Chicago and have a whole new set of friends in his new life.

I know my dad will worry the most. The news in Bosnia hasn't gotten better. We don't talk about it much, but I can feel the anxiety and quiet sadness in his eyes.

I've tried to make up for a little lost time by coming up and seeing him the last few weeks here and there. We play guitar. His own songs. The Beatles. The Smashing Pumpkins. It doesn't matter. It's a good distraction and good to see him.

"Be careful. We'll write to you. Write to us too?"

We hug.

"When are we going to see you?"

I have no idea. Honestly.

"I think I have some leave time after training? This summer probably. I'll let you know."

It seems like light years away. I can't fathom coming home after being trained to fight, protect and cook for our country.

My dad hugs me again. He hands me a guitar pick.

"For good luck."

"Thanks, Dad."

I put it in my wallet where it will stay.

After many more hugs and "I love you's," Nana took me home. She's letting me have the car today so I can say one more goodbye. My mom.

The car is finally warm enough. I'm a mixture of nerves.

This is it. I drive.

I think about what's to come. In the movie version of my life, this last meeting with my mom would be one where I knock on the door and my mom would open it, stopping to stare at me, her son. She suddenly realizes I'm about to leave for a very long time. I do too. We hug. She invites me in where we sit at the kitchen table and talk over coffee and cigarettes about the last five years. A montage of every major moment. There are apologies, tears, memories, misunderstandings, epiphanies, laughter, understandings and promises. The camera pans out, leaving the viewer hopeful for both mother and son.

When I arrive, not my mom, but a woman I don't recognize answers the door. Aaron's sister? A friend of his sister's? She doesn't even say anything, just walks away and yells, "Aaron!" I'm not sure what to do, so I walk in slowly.

The house is fairly clean. Dark. Smoky. It feels like walking into our old house, late at night, with my mom talking on the phone at all hours, lighting one cigarette from another.

My mom's sitting on the couch. The TV isn't on.

"Hey, Mom."

"Oh, CJ, what are you doing here?"

She's a little drunk. Or a lot. I don't know anymore.

"Didn't Aaron tell you? I called. I'm leaving in a few days, remember?"

"Aaron's been asleep all day."

I'm confused. I talked to Aaron this morning. This is my mom though in her own world. Reality is foggy.

"Are you still doing that Army thing?" She says, not looking at me.

"Yeah, Mom. I actually leave for South Carolina soon, and then - "

She just shakes her head. Not listening. She isn't interested in me. Instead, I hear about how she's getting disability checks now because of the car accident, but it's not enough. She still wants to get a lawyer and sue the truck driver that hit her.

"It's all his fault I can't work and I get these headaches. That on top of my stomach problems. CJ, you have no idea."

I just nod. I sit and stare at her while she talks. The disheveled hair. Pale skin. Glassy eyes. Dirty clothes. Yellowed fingernails. A shadow of the most important woman in my life.

I know there is absolutely nothing I can do in this very moment to get her to not take another drink, but dammit even after years and years, I can still hear and see the mother I've loved more than anyone under the thick layers of the disease and I want to take her by the hand and set her free.

But I can't. She needs to do that.

I hope for the best, whatever that is. When we finally say goodbye, it's like any other time. No fade to black. No tears or "write to me" or "stay safe." Just a hug and "a see you soon." No uplifting music.

As I leave, I think and know this isn't a movie. Or a novel or a play. It's my life. My mom's life.

With my story, this is the appropriate ending to this part of my life. The only way it could have ended. Or begun? Are there happy endings to sad beginnings? Or happy beginnings with sad endings? Or just endings?

As usual lately, I feel both sick and relieved at the same time.

❋ ❋ ❋

It's morning. The morning. My last morning.

I've been sleeping slightly better lately. The drowning nightmares have stopped, but it's still hard to sleep through the night completely. Nervous energy I suppose.

Nana tearfully watches me make and drink coffee for the last time.

"It won't be the same without you here," she says.

"I know."

I look at her and know it's probably for the best. It won't be the same sure, but she'll have her condo back to normal. As normal as it can be.

"Don't worry, I'll keep your room exactly the way it is. When you come back to visit, you can always stay here."

"Thanks, Nana. Thanks for everything the last year or so. And sorry for everything too."

We hug. I am more emotional than I thought.

"I love you," I tell her. "Don't forget to write. I'll send my address. Let me know how all these crazy animals are doing, especially E.T."

Through tears, my Nana says, "I love you too. It's not a goodbye, it's just 'so long.'"

I grab my bags, smile and take one last scan of Nana, the dining area, the living room. I feel like I'm outside my body a bit.

I go outside where Sergeant Moore is waiting and helps me with my bags.

"Hey, this is it! The first day of the rest of your life."

"Ha! Yep, let's go."

We don't talk much on the way there. The "new" Beatles song is on the radio, so I'm glad he doesn't change the channel. "Free as a bird" indeed. I just stare out the window. When will I see all this again? I can tell I'm a little raw emotionally that this is actually happening. The wheels are literally in motion.

We arrive at MEPS again. This time Sergeant Moore is just dropping me off. His work is done. He's successfully recruited a new soldier and I just helped make whatever quota he probably has.

"Good luck. You're going to have an interesting time and don't forget that you made the right choice. I'm proud of you."

It seems odd to hear something so nice from essentially a stranger. I'll take it though. I haven't heard anyone say they were proud of me in years.

I shake his hand.

"Thanks, Sergeant Moore. Appreciate everything you've done. Take care and thanks for the ride."

At MEPS, there is a lot of "hurry up and wait," which someone else in line says is kind of an un-official military practice. There are more forms, checks and contracts, then we take another Oath of Enlistment to make my active duty official. It's more anticlimactic than last time, since I'm actually ready to go. The whole day has been a little boring, but then I think about how I don't have to go back to McDonald's, to my sad bedroom or my toxic life. I just take a breath and wait for my name to be called.

I'm handed a sealed envelope with all my orders and necessary papers to turn into folks in South Carolina. I get instructions, a plane ticket, and more information that I don't understand quite yet. It's all in my hands.

I walk outside and find a bench. I light a cigarette and instantly wonder how I'll live without cigarettes in my life. Starting tomorrow. I take a long inhale and my mind drifts. Just four years ago, I was sitting in a bed in a psych ward after cutting my arm to get my mom off the phone. Now I'm sitting, waiting to leave for the United States Army to escape my mom, my life and start over. What a difference. All the drugs. The near misses, the near accidents, the girlfriends and replacements for girlfriends, the friends and friends of friends. It's all been unreal.

But I survived. And now I'll have to survive some more. That's all I can do.

I'm ushered back in and suddenly on a bus to the airport with my bags and papers. At O'Hare Airport, I mingle with the other new recruits. We all look a little shell-shocked. There is an official looking military sergeant or officer or counselor in front of our group.

"Alright, soon we'll find your gate and you'll report to the Military Reception Counter at the Columbia Metropolitan Airport by Fort Jackson. Remember the code of conduct you discussed at MEPS. You're in the Army now and you'll behave as such in the airport, on the plane and when you land. Understood?"

"Yes, sir!" We all shout. Wow.

"Good, good. Now, is everyone here? Private Adams . . ."

He calls everyone's names and we take roll call but unlike in high school, he doesn't call mine. Panic sets in. Is this a dream?

The drug test. Damn, I knew it. It would come back to bite me at some point.

Will I not get on the plane? I raise my hand.

"Um, sir? You didn't call me. I'm on the list right? I do have my ticket, papers and every-"

"Yeah, calm down. What's your name?"

"Morris, Christopher Morris."

He looks through his clipboard. My body feels dizzy. He shakes his head and then makes the universal "a-ha" look and checks his bag. He pulls out another form and nods.

"Morris, yes. Food Service Specialist?"

"That's correct, sir."

Relief.

"You're all set, Private Morris. Alright, soldiers, now follow me."

Regular passengers look our way.

Some of us just stand there, unsure of what to do or in disbelief. The man looks back.

"C'mon, let's hustle! It's time."

I follow him, gripping my ticket to the future tightly.

RISE

Epilogue

Dearest,

I'm sure you have a lot of questions.

First, no, my stepdad never did mention the big burn on the carpeted floor of my old bedroom from foolishly lighting love letters on fire. Big props to you, sir.

More importantly, the Army. Yes, well, the recruiter was wrong. Being a cook was not one of the easiest jobs in the Army. Far from it. I was able to take just one college-level class, not quite the associate degree I was expecting.

The thing is that soldiers always have to eat. Weekends, I worked. Holidays, I worked. Sometimes we did double back-to-back shifts in the dining facility on base. In the woods on training exercises for weeks at a time, we worked almost non-stop, never sleeping it seemed, except to take naps, making coffee and breakfast in the night. All while hearing the boar hogs outside your tent.

But, but, but . . . I always ate well. I made friends from all walks of life. I was stationed in Germany and traveled all over Europe. It was the right choice in the end. I needed that kind of isolated and unique behavioral therapy.

I learned to find the meaning in our work. One time a sergeant said to us after a long day, "Guys, I know we've been at it hard, but you should be proud. There are three things that boost a soldier's morale: pay, mail and food. You all are part of making everyone on this mission happy."

That stuck with me. I had a purpose. Some semblance of meaning in my life. A new start.

It felt impossible at times, but I soldiered on. I tricked myself into thinking that it was just three years and to get through at all costs. It was insane at times, but I didn't take it as seriously as some of the others and just laughed off the absurdities. After making jokes and doing my best to fit in at basic training and then cook school, I ended up in a field artillery unit across the world in a small town in Bavarian Germany. I immediately loved it. The people, the history, the cobblestone streets. It felt like I was in a different world. A beautiful, enchanting one. And I was.

To my dad's disappointment, I found out fairly quickly that I would be deployed to Bosnia after arriving in Germany. Apparently, my unit had taken part in almost every military conflict ever. See? You've just got to laugh! In 1997, I spent six months near a town called Doboj as part of NATO peacekeeping operations, living out of a bombed out warehouse that was converted into a small Royal Danish Army base. Myself and two others cooked for the small contingent of fellow U.S. soldiers there, alongside our new Danish friends.

The Danish guys were awesome. They made the best pastries and they let me DJ on their radio station on base, playing my favorite songs every Monday night for "Morris's Monday Madness." I would insert a few of my dad's into the playlist to get him some international airplay.

My perspective was slowly changing. New places. New situations. New challenges. New people.

For example, the Bosnian people revered me, both on and off base. I quickly realized it was because of the American flag on my uniform. They knew the idyllic U.S. only from TV and movies.

"Do you have a wife at home? My daughter is very pretty," I'd hear a woman say, before suddenly showing me pictures of her daughter maybe around my age.

"Do you know Tom Cruise?" A kid asked me on the side of the road.

I struck up a conversation with another kid and after answering his questions about Chicago, I asked him how he was. He smiled.

"Things are good. Last week, my dad just made a well in the backyard! We have water now and have been waiting for so long . . ."

Water! I had taken so much for granted. I had endured hardships, but always had a roof over my head, food and clean water. It put the trailer park in a new light.

The women who helped us cook and clean on the base were the nicest women I'd met and they had just come out of an actual war. One older lady would take breaks to sit when washing dishes. She told me later that a bullet had gone through her legs. But she said it with a smile. They all smiled. They were all happy to work and provide for their families. After losing everything, that was all that mattered and they realized that the hard way. They had been to hell and back and came out the other side different people. I learned so much from them. I think about those women often and remember their kindness, warmth and stories.

I spent another year in Germany after that and refused any and all attractive offers by the Army to re-enlist as my three years came to a close. I came back to Chicago a new version of the Chris who left. I had some money saved. I had four years of college just waiting to be put in my head. A lot of the darkness had subsided.

Everything felt different. For my family and friends too. During the three years I was gone, I only came home twice. Once after my initial Army training, and then again a year and a half later for Christmas after Bosnia. Instead, I often took leave for places like Amsterdam, Paris or Munich, fully taking advantage of my circumstances.

Once I was back to Chicago for good, I ended up in a one-bedroom apartment in Rogers Park for a year, working full-time and going to college full-time on the GI Bill. I was busy, but I put my head down and almost never missed a class or assignment. I worked for three years to get to where I was and I was going to do my best. I quit smoking too after realizing I could get a bigger apartment with the money I'd save. I had a beer every now and then, but that's it. I can count the number of times I've been drunk on one hand.

My dad helped me move in and we saw each other a lot, with him and my stepmother Nancy - still together and happy as ever - living only fifteen minutes away. We made up for lost time. I hardly saw him as a teenager or in the Army, yet I never doubted his love. He could've easily washed his hands of me since I didn't appreciate him as much as I could or should have as a teen, but he was the one who wrote to me the most when I was in the Army, in the woods and especially in Bosnia. Those letters, postcards and little slices of life from Chicago made a world of difference. I let him know that and also apologized more than once for being such an asshole as a teen. I still feel bad about it. In fact, I've made amends to a lot of the people you just read about, believe me.

I met a beautiful and witty woman at Crate & Barrel on Michigan Avenue in Chicago where we both worked. We quickly fell in love and into each other's lives, moving into Lakeview, not far from Clark and Belmont, where I always thought it would be cool to live when I was a teenager. After making so many mistakes with so many girls, she came into my life at exactly the right time and was the anchor of our lives.

We got married. My first daughter was born. Both of those events gave me new drive. I had even more purpose. I had to provide. I had to succeed. Lots of late days and nights both working and going to school full-time. Then, impossibly, this high school dropout graduated college with honors.

My degree was in teaching high school English. I taught for a semester, always thinking of that piece of GED paper I had filed away somewhere. The irony made me smile sometimes when I'd stand in front of the students.

We moved to Madison, Wisconsin to escape the noise of the city and settle down. After no teaching jobs arose, I ended up at a non-profit as a temp, which turned into a full-time job, lots of opportunities, travel and even more positive changes since then. I get to help people through my work and volunteering now, which is awesome. It's all been unexpected and wonderful.

My second daughter was born the second year we spent in Wisconsin. It was the first week in our first house too. After a while, we were basically living the dream. My dream. My own delightful family in our house in the suburbs. Amazing wife. Two fantastic, smart, beautiful, all-around inspiring daughters. Good paying job. Vacations. A dog. Karma came back in the form of my mailbox being destroyed. Twice. Regardless, I was thirty-four and life was ... normal?

Until it started to fall apart. Me. I did. You see, normal is a great goal, but then you get your version of it and you realize you don't know how to do normal. You've grown up in chaos. In survival mode. Then life is fine and steady, but your brain is just waiting for something bad to happen. But those bad things don't happen.

Unfortunately, that doesn't stop you from endlessly thinking of all the ways that it could. Hell, you start to actually manifest those things.

You try to control everything. You don't trust anyone, which doesn't lead to any close relationships outside of the home. You're addicted to excitement. Slightly perfectionist. You're sometimes isolating. You're cynical and negative almost all the time.

Of course, these behaviors caused a lot of problems. At work, I was still doing fine, because some of these traits were strengths in some way, things like being rigidly organized, a perfectionist and so on. At home, I was driving my wife crazy. Nitpicking over anything and everything, slowly pushing her away for no apparent reason in a myriad of ways. It made no sense. To her and especially to me. In a lot of ways, I was still emotionally immature.

"What is wrong with you?" She would ask through tears at night.

I didn't know. I thought I was having a mid-life crisis. I couldn't stop the behaviors. I was spinning out. I would get mad at myself, which would just make it worse. An endless, shitty cycle.

I saw a therapist. He suggested I make new goals since I clearly was having a hard time with getting to the big goal I was shooting towards for so many years. I had plateaued. It made sense intellectually, I just didn't get it. I was living an amazingly charmed life, but was a bit hard to be around sometimes. I should've been happy, right?

Thankfully, my wife was unbelievably loving and understanding, so she suggested marriage counseling, which turned things around. Not the counseling, but one particular session. One conversation. One question and one suggestion changed it all for me.

"Chris, tell me about your background. What was it like growing up?"

I laughed nervously.

"Well, my mom is an alcoholic and it was a little crazy . . ."

I hit the so-called highlights of everything in the preceding pages, my voice cracking while pulling up so many events I had filed away in shame.

"Interesting. I think I know what could help."

She took some brochures out of her file cabinet and handed them to me.

"Have you ever heard of Al-Anon or Adult Children of Alcoholics?"

I read the pamphlets and it was if I had found the key to unlock much of my dysfunctional thinking.

Al-Anon is for friends and family members of alcoholics, a grown-up version of the Alateen meetings I attended a few times freshman year. Adult Children of Alcoholics is a recovery program for adults whose lives were affected as a result of being raised in an alcoholic or other dysfunctional family. That brochure listed fourteen traits of an adult child of an alcoholic and I could identify with pretty much all the bullet points. It was a watershed moment.

It turns out that there are long-term effects of living in the environment around my mom's drinking! I was hardwired to react in a profoundly not-normal way to my perfectly normal life. My life had become unmanageable. Not nearly as bad as when I was nineteen, but it still threatened my whole nature of being.

After fifteen years, it never occurred to me that my childhood chaos could affect my behavior in the present. I always thought, "Hey, I survived! Just don't become an alcoholic." I didn't look back much either.

I started going to meetings for both groups and found a whole bunch of people just like me. I would cry so hard in my car on the way home. I inhaled the program literature. My self-awareness increased. I finally knew why I was acting the way I was.

It caused me to also reflect on my teenage years. Alcoholism not only affects the drinker, but those around them too. A loose set of boundaries and independence mixed with my mom's behavior caused me to react in ways I shouldn't have. I'm not blaming her. I probably did at the time, but don't now. As you've just read, I made a lot of mistakes. I was very complicit and those were my bad choices and actions, leading to my first bottom.

I mean, I cut myself to get her off the phone? I've learned that when you are around alcoholics, you tend to think they are the unstable ones. But often those closest to the person drinking start to act even more unhinged as a reaction. Acting out of love, impulsiveness, anger, helplessness or just to get attention. It started my descent right alongside with my mom. I got lost into drugs. I latched on to girls and friends, but yet had no empathy for anyone either including my family. The immature, teenage version of me took advantage of having no boundaries, yet was so jealous or resentful of other people's normalcy. It changed on any given day back then. I navigated those rocky waters and sometimes fell off the boat myself, sinking. Even though I look back and shudder at some memories, at least I can make some sense of it. Without a nurturing, loving system of support, medication or therapy, what other choices did I have?

I'm thankful that I had that moment when things hit bottom to make a hard, bold, crazy decision to join the Army and escape my life of living day to day with no hope. As noted in this book, I don't think I would've lived to be thirty if I stayed on that path and if I did, it would have been dark.

I wasn't alone either. I've heard all kinds of stories similar to mine. The more I read and heard other people share about their childhood and alcoholic parents, the more I started to look at my mom's drinking in a new light and gave me a new perspective. It started to make sense in a very strange way.

Anger and resentment turned slowly into forgiveness and understanding. I know. I couldn't believe it either. Let me explain.

There are alcoholics dripping from both sides of my family tree. Some grandparents, some great-grandparents, some uncles and aunts all had long periods where they drank endlessly. Throw in mental illness here and there too. Some drugs. It's their story to tell though, so I won't try, but I feel like I was born with scar tissue sometimes.

Many of my fellow adult children of alcoholics turned into alcoholics themselves, married one or both. I thought of my grandfather. Papa. I knew he was an alcoholic, but never thought much more about it. He was larger than life to me and could do no wrong. I remember my mom mentioning once when I asked why my Nana Dody and Papa divorced and she said he got into trouble drinking. That was that.

I don't remember him drunk as he clearly was a high-functioning alcoholic by the time I was a kid. It wasn't always that way though. Thanks to Al-Anon and hearing other people's stories, I started asking questions. Nana and my uncle filled in the gaps.

Papa was a charming, handsome man in his younger days. First, as a WWII veteran and then at his big sales job at Philip Morris. He was successful and reminded people of Jackie Gleason. He married my amazing Nana and they had two kids, a son and a daughter, all living in a nice house in Oak Lawn, a south suburb of Chicago.

They were living the American Dream.

Papa soon moved on to Consolidated Foods and found even more success, helping them acquire Shasta beverages among other things. He traveled a lot, which in the sixties was the Mad Men era for sales executives. Drinking, meetings, lunches, dinners, cigarettes followed by more drinking. He started drinking at Philip Morris, but now he was drinking all day and was almost always drunk at home.

Papa was a good person at heart and helped people when he could. He was a mentor to his kids, but when his drinking got worse, he didn't know how to be a dad or a husband for that matter. He would feel guilty about his drinking and spoil my mother. As a teen, my mom was insecure about her weight and the way she looked in general. Her dad doting on her helped ease it, but she was still mad and confused about his bad behavior.

Then Papa hit his bottom, imploding and exploding everything. The drinks never stopped. He started hallucinating, hearing voices and becoming delirious. Once he brought my mom into the garage because the golf clubs wouldn't stop talking to him. He was scaring the family. Co-workers. And by the time he drunkingly threatened the family with a shotgun, it was over.

Nana left him, taking the kids. He lost his job and his idyllic life.

My Nana later met Hal, the opposite of Papa in many ways, who took care of her until his death. She's one of my favorite people and lived until she was ninety-one. She became a mother to me as an adult, always boundlessly kind and cheery in spite of her own scars.

At the end of Papa's life, I think he could see the writing on the wall with my mom. A family member told me recently that he was upset when my mom started drinking regularly, likely drawn from his own experiences. They would argue about it when I was in middle school. I remember my mom being upset when she got off the phone sometimes with him and now I know why.

He had regrets too. When he was going through chemotherapy, he once told someone, "Don't let pride and anger ruin your family." I could probably write another page decoding that, but I think it speaks for itself. I think about those words a lot.

Papa got lung cancer when I was in eighth grade. His health deteriorated fast and he looked so different after he lost his thick black hair because of chemotherapy. It hit my mom hard. Too hard. I knew my mom was always "daddy's little girl" in some ways, so she was already feeling guilty about drinking and then he passed away. As you just read, that's when the drinking got worse, right before my freshman year of high school and right before I decided to go off the deep end myself.

Whether or not Papa dying was a catalyst for my mom's descent into a life of binge drinking, I'll never know. It's possible it would've happened regardless. A few years ago, I was pleasantly surprised when talking with Nana Dody, I decided to mention Al-Anon and she said that she used to go to meetings and still reads a lot of the literature, with so many of her books worn and tattered. I never saw her drink and she seemed to have learned so much having lived through the pain inflicted by Papa and then my mom.

Nana and I would talk about my mom and try to figure out what happened. We compared notes about her drinking and how it got progressively worse. Was it the stability of suburban life she strived for? She turned to drink as many do in that situation. She didn't know normal. She had her own scars, but they never really healed. When I reached a similar period in my life, I didn't drink, but just unraveled and spiraled mentally. We were more alike than I had ever thought.

Hearing, thinking and seeing this different side of my mom's story, along with my own parallel experiences, helped shift my thinking. I didn't talk to my mom much after the Army and didn't see her almost at all, even after my daughters were born. She was still drinking, and I was still mad, looking back at her as some type of villain in my story, when in reality, I was my own villain at times. When I would talk to her, it would be a lot of the same. Asking for this or that, new lies about a sudden illness, a terrible circumstance and even that she was pregnant again.

Not long after that fateful marriage counseling appointment and some months of Al-Anon meetings, I called my mom. Through tears, I told her I loved her and forgave her. I meant it. I didn't go into all of what I just have written, but I said I wanted to clear the air and put that all behind us after thinking about it all. I realized I was more upset with the disease of alcoholism, not her.

She was appreciative and cried too. She loved me deep down, even when she was at her worst, but I was now open to letting it in a little more. I didn't think we'd ever have a perfectly healthy relationship and she probably didn't either, but at least we were on good terms.

It was a start. But it didn't last.

✳ ✳ ✳

Just a month later, at fifty-seven years old, my mom died. Given her lifestyle, I knew she wouldn't live that long, but it still was a shock, getting an early morning voicemail from my stepdad Aaron to call him, which was concerning.

She went to sleep and didn't wake up. No autopsy was done. We all knew the cause of death.

My mom left the earth on February twentieth. I realized later that it was the exact same date that I left Chicago for the Army. An eerie echo.

At her sparsely-attended funeral, I worked up the courage to speak. I talked about the family that was there and how much she loved us all. I talked about her humor. Her kindness. How one time as a teen I walked in the door from somewhere and she was on the phone talking as usual. I thought she was chatting with an old friend the way she was speaking, saying nice goodbyes and then she hung up.

"Who was that?" I asked.

"Oh, that was Stacy, she was looking for you and we just got to chatting. Sorry, did you want to talk to her?"

That was my mom. At her core. She was a lovely, beautiful woman - friend, sister, wife, daughter and mother - who couldn't escape the disease of alcoholism.

The timing of her death was hard. I felt like I had just unlocked some understanding and recovery for myself, with my mom being a huge part of that. I cried a lot. Sometimes when I'd finally be in a moment of distraction in the car or at a work event, a song like "When Doves Cry" would come on and I'd instantly be transported to driving around with my mom in Chicago Ridge, her singing along to it on the radio with me in the passenger seat. I'd have to fight to keep it together. I was still coming to terms with so many new feelings. My wife was surprised at how much the death affected me. I was too.

A few months later, I was getting better and in a book I was reading about my situation, it recommended writing a letter to your alcoholic parent, forgiving them for everything you can think of.

I sat down and wrote four pages, filling up almost every piece of white space, letting any and all resentments pour out of me and onto the paper.

"I forgive you for drinking.
I forgive you for admitting me into a psychiatric ward.
I forgive you for saying that I was ugly that one time.
I forgive you for saying you hated me that other time.
I forgive you for losing or selling all my childhood

mementos.

I forgive you for running out of the car and away from me on Thanksgiving.

I forgive you for jumping in front of that truck.

I forgive you . . ."

It was a simple yet powerful exercise. Following the book's instructions, I put the paper into my fire pit in the backyard and burned it, with the smoke far reaching into the heavens and into my mother's hands.

As time went on, I got better. I started the process of forgiving myself and how to live a healthy life with my faulty wiring. Progress - not perfection - became the goal. I eased into regular Al-Anon meetings, participating, being of service and making great new friends. The program gave me - and continues to give me - powerful tools to work through my issues. I even started helping out at Alateen meetings, sharing my experience, strength and hope to kids struggling like I was at that age.

Other Al-Anon members invited me to attend "open" Alcoholics Anonymous meetings, which are meetings for alcoholics that non-alcoholics can attend, usually centered with a speaker or two telling their story. Again, their stories and even reading AA literature deepened my knowledge and I sympathized with my mother even more. It also gave me more courage and inspiration in my own life to become a better version of myself. Hearing an alcoholic talk about their journey and struggle to remain sober is very humbling.

"When I focus on what's good today, I have a good day.

When I focus on what's bad, I have a bad day. If I focus on the problem, the problem increases. If I focus on the answer, the answer increases."

- Big Book of Alcoholics Anonymous

✳ ✳ ✳

It's not always easy. The effects of growing up in an alcoholic household last a lifetime. Yet, I'm doing alright. I have such little artifacts of my teenage years, but by some small miracle, the plaque with the Serenity Prayer I made in the hospital so long ago survived. It's now the cornerstone of my daily life, sitting on my desk at work:

God, grant me the serenity to accept the things I cannot change,
Courage to change the things I can,
And wisdom to know the difference.

When I'm anxious, I reflect on this. Can I change what's happening? What can I change? If I can change it, how do I do it? That simple prayer and concept is at the core of my growth.

Shedding shame has helped too. I've slowly let go of the shame of dropping out of high school. Of being poor. Wetting the bed. Doing drugs. And of course, growing up with an alcoholic mother. They were all dark, dirty secrets to me. I didn't talk about any of this for years, but then I realized how freeing it was to let it go. I started sharing a little about my past here and there, at meetings and with friends, even in work presentations. I'd be riddled with anxiety, but the response was always unexpected. I'd hear stories of other people's scars, hardships and dysfunction.

Many years after escaping my situation and joining the Army, this realization is one of the most profound things you can learn: no one had a perfect childhood. Besides, what is normal, other than a setting on a washing machine, really?

As a teen, you feel like you are the only one struggling. I know I did. It's a self-centered time, figuring out who you are and why your world is the way it is. Being a teenager is hard in any situation, but it gets better. I've learned that at any time in your life, no matter what, don't let your past define you, but refine you. Don't let the past, or any limitations or assumptions define your future. *You* define your future and you can reset at any time. There is always hope.

I focus on the positive and reflect on any success, big or small. I'll give you an example from my life that set me on a gratitude journey.

In 2014, I found myself standing on a cliff in Australia. I had won an international scholarship for an industry conference and stayed in Sydney for a few days and I found myself on a beautiful walk down from Bondi Beach overlooking the ocean. It was mid-day, during the week and I was alone with my thoughts. Suddenly I was overwhelmed with emotion, breaking down in tears on the rocks, staring at the most beautiful expanse of water.

I was so confused, but then it hit me, thinking, "Is this actually happening? If only my sixteen-year-old self could see me now, sitting on the other side of the world for an international event. He would be so proud of me." And he is.

Gratitude is a powerful thing. Sometimes, you need to slow down and celebrate the achievements, the progress and the good in your life, both at work and at home. We don't do that enough in such a busy world. I've made it a habit, with things as simple as keeping a gratitude journal and writing a few good happenings from my day. It's helped to slowly rewire a brain that has only focused on the negative for years.

I look back sometimes, as we all do, but do so as I move forward. I'm so thankful that my children have a mother who has helped raise them into smart, kind, caring, confident people who don't want to escape anything except homework, chores, vegetables and bedtime. In 2018, we decided to divorce amicably after sixteen years of marriage. We co-parent well, talk almost every day and I'm grateful for the time we had.

I focus on what I'm passionate about. I have a great job where I get to help people improve their financial life. I think about the hungry boy I was, sitting in our little trailer. I think about my Army sergeant who talked about how food is so important. Now, I donate and volunteer in multiple ways at my local food pantries.

I've learned that everyone has something they are passionate about. Your passion could be to work at

McDonald's! It doesn't matter, as long as you're happy. Everyone has a story. I've been able to look back and find the inspiration and direction in my own story, channeling it to take my talents to make a difference in any way I can. Someone once said that, "The meaning of life is to find your gift. The purpose of life is to give it away." I think that's absolutely true.

I hope you understand a little more about me. You had to experience my story first. I'm sure that's true for most people and their own stories and scars. We don't really know what heaviness they are carrying with them. When I meet people these days, they don't know my backstory, it's just an invisible scar. A memory. A wound that healed. Just me as I am now. Moving forward, yet loving, even missing my mom along the way.

I still have a faint scar on the top of my wrist where I foolishly cut myself to get her off the phone long ago.

Strangely, I have a bigger scar on top of it now. I have a larger crescent moon over what looks like small cat scratches from that steak knife. My first job after coming home from the Army was cooking for banquets at a hotel restaurant in downtown Chicago. I had just started college and I worked the early shift. One morning in the kitchen by myself, I absentmindedly brushed past a trash can and felt a slight scratch. I looked down to see my wrist cut open to the bone. Someone left a broken beer bottle in the trash that was sticking out too far. Twelve stitches later, I had a new scar in the exact same spot.

It was like some higher power was trying to erase my other scar. The first scar, in a way, started a descent into darkness, but this scar cut into those wounds and healed over them. In more ways than one.

I see the scars on my wrist now as a physical reminder of just how far I've come. We are all made of scars, this is true, but don't forget we are all made of beautiful stars too.

A portion of the proceeds of this book are being donated to alcoholism treatment centers and Al-Anon groups in the area where the author resides.

In Loving Memory

Linda Sue McCollum

July 2, 1954 - February 20, 2012

ABOUT THE AUTHOR

Christopher Morris

Christopher resides in Madison, Wisconsin and has been working in the credit union industry since 2005 holding various positions, including Director of Communications. He has won many industry awards and holds a bachelor's degree in teaching English in secondary education from the University of Illinois at Chicago.

An active community volunteer, Christopher enjoys working with local food pantries and organizing frequent group volunteer opportunities.

Christopher is also a veteran of the United States Army, including NATO peacekeeping operations in Bosnia-Herzegovina.

Twitter & Instagram: @morrischris

weareallmadeofscars.com

Made in the USA
Monee, IL
06 November 2023